WE ASPIRED: THE LAST INNOCENT AMERICANS

We Aspired: The Last Innocent Americans

Pete Sinclair

Utah State University Press
Logan, Utah
1993

Utah State University Press
Logan, UT 84322-7800

Cover and book design and art by Mary Donahue. Cover photograph by Dennis Turville

Library of Congress Cataloging-in-Publication Data

Sinclair, Pete.
We aspired: the last innocent Americans / Pete Sinclair.
p. cm.
ISBN 0-87421-166-2
1. Sinclair, Pete. 2. Mountaineers—United States—Biography. 3. Mountaineering—United States—History—20th century. 4. Grand Teton National Park (Wyo.)—History—20th century. I. Title.
GV199.92.S58A3 1993
796.5'22'092—dc20
[B] 93-3859
CIP

Contents

List of Illustrations

THIS ACCOUNT IS MADE IN MEMORY OF . . .

TIM BOND
BILL BUCKINGHAM
JAKE BREITENBACH
GARY COLE
DICK EMERSON
MARK EMERSON
JOHN FONDA
HARRY FRISHMAN
GARY HEMMING
JOHN HUDSON
LEIGH ORTENBURGER
DICK PITTMAN
DEVI UNSOELD
WILLI UNSOELD

. . . FOR ALL WHO REMEMBER THEM.

CHAPTER 1

NORTH

t. Sanford, though not a big Alaskan mountain, was the biggest mountain I had ever seen. We had changed drivers in the pink and gray dusk of the approaching solstice about an hour before, at Tok Junction, so I hesitated to wake up Barry. There were four of us in two cars: "Millicent," Barry Corbet's '40 Chevy, and "Bulldog," Jake Breitenbach's '50 English Austin. (Jake wore Italian racing gloves when he drove.) Bill Buckingham and I rode shotgun. June 5, 1959, the last year a person could light out overland from the States to a U.S. territory; we were headed south, which was strange after three days of going north over two thousand spine-shrinking, tongue-dusting, mosquito-slapping, windshield-nicking, tire-popping miles. Bulldog and Millicent were as festooned with used tires as tugboats are. At Jake's suggestion, we stopped counting flats and timed tire changes instead. Four and a half minutes was the best we could do on Millicent, but we got a doorhandle-to-doorhandle time of three minutes fifty-eight seconds on Bulldog's left rear tire.

Much of the gravel highway between the northern mountains was long, level, and straight, logical if you thought about it, but I hadn't. Down these interminable stretches, holding the jiggling wheel at top dead center, we felt the road at work dismantling the cars. The trees were recent second growth. There was a limit to how long we could hold our breath at the vastness and the dust. When we exhaled, we found that we were tired, dirty, stiff, bored, and unenvious of the pioneers. The Alcan equivalents of old Fort Bridger combined filling station, garage, wrecking yard, general store, diner, bar, post office, and community center. Their construction was log or rough-sawn board and batten, your basic abandoned early logging camp. They all looked rustic and homey to us. We stopped at one about every four hours for gas. Twice a day we'd stay for an hour to get our tires patched and to eat ham and eggs. Due to some mysterious economic principle, the further up the highway we went the cheaper the ham and eggs got. The price bottomed out at eighty-five cents between Watson Lake and Whitehorse, then rose gradually until we crossed into Alaska, where it jumped a dollar. In Alaska, you have to be a high roller just to eat breakfast.

Beside the summit of the mountain a rainbow formed, a double rainbow, a truncated double rainbow: not an arch but a square as big as the upper part of the mountain. There was the square rainbow to the left, the white Mt. Sanford triangle in the center, and to the right were dark foothills shaped to a rectangle by clouds above and ground fog below. Sorry Barry, you've got to see this.

He looked, didn't get it, was polite, tried to work up some enthusiasm, fell asleep again. I understood. The membranes in my eyes, too, felt like rice paper dusted with talcum powder. I was embarrassed by my aesthetic gush. Still, a square rainbow, a mountain for a triangle, a forest for a rectangle, a night without dark. I'd expected big things of Alaska and here was God doodling in color.

Even allowing for the years since having scoured off the memory of the spines and sharp edges of youth, 1959 was a special year. Jake was still alive and Barry had his legs. Life was sweet and we could taste it. We were twenty-three to twenty-five, too young for World War II, too privileged for Korea, and too old for wars to come. We had been children before Hiroshima. Like Robert Frost's bird singing in its sleep, we had come through the interstices of things ajar. We were the high school and college generation of the 1950s, as it seems to me now, the last innocent Americans.

We were in Alaska to climb Mt. McKinley. The bulk of our gear had come up by barge from Seattle. A friend of Jake's in Anchorage (Rick Smith) gave us the use of his basement for sorting and repacking, as friends of Jake's in Seattle (the Kammerers) had given us the use of their lawn, kitchen, and sewing room. There weren't many climbers in the country then. We all pretty much knew or knew of each other. We also knew or knew of folks like Rick Smith and Kent and Sonja Kammerer, who offered floor, shower, and spaghetti feed—people who made for us a sanctuary of ordinary life. That the country could have been that small only thirty-four years ago!

The next day the barge with our baggage came and we went from Anchorage to Talkeetna on the Department of Interior train, stopping to let passengers on or off at what appeared to be trail crossings in the bush. The Matanuska and Susitna valleys were surprisingly lush, cool jungles giving off soft, green light. We drank beer in the dining car in the morning, feeling just slightly sinful; nearly everyone else in the car was joyously drunk. Also, we'd read Hemingway and Homer. Drinking is part of adventuring: one last round, boys, a libation to the gods, boys, before we go off in search of the Great Death.

We chose to use the Athabaskan name, Denali, for Mt. McKinley. Of the four of us, only Jake had been on Denali before. From the airstrip in Talkeetna, we got glimpses of it among the clouds over the Alaska Range. Unable to distinguish mountain from cloud, I took the short view, concentrating on sorting our gear into drop loads and plane loads. The mountain would wait.

After we sorted our gear, we cut fir boughs to drop on the glacier to give the pilot, Don Sheldon, something to judge depth by. Sheldon flew Jake in first. He found a slope on the glacier that was a hair steeper than he could taxi up at almost full throttle. He landed by cutting back until he touched down and then giving it almost full throttle. The Super Cub roared up the landing site, gradually losing way. Just as the plane was about to stop and start sliding backwards, Sheldon turned so that his skis were across the fall line. He kept a little power back in case he fell into a soft spot, as in fact he did while landing Jake. The glacier was almost too soft to land on, so Sheldon put Jake to work packing a landing strip while he returned for me. This was my second plane ride, the first had been in an Air Force jet fighter. Packed in gear up to my neck, I peered left and right at unnamed, unclimbed, Rocky Mountain-size peaks lining the Kahiltna Glacier. Denali was out of view beyond the clouds above these peaks. It was as if we were tunneling our way up to the mountain. Sheldon said that the clouds had been higher on the first flight and they'd been able to take a look at the lower part of the route and pick a drop site. Good news which I would have received with more enthusiasm if Sheldon had been able to give it without turning around and looking at me. I wanted him to look the way the plane was pointed, toward the rising glacier and hemming walls.

It looked like we were going to run out of clearance between glacier and cloud, with no room to turn around. It looked like we were flying into the toe of a giant white sock. Then we came to a wide place where the glacier had arms branching off both sides. We circled right and there was Jake, the evergreen cuttings, and the track he packed.

We drop down and drift over a large crevasse, and another, and then we are on the track, and then we run off the end of it because we went faster on the packed snow, leaving Jake behind. And now the turn, and then the snow gives way under the right ski, and we sink down until we are held up by the wing resting on the snow. With the engine off, it is very still. I can hear Jake's snowshoes as he approaches. Sheldon is grinning, which I understand to mean that we are in a hole and not in a crevasse. Jake laughs as he begins to dig out the door for us. I think that it takes a lot to get someone nervous around here; then I too laugh and decide that I'm going to like it here.

By careful tilting and tugging and by placing a pack frame under the ski, we got the Super Cub back onto the surface of the glacier. Sheldon decided he had to have one of those pack frames, an invention of Jake's.

After taking off, Sheldon circled and waved his wings. We guessed that that was it for the day, but waited up until midnight anyway. Jake talked about logistic possibilities: how many loads from Landing Camp to Base, how heavy, in what order, how long. I tried to pay attention. Soon it became apparent that Jake wasn't paying attention either. He was just saying the words that he, as leader, was supposed to say. We had been in a state of anticipation for almost a year; it had become a habit. It took a while for what was there to assert itself.

Our chatter about what we were going to do stopped. We got in our sleeping bags, put on our wool caps, stuck our heads out of the door of our orange tent, and took a look around. We picked out climbing routes on the rock above us. Our route started from the next arm up on the glacier. We were picking out routes on a ridge that divided that arm from the one we were on. We didn't have to climb the ridge; we'd just walk around the end of it. Picking out routes was just a way to make ourselves feel at home. After a bit it dawned on me that this ridge, on which I had been selecting rock-climbing routes as if it was a practice cliff, was the Kahiltna Peaks, as high off the glacier as the Tetons are above Jenny Lake!

By midnight next (June 8, 1959), Bill and Barry had landed and we had moved most of our gear five miles up the glacier. In another twenty-four hours we had established Base Camp at the foot of the ridge we wanted to climb. It was a miserable two days. The heat on the glacier was intolerable. I was treated for heat stroke during a lunch break. Our loads were enormous. My intestines lost their grip. But the tedious work ended and soon slipped from memory; the climb proper was about to begin.

The ridge we wanted to climb was the southwest spur of the South Face, now called the Southwest Rib. We were on the west side of the spur and had to climb through the icefall formed by the glacier squeezing around the protruding spur. Our camp lay below the line where most of the ice and snow cascading off the icefall came to rest. Nevertheless, our tents were surrounded by debris that came from a hanging glacier on the north wall of the Kahiltna Peaks.

Because of fine route finding by Bill and Barry, the icefall turned out to be a minor problem. From high up on it, on our last carry out of Base Camp, we watched impassively as an avalanche washed over our abandoned camp. It was as difficult to attend to such past dangers as it was to attend to the magnificence of the terrain. The long view was the length of a rope, the short view was just in front of our feet. My foot went through a snow bridge over a crevasse, and I felt a surge of adrenaline (panic). I shifted my weight to the other foot, planted my axe, and that was it. Within two steps I forgot the incident. I was forgetting how to worry.

From Base Camp, we could see the upper mile of the rib, but it was like looking through binoculars at mountains on the moon. The route through the icefall took us eastward, past the base of the rib, then made a left turn around the bottom tip of the rib, and headed us north toward the face. From the top of the icefall, twelve hundred feet above Base Camp, we took our first clear look at what we had come to climb.

The South Face, two and a quarter miles across at the fifteen-thousand-foot contour, has two facets divided by a central rib.[1] We could see only the left (west) facet, that portion of the face bounded by the Southwest Rib and the Cassin Ridge. We made our camp, Icefall Camp, over against the rock of the Southwest Rib and looked up.

The ice sloped down to form a swale and then ascended to the base of the face, three-quarters of a mile away. We were at the left edge of a semi-circular amphitheater, a mile and a half in circumference from our rib around the top of the glacier to the base of the Cassin Ridge. The wall of the amphitheater, from its base at the top of the glacier to the summit of Denali,

---

[1] This central rib of the South Face is now called the Cassin Ridge after Riccardo Cassin, who, leading a party of five other climbers from the Lecco Section of the Italian Alpine Club, climbed the rib two years later, July 19, 1961.

was just under nine thousand feet high. We had before us an honest-to-God awesome prospect.

We were there because no one had done anything on the South Face before. Our reason for thinking that we could do something was that any route up the face appeared to require rock climbing, and, though we had little experience on mountains like Denali, we were Teton rock climbers. Bill, Barry, and Jake were Teton guides. Jake and Barry had a fantastic season in 1957. Bill had grown up in Jackson's Hole and had climbed every major peak in the range solo at the age of thirteen. I had started climbing with Jake and Barry at Dartmouth in 1954 but, because of various dealings with the military, had never been in real mountains until I went to Jackson's Hole in August, 1958. There, Sterling Neale, another Dartmouth climber, gave me a crash course in Teton climbing. He got me in good enough condition so that I was able to join Barry, Jake, and Bill on the second complete ascent of the South Buttress of Mt. Moran. Southern exposures are so much pleasanter to climb than northern faces that, after five beers in Jackson after that climb, someone suggested that we have a go at the south side of Denali. As is usual with projects like this, it grew rapidly in the early stages, until it included a fair portion of the climbers and skiers wintering over in Jackson's Hole, and then began to shrink. Ultimately, there were only the four of us who had made our boast in the Jackson mead hall. We weren't really an expedition any more, just an alpine climbing team. Well that was all right we decided. Hermann Buhl thought it was good to go to the big mountains in small teams; we'd give it a try.

All of these plans, and our implied boasts, had been made in the valley. Now we were face to face, so to speak, with the consequences. From our point of view, near Icefall Camp, the face itself was unclimbable. Up across the middle of our facet of the wall was a rock band with blank sections in it. It was hard to judge how big these blank sections were. The map showed the rock band to be twenty-nine hundred feet, almost the height of El Capitan. The blank sections in the rock band could easily be as much as five hundred feet. But that alone only made the face almost impossible. Someone who could climb the Eigerwand could somehow find a route up this band. We judged the route impossible because of the two great glaciers which framed the El Capitan-sized band above and below. The two-thousand-foot glacier plastered to the face above the rock band sent down chunks of ice that did not seem big, in the scale of the face, but were actually the size of log cabins.

The view to the right of the face ended at the Cassin Ridge, obscuring the facet to the east. This central rib did not look unclimbable, but it looked unclimbable by us then and by any standard of competence we could then imagine aspiring to—even after five beers in the Log Cabin Bar.[2] There was something about looking at the face that I must have experienced when, prior to memory proper, I looked about me and realized that the world had not been constructed for a person my size, that a person was going to have to get bigger if he wanted to get along around here.

When we finished contemplating the "brutal immensities," as Buckingham called the features of Denali, we turned to our own project, the Southwest Rib. We spent a day and a half searching for a way to get to its crest. To us, the rib appeared to be a ladder placed against the wall to carry us past the two glaciers and the rock band. Jake and I searched the rock immediately above the camp. We hoped to make an ascending traverse back southward across the flank of the rib to the crest. After days of snow-slogging, the rock climbing was fun and relatively easy, but the flank of the rib was, in effect, a face. It only took us thirty minutes to climb it to the crest, but it wasn't a way to go because the technical work needed to ferry loads across and up it would be slow. Also, we'd run into a small blank section. We'd have to hit the crest further up.

---

[2] The life history of a difficult mountain route has seven stages: (1) invisible or un-image-able, (2) unclimbable, (3) possibly climbable but suicidal, (4) first ascent, (5) difficult route, (6) a classic route, and (7) once considered a classic route.

The next day, Bill and Barry did that, climbed to the crest by a route closer to the South Face, and discovered, yet closer to the face, a giant couloir that appeared to lead all the way back down to our glacier. Above, there seemed to be only two large snow hummocks to climb to bring us to the place where the rib leveled out and abutted into the face, five hundred yards to the left of the El Capitan-sized rock band.

We did not welcome this opening up of the route as joyfully as we ought to have. We had been expecting to gain the face by the rib ever since we saw the first photographs of the face. It was unnerving that our first move was a wrong move. And, in abandoning the rock of the rib for the snow of the couloir, we gave up our special qualification for attempting the route. But there was no way to avoid it, it was too obviously the way to go. By the evening of June 12, Bill and Barry had placed eight hundred feet of fixed-rope in the bottom of the gully, which turned out to be not a snow but an ice gully. We would attempt the mountain not as a team of specialists but as one of fairly young climbers with just over the minimum qualifications.

I had not participated in the discussion that led to the decision to use the gully. The first time I looked up it, it seemed to sway, making me the first climber to get vertigo by looking up an exposure. The bottom of the gully was steeper than the top. When Bill and Barry went out to fix rope up it, having seen only its upper section, they passed it by as being too steep to be part of the gully they had seen. This gully they'd lost track of, much wider, longer, and steeper than the Teton Glacier, was but a minor feature beneath the great South Face. Jake, Barry, and Bill called the angle of the ice sixty degrees because it was steeper than the ice wall on the West Buttress that was called fifty degrees. The exact angle of the ice was a matter about which I could feel complete indifference since this was to be my first ice climb.

With a minimum of internal hysteria, I made my first carry up the eight hundred feet of three-eighths-inch manila rope that Bill and Barry had put in. I climbed the gully as if the fixed rope were not there—which, as far as I was concerned, having never trusted my precious body to anything smaller than seven-sixteenths-inch nylon, it wasn't. After surviving the first 120 feet of descent for the second load, I stopped imagining myself hurtling down the gully and trusted my weight to that puny thread.

So this is how it is in the big mountains, I thought to myself as I waited at the top of the lowest section of rope until Jake cleared from the rappel. What else do you have to do to be ready for Annapurna? Bill and Barry were fixing the upper section of the gully. They were hundreds of feet above, but I had a comforting image of being connected to them by the ice chips streaming down from where they were cutting steps. Little shards of ice danced and tumbled down the surface, glittering like bubbles on a brook. I followed them with my eye to their source, reading the surface of the ice by their path. Bill's axe rose and fell like a fly rod casting into the depths of the ice. Barry looked around from his relaxed belay. Above them a black dot was bounding gaily on the surface of the glacier like a water bug.

"Rock! Rock! Rock!," I yelled. I hugged the ice, trying to melt my way into it. At last glance the rock had almost reached Bill and Barry. By the time it got to me, it had reached terminal velocity. The corners and edges of the rock ripping through the air hummed a terrifying tune. Missed. I lifted my face from the ice to glance at Bill and Barry. Jake! No, the rock had exploded a small crater in the snow a few feet in front of him. The rock had passed within twenty feet of each of us.

The gully, the fixed rope, the falling rock, were to me an examination. I wasn't sure that I had passed. I wondered if the others had also worried about themselves first. But I hadn't quite done that; I did yell a warning before taking cover. Did I think, "Him, not me?" No, I did not have that thought. Did I have that wish unspoken? I might have. If Jake had been killed, I would have been certain that I had permitted it.

We went on to the top of the gully. And there we stopped. The top of the gully was not a col or saddle or cornice, it was a large double mound of ice of uncertain origin. We spent most of the next three days of perfect weather at these "snow bumps," as we had named them from below, stuck as effectively as if five feet of snow had fallen. Perhaps it was the rattlesnake whir of the rock. Perhaps it was the steepness of the ice or the fact that in deciding to abandon our snowshoes we might have cut off our retreat. Maybe things had gone too well. Some wyrm of unconfidence found its way to our courage-hoard. We named this camp Concentration Camp.

The next day, the eighth straight of good weather, Bill and I climbed the first bump, to be stopped by a level area on top. Although it was level, the snow was crisscrossed by a confusion of snow and ice structures whose logic and origin escaped us. To the east was the ice gully; to the west was a three-thousand-foot drop. There was only forward or back. Bill had barely started to cross when he sank to his waist.

"What is it?" I asked.

"I don't know, but I'm getting out of here," came Bill's ominous reply.

But, before he could reach the camp, Bill had one more problem to deal with: my very first experience descending ice had happened within the past twenty-four hours and that was with a fixed rope. In those days there was no such thing as adequate protection on ice. Our axes were of no use, so I had to go down on crampons only, facing out from the mountain. And there would be no practice tries. When my body was properly in balance over my crampons, my mind was of the opinion that I was leaning forward, about to go down, down, down two thousand feet of hard, blue-white ice. It did not look right, this descending ice; it didn't look like something a person ought to do. Like Christ leading a disciple across the water, Bill showed me that it could be done. He said it was like friction climbing, which is exactly what I feared it was like, but I did what he told me to do. I made the first step correctly and the subsequent steps also, so that when we got back to the tent I was feeling a little bit chipper.

It didn't last. That evening a gloom heavy as remorse after sin weighed us down to thoughts like "If we leave now, tomorrow morning, maybe we can still get out alive."

Our climb was a deliberate experiment in climbing on an expedition-sized mountain with an alpine climbing team. We had to talk the Park Service into letting us try it. Nearly everything had gone as we expected. Any size expedition, the bigger the better, could have gotten to the base of the gully. To get to where we were and to where it seemed we had to go, we were just the right number. We had abandoned materials all along the route until we were down to what we could carry in four enormous loads. Of the 1,725 feet of fixed rope that we had brought, 1,600 feet were gone, fixed in the gully below us. Our snowshoes were stuck heel first into the snow at the base of the fixed rope. Not one snow bridge that we had used in the icefall was still intact. Retreat would not be easy.

When Bill turned back that morning, I feared that it might be because he couldn't trust me to do my part. But that was not what was going on, at least not that any more than the dozen other things we randomly chose to worry about. What had happened is that we had encountered precisely the difficulties we had told each other we would encounter, while we had secretly hoped that things would turn out to be easier.

Just as the maps and photographs indicated, the south side of Denali was steep. Rocks fell off the mountain when there were people in the fall line as they did when there were not people in the fall line. There might be a good campsite where we wished one to be and there might not. Manila rope three-eighths inch in diameter is exactly as it appears, not nearly as strong as seven-sixteenths-inch, nylon rope. The fact that we had surmounted with ease the difficulties we had made extraordinary efforts to find did not increase our confidence. That just made us wonder when it was going to happen. "It" was . . . what? A storm.

We first decided that we couldn't go up because there would certainly be a need for fixed ropes ahead. All the fixed rope we brought was already fixed and had to stay fixed so we could retreat in case of a storm. Later we argued that there were probably four thousand more feet of ice ahead, which would be easier if there were snow on it, so we could kick instead of cut steps and could do without fixed ropes. Therefore, further progress could not be contemplated until a storm brought snow. When Buckingham had enough of this creative speculation, he stopped it by observing, "We came here to climb. It would be ridiculous to retreat with the report that we couldn't do the route because the weather was too good."

That stopped the silly talk, but it didn't get us going. On the next day, when it was Jake and Barry's turn to lead, Jake insisted on turning back before they even got to the high point Bill and I reached.

All the gloomy talk scared me, and I would have been happy to turn back. So far I had had a wonderful time. I was willing to take that back to the valley. I had the least idea about how to read the terrain for foreseeable dangers, but when Jake and Barry turned back from terrain that *I* found easy, I knew that it was the geography of the soul that was holding us up.

Jake had had me as his partner since we landed. I suspected that sending me up with Bill was a subtle move by Bill and Barry to release Jake from the grip of his depression, that they felt that it didn't help Jake to have to look after me. I had done my share. Any worries I had I kept to myself. I cleaned the dishes without complaining. But if they knew only half of what I knew about what I didn't know, they had something to worry about. I didn't mind not having major responsibilities until Jake turned gloomy. I ought to be helping, but I knew not how.

The only worry Jake spoke about was that we might "extend ourselves" beyond a point from which we could retreat. He had climbed Denali before and felt, justly, that we didn't know what it could be like there in bad weather.[3]

---

[3] Some years later, Barry, back on McKinley for a rescue, returned with a tale of their six- foot high Logan tent being buried in one day's snow.

It might have been our unorthodox expedition that bothered Jake. It was as much his plan as anybody's, but it might have appealed to his logic and not his heart. We were unorthodox in that we did not really have camps; we bivouacked in tents. We weren't living right. The British had invented mountaineering in the first place. The philosophy of expedition climbing was a product of their military and colonial genius. We were a guerrilla band. The distinction isn't one of safety versus risk; no one matches the British for sheer daring. The issue is more one of style. The classic mountaineering expedition is large not because it's safer that way, it isn't, but because it takes a large expedition to carry the necessities. Going into the jungle is no trick. Having an afternoon tea in the jungle is. The touch that the British carried into the darkness was gracious living. It was not enough to drink tea from china cups, to present a good show; the tea actually had to taste good. Jake was American and therefore informal. He wore suntans and rolled shirt sleeves for all occasions, a jacket over the rolled sleeves for formal occasions. But his trousers were always unwrinkled, and his shirts always white and fresh. There was a crispness to his informality.

Jake had been talking about us overextending ourselves since Bill and Barry found the gully. Now, at the top of the gully with all our fixed rope below us, we were certainly at least extended. We all talked superstitiously about the phenomenal weather. We all had seen the avalanche cover our base camp. We all had been near the falling rock. We all wondered if we could do what we'd been doing if the weather went bad. Doubt drained our energy like a low-grade infection.

When Barry and Jake returned to camp on June 15, it seemed to mean we were defeated. Then Barry asked me if I'd like to go up with him. He just couldn't give up without taking a look himself. I worried that his asking me might be a little hard on Jake, but by the code of the mountains, Barry not only had the right to make the request, he had a right to expect support. If he regarded me as adequate support, that was his affair.

SOUTHWEST RIB OF DENALI
T: Traverse
C: Cache
F: Camp Fatigue
P: Paradise Camp
CC: Concentration Camp

Photograph by Bradford Washburn, courtesy of the Museum of Science, Boston, Massachusetts.

The first bump went easily. This was my third day of ice climbing, and I was beginning to get the hang of it. I was in a perfect environment for quick learning.

Barry diagnosed the weird area between the two bumps, where Bill had sunk to his waist, as "an area of fossilized cornices." Giving it a name helped. No one but me appeared to think that if the name was a correct description, it was possible that we would sink up to our armpits and find our feet hanging free in the air.

We crossed over to the second bump. It was steeper than the first bump, and getting onto it required traversing a small, yet steeper section of ice. I realized then that we might not be defeated after all if I could fill in for Jake. We could go on if I could lead the pitch. Barry could establish a bombproof belay on the level section. If I couldn't climb the pitch with that degree of protection, then we probably ought to turn back. None of this was stated of course, but for the first time since we left Seattle, I understood that I had a contribution to make.

A person can sometimes climb pretty well when he knows he can't get hurt. It's like playing poker with a pat hand. It's not really poker, but it sure is fun. I did the pitch in good style for a first lead on ice. Then Barry led a pitch and it was my turn again. The protection for my second lead was practically worthless, but I'd learned what crampons would do. I was half a rope length out on the lead when it began to snow. We turned back because we already had what we needed, a way over the bumps. The sky had cleared again when we reached the tent.

We began the discussion again, this time knowing we were going to decide to go up. The retreat might be impossible, "So," said Buckingham, "the only way back might be over the top." That did it. Retreating up the mountain was exactly the right idea. This gave Jake the opening he needed to recoup his leadership. We didn't literally have to go over the top with our camp. There might be a route from our rib over to the West Buttress Route. Jake thought he had spotted a traverse when he climbed the mountain by the West Buttress Route. The photographs also indicated that there might be one. Jake had thought of the traverse as a possible way to the summit if the upper part of the rib stopped us. Since the traverse was below the level of the ice wall on the West Buttress, it might even be an easier route down than the standard West Buttress Route, allowing us to avoid the danger of descending that ice wall without having fixed it with rope. It really was all a matter of how one looked at things. The whole climb had a new gestalt. Someone casually mentioned that we still hadn't figured out how we would get down the Kahiltna Glacier without the snowshoes we left at the base of the gully. After thinking about that a bit, we pretended it was never said.

Barry was so delighted with the decision to go up that he volunteered to go down into the gully to retrieve eight hundred feet of our fixed rope. Buckingham asked to join Barry because he hadn't been out of the tent all day. I didn't object; neither did Jake.[4]

The weather was perfect, the route was perfect, we were not perfect. Jake probably experienced both joy and fear in the mountains more purely than the rest of us. We all felt some fear. Bill's weapon against it was calculation and wit. If he couldn't think his way through it, he'd disarm it with a phrase. Barry's weapon was action. If Barry was on a climb that scared him, he got up earlier in the morning. My trick was to leave a piece of equipment behind, nothing serious enough to stop the climb, but a plausible excuse if I couldn't do it. Jake didn't have a trick. He had to wait it out.

The two bumps took nearly a thousand feet of fixed rope, requiring the use of a climbing rope in addition to the three-

---

[4] A year or two later, Yvon Chouinard told me that this moment, the moment we decided to go on, was a historic moment in the history of American mountaineering. The climb was not terribly difficult even by the standards of that time, but, said Yvon, "It was the first time an American team committed itself totally to a mountain route." Yvon might be right. It might be that what stuck us at Concentration Camp through three days of gorgeous climbing weather was the thought that we were at a threshold that hadn't been crossed by anyone we knew.

eighths-inch manilla. We emerged from the top of the second bump onto a sun-lit snow meadow several hundred feet across. We were high enough now so that we could look across the shoulders of Mt. Foraker to the Susitna River Valley ten thousand feet below us. Nobody but us had ever looked out on the world from here. That had been true all the way up the route, but this was the first place that made us think it. We named the camp Paradise. We had cut a Jacob's ladder of about five thousand steps to get there.

Then there was Camp Fatigue. The day was hot. The altitude was getting to us. Our loads were over eighty pounds. Another day like that and we would have started thinking about going home again.

The climbing the following day, from Fatigue to Balcony, was on rock, and it was great fun because we lightened our loads. At the point where the traverse over to the West Buttress could be made, we cached all supplies not needed for the three days we gave ourselves to get to the summit and back and climbed on. We were high enough to see approaching weather and it was certain that a storm was coming, but there was no talk of retreat. It was a great relief to have made the commitment. For the first time since childhood, I was where I wanted to be, doing exactly what I wanted to do, with the people with whom I wanted to do it.

CHAPTER 2
BREAKING OUT

hat am I doing here? and How did I get myself into this? are questions which every climber comes to sooner or later. The standard occasion is some petrifying situation, and no answer is forthcoming because the climber is busy trying to get out of there. Once out, the climber finds he has other interests, particularly if he suspects that there is another situation in his immediate future where the question might again arise. It is rare but sometimes happens that the question comes to him when he has done something right.

We made Balcony Camp on a small step in the rib, a rock fin half a lead high, which had, of all things, a bed of fine gravel just large enough for a tent. We still had over three thousand feet to go to the summit, more than we had been able to make in either of the two very hard days since Paradise Camp. But there could not have been on Denali at that height any other such place, a level, graveled platform on a ridge, while there were hundreds of such places in the Tetons. We were almost home.

After supper, I stood on the outward edge of the balcony, my back to the mountain. By peering over my right boot, I could see where Base Camp had been, seven thousand feet below. Six thousand feet below my left boot was Icefall Camp. Down the Kahiltna, through holes in the low clouds, I could see the river valleys and forests to the south. Moisture-laden air gave an aquamarine cast to the world under the clouds, as if everything below snow line was submerged. Above, the mountain snow and the cloud tops had hues of purple and pink kneaded into their whites and grays. We were almost to the solstice; the light went on and on. It was just what a high camp should be.

Although we were calmer than we had been since we landed on the mountain, it was not easy to sleep. Nor did we talk. I thought of the efforts that had brought me to this place.

The assistant dean of freshmen asked me what I wanted to be.

"An explorer."

He smiled and said that there wasn't much demand for explorers any more. I smiled back and shrugged. Why else would anybody go to a college in the North Woods?

I could afford to go to Dartmouth because I had a navy scholarship. At least I regarded being a "regular" in ROTC as having a scholarship; the navy regarded me as having joined up. It took me a while to discover that the navy had the correct view. What was important to me was that the navy paid my tuition, supplied my books, and gave me fifty dollars a month. What was important to the navy was that they prescribed about a third of my education and that I went to drill once a week, wore a uniform once or twice a week, and went on a cruise every summer. This was all right with me. I liked the uniform, especially the navy-blue wool shirt. I looked forward to the summer cruise.

I was assigned to a voyage that went from Norfolk, Virginia, to Oslo to Stockholm to Guantanamo Bay, Cuba, and back. Forty-eight hours out of Norfolk, I was surrounded by vomiting midshipmen. Although I didn't get seasick, I skipped lunch, and after receiving someone else's used lunch in my lap while sitting on a garbage can, I stood. Whatever fantasy I had about shipboard life soon dissipated in the steel compartments and passageways of the USS *Albany* CA123. The navy seemed to believe that the warrior virtues were best induced by boredom and sleeplessness. That was a surprise though, when I thought about it, not unreasonable. The worst time for an enemy attack would be when we were tired; better to be practiced. What I could not warm to was the ship's utterly mechanical being. It might have been easier if I had been on a destroyer instead of a heavy cruiser. During a storm I'd seen the little destroyer escorts shudder their way up out of waves that broke against their bridges. A person could have some fellow feeling for vessels like those. The *Albany* was just a huge machine. In the parts of New England where I had lived, tending a machine was what you did when you could not think of anything better to do. But the thing that galled me most was the requirement that I remove my hat in the parts of the ship called officer's country. I couldn't see myself as a person who took off his hat because the paint changed color.

Off the Azores, a friend and I formulated a plan to jump ship, just to see if it could be done. We'd heard the sailors use the expression, and we imagined doing it literally, swimming for the islands. We liked to believe that we had an option. It looked as if we were steaming by the islands about three miles off; we figured it was probably five. After we had our plan all worked out, we checked the radar. It showed twelve miles.

A beach officer in Stockholm pushed me while I was part of a drunken crowd of sailors and midshipmen waiting for our ship's boats. Before I had time to think, I pushed back. It was just a reflex action, but having done it, I decided that I was in the right and told the officer so in impolite terms. He, in return, ordered me to detach myself from the mob and stand to one side in plain view. I did not stand but paced, giving the lieutenant my best version of a murderous glare. After I cooled down, the thought came to me that I might be able to get through life without becoming a naval officer.

By captain's mast the next day, that thought faded before the more pressing need to avoid complete disgrace. I also lost any righteous fervor. The lieutenant was technically wrong to push me. I was drunk, abusive, and where he had been merely irritated, I had been self-righteously enraged. I was more wrong than he. Fortunately, somebody mixed my case up with that of another middy. I was able to prove that I didn't do what he did, and he was able to prove that he didn't do what I did. We both got off with a mild punishment.

It took almost a year for me to return to the thought that I might somehow get by without the navy and its money. The dean helped me get out of the navy without being dismissed from school. Not getting kicked out was for me mainly a point of honor since I no longer had the means to go to college. The navy notified my draft board that the army could have me.

"Sinclair," said Captain Bull, who was a short Texan, as most of the officers at the Fort Sill officer's candidate school seemed to be, "I've seen a lot of men in this army and I can tell about them. You're never going to make it through this program because you don't have the guts." I had applied for OCS after basic training because of, what else, a woman. Twelve weeks later, after detecting a change in tone in her less frequent letters, I discovered that I only wanted to serve the required two years, and thus made a prophet of Captain Bull.[1] I most hated the thought that Captain Bull would continue through life proud of his ability to judge character. Since of the entering class of sixty-eight, twelve remained after I left and since the first to drop out was a first sergeant who'd earned the Medal of Honor in the Korean War, I wasn't persuaded that guts were the essential ingredient. After the first three days of hazing, the sergeant sat down on his bunk and started crying. He continued to cry almost all night. We knew why. He needed to kill one of these little fuckers who stood us at attention, their tilted-up faces inches below ours, screaming and spraying us with saliva, and he could not. All he had ever wanted was the dignity of being an officer, and they had found the one way to prevent him; they took his dignity away from him in the first hour, and then his honor as well. I was quite sure that I had no business being in the army, never mind being an officer. But clearly there was something

---

[1] A friend recently pointed out to me that I may be the only person in America to have washed out of both the navy's and the army's officer training programs.

odd about me. The skill I needed to acquire was avoiding getting into places where I didn't belong.

I finished my hitch on August 6, 1958 and hitchhiked to Jackson Hole, Wyoming. I heard of the place while at Dartmouth. It had been a Mecca of Dartmouth climbers since the days of the Durrance brothers. While I'd been on the navy cruise and in the army, Jake and Barry had been burning up the peaks. Glen Exum took them on as guides. They were busy guiding when I arrived, so Sterling Neale introduced me to the Tetons. In September, Sterling and I returned to Dartmouth. Barry had decided to drop out. He stayed in Jackson. Jake had given Dartmouth his third and last try that spring. He went on to Seattle from the Tetons. Dartmouth brought us all together; Dartmouth got us into the mountains; but Dartmouth had a hard time holding us.

I proved to be unexceptional in this regard. The tuition at Dartmouth had doubled while I was in the army. My savings were exhausted in less than a month. But I had learned one vital skill in the army. By working as a dishwasher at the hospital, I was able to live on food I got off the trays. Barry's life in Jackson, as he described it to me in a letter, was enviable. One phrase in particular caught me. He described Jackson in the winter as the closest thing to a classless society he'd ever seen. Suddenly it seemed that this was exactly what I'd been looking for. Around Thanksgiving I wrote to Barry saying that I'd about come to the end of my string at school, I missed the mountains, and I envied his life. He telegraphed me suggesting that I give up this nonsense. He had a job as a ski instructor, would support me until I got a job, and would teach me to ski. It was like a message from grey-eyed Athena. I wasn't getting anywhere trying to make something of myself. And the world had failed to notify me that it would be upset if I dropped out.

Before going west I considered something else. In those days Al Lowenstein was touring college campuses trying to raise political consciousness. Al had come to Dartmouth to look for people to go to South Africa with him. Kurt Webering, president of the student body and member of the Dartmouth mountaineering club, knew that Stu Rice and I were dropping out and put us in touch with Al. We went down to New York to talk with him. We went on a motorcycle, in December, drove all night in a snowstorm, drove down Manhattan into a rising sun. The newspapers I had wrapped around me under my Harris Tweed overcoat to break the wind crackled as I huddled behind Stu. Al's mother greeted us with the comment that she enjoyed meeting Al's unusual friends. She invited us in, fed us breakfast, chatted with us, and suggested we take a nap.

Al's project had some attractions. There was a chance of getting thrown in jail. There was the certainty of playing hide and seek with the South African police. There was the opportunity to meet chiefs of Southwest Africa. Also, I would meet Reverend Michael Scott and others who were fighting apartheid. I was tempted. My decision would depend on whether I could make enough money to pose as a student on tour by the time Al was to leave in the spring and whether or not the McKinley plans went forward.

As things turned out, I was at Balcony Camp when Al sneaked into Southwest Africa to tape the pleas of the tribal chiefs, a tape which Michael Scott later presented to the U.N.

From New York, Stu went to the D.C. area for Christmas and I went home to Connecticut. In January, 1959, still wearing my long Harris Tweed overcoat, army dufflebag shouldered, I hitchhiked to Wyoming. Stu followed two weeks later.

The three of us, Barry, Stu, and I, dropouts from the Dartmouth Class of 1958, were among the pioneer ski bums in Jackson Hole. We had been preceded to Jackson by a year by Frank Ewing, a Yale dropout. There was also a couple, Dick and Angie Pittman, trying to see if it were possible to choose not to have a respectable career after attending good eastern colleges. They built a one-room cabin in a cottonwood grove and began raising a family. They worked for wages to buy things they could not grow, make, or barter for. They were getting by. If you worked hard at what you did, the local people accepted you.

I couldn't ski, but there was a possibility of getting a job on the professional patrol if I could learn fast enough. For thirty days I was on the first chair going up, and I skied all day. Barry gave me instructions between his classes and while we stood in the lift line. He used me to figure out a way to teach parallel skiing directly, without having to retrace the evolution of skiing. At the end of the month, Neal Rafferty, the manager of the area, decided he could risk hiring me, and he and Stearns Morse taught me how to be a patrolman.

Until I got my first paycheck, we lived on Barry's small earnings. If Barry got a big tip, we would go to a movie and have one beer at the Silver Dollar Bar. We skied all day, talked in the evening, went to bed tired, and woke up feeling wonderful.

The job I liked best on the patrol was "sweeping the hill," checking every run to make certain no one was left injured or stranded. (Snow King mountain, at that time, was the ski area with the steepest average slope in the country.) On weekends, five to ten people from the volunteer patrol would sweep the hill by sending someone down every run. On weekdays, the professional patrolman on duty did it alone. Often, I would get to the top of the mountain just as the sun went behind the Tetons. Then, in the deepening twilight, I'd traverse the face of the mountain in four long sweeps which covered every slope and gully. The only sound I heard was my skis brushing through the bluing snow. Lights shone in distant kitchen windows, the silhouette of the Tetons sharpened in the west, and the alpenglow faded from Jackson and Cache peaks to the north. Nineteen fifty-nine was beginning to look like a vintage year.

Word came from Buckingham, who was at Princeton, and Jake in Seattle that the expedition was on. We needed to get serious about money. When the ski season was over, Barry, Stu, and I headed a hundred miles south and two thousand feet higher to Big Piney and the oil field.

Big Piney was a town of about six hundred on the high plain south of the Green River and near the site of the Green River rendezvous, where Bridger, Jackson, and other mountain men had their annual drunk with the Indians. The town was a mixture of log cabins, modest frame houses, and trailers. Why exactly Big Piney or its older suburb of half-a-dozen buildings,

Marbleton, came into existence before the development of the oil field has never been clear to me. I guess the ranchers who lived in grand houses scattered thinly in the surrounding five thousand square miles needed someplace for a post office, cafe, and headquarters for the Forest Service. The cabins and frame houses were the permanent core around which the trailer courts expanded or contracted as the wells came in or failed. I got the feeling that someday the trailer houses would all disappear; they'd either be towed to Bakersfield or be blown into the Wind River Mountains by the relentless western wind. (I stopped by there recently. The trailers that had been blown or towed away had been replaced by mobile homes waiting their turn.)

Most of the oil rigs were located between eighty and eighty-five hundred feet on the great plateau south of the town. It's not the best climate for outside work in the early spring. None of us had any oil field experience, but we'd heard we might be able to get jobs because experienced roughnecks from Oklahoma, Texas, and California were not eager to work there at that time of year.

We rented a log cabin. I got a job on a rig. Stu got a job on the pipeline. Barry didn't get a job and went home to Vancouver. He had enough money saved for the expedition and had a job as a guide after the climb. He used the time to do some writing.

I stayed in the oil patch for two months. I liked the work, my fellow roughnecks, and the country. As an eastern college boy I was something of a curiosity. The men I worked with were from Wyoming, Oklahoma, and California, often uneducated, but of above average intelligence, and restless. The work was dangerous. One day I climbed up on the rig tower to tighten a bolt, when I noticed a change in the sound of the drill. Everybody was looking at the pipe. The driller disengaged the clutch, and the pipe started to rise and fall in the hole. I couldn't believe it. The pipe, filled with water, weighed more than fifty tons. Then the well blew. A piece of metal shot past my head. The metal hit something high on the rig and came back down, this time closer. Everybody was heading for the sagebrush. They had a head start on me but I soon caught them. All those years on the track team hadn't gone for naught. Fortunately, the driller got the machinery shut down before a spark could ignite the escaping gas. Unfortunately, we had to go back and turn a valve to shut off the well. It probably took us four minutes to close the valve, but with gas screaming out of the well, it seemed much longer. This incident occurred about two weeks before I was due to leave. I began to look longingly at the mountains on the horizon.

Finally the last day came. About an hour before quitting time, the pin came out of the kelly hook, also called the grief stem, thirty feet over my head and landed beside me. I stared at it for a moment, trying to remember what it was. I jumped just before the jaw of the kelly hook landed. It tore my pant leg open on the bounce. I wasn't conscious of ever having noticed that pin in the kelly hook, but I quickly figured out that a pin that big must have secured something very heavy. I told the driller to dock me an hour's pay because I'd just quit.

Not all the dangers in the oil patch were at the rig. I decided to have a couple of beers at the local bar to celebrate my last night in town and to collect five bucks that an Okie roughneck named Charlie owed me. The bar was full of cowboys as well as roughnecks. Charlie told me to be ready to get out of there. The cowboys were real. They'd come into town to have a few before going out to cow camp for the summer. The drive into the mountains was to start the next day. They were a quiet and affable bunch; I couldn't see trouble. Charlie said that there were new roughnecks in town who'd never worked this patch before and might take it into their heads to take one of these cowboys on. These weren't Oklahoma, Texas, or California cowboys, Charlie pointed out; first, this was their country. Second, these cowboys had spent the winter loading tons of bales of hay onto sleighs and then pitching the hay off the sleighs to feed the cattle, bales which weighed over a hundred pounds apiece because they were saturated with frozen snow driven into them by the winds of a dozen Wyoming blizzards. Now they were about to chase cows through the mountain forests for a summer. Charlie figured that three roughnecks to one cowboy would be even. I drank carefully and smiled until my cheek muscles ached.

Before I got a chance to mention the five bucks to Charlie, there was a phone call for me. It was the waitress from the cafe where I ate. She had been nice to me and I joked with her. She told me about problems with her boyfriend. She called to invite me over to her house to say good-bye. She told me how to get to her house, and when I got there, I found that she was alone. She welcomed me with something more than ordinary warmth. I couldn't understand it. She knew I was leaving the next day, and her problem with her boyfriend was that he hadn't asked her to marry him and she thought it was time he did. But I didn't ask any questions; it sure beat a bar fight.

Then there was a phone call. It turned out to be you know who. I began to understand; she began watching the window. Every few minutes, a pickup drove by. I asked what was up. She said that it was her boyfriend, that he was real mad but didn't have any right to be, and that he could go to hell. He had other ideas, however. The pickup stopped. "He's coming to the house," she said in a tone that was half frightened, half joyful. "What are we going to do?" she said. Honor required that I stay and explain. But on the other hand, all I had holding me to this town, beside honor, was the five bucks Charlie owed me. I said, "I'm going to Alaska to climb a mountain," and slipped out the back door I'd located while she'd been looking out the window.

I remembered her while standing outside the tent at Balcony Camp. I smiled as I headed for my sleeping bag. She had helped two guys figure out what we most wanted. There was a good chance she'd be married before snowfall, I figured, and I had a pretty good shot at getting up this mountain.

CHAPTER 3

GETTING THERE

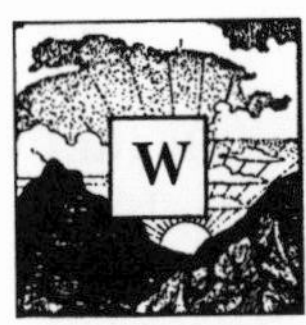

e left for the summit at 7:40 A.M. By 8:10, I was thinking about explanations for not making the summit. I had a fierce headache; I wished I hadn't forced myself to eat breakfast that morning. The others seemed beastly strong. We climbed about a thousand feet of very nice rock that I could not enjoy. The clouds closed in below us and crept up the mountainside. We paused at eighteen thousand feet to put on crampons. The snow was hard, just right for crampons, but as the going got easier, the breathing got harder.

We moved to different rhythms. I tried to keep pace with Buckingham. If the pace is right, two can move easier together than each can alone. Each step is then not a separate act of will. You lift your foot because your partner is lifting his foot, and he lifts his foot because you are lifting yours. I learned that as a miler. Pacing together cuts out cross-purpose chatter between the mind and the body.

Barry stayed a little ahead, just far enough to urge us on without breaking from the pack. Jake moved back and forth between us. When I lagged behind Bill, Bill would pick up Barry's pace, then I would catch up. So it went, not for the sixty-five seconds of the fourth lap of the mile but for nine hours, every minute of which felt not like the thank-God-it's-almost-over fourth lap but the horrible I-can't-make-it third lap.

Barry seemed to have the least trouble, but it was shocking to listen to his breathing. We all were gasping and fighting for air. By nineteen thousand feet, it became an individual battle. We each fought for every breath and every step.

One, two, three . . . at twenty I'll stop . . . six, seven . . . how does Barry do it . . . eleven, twelve, thirteen . . . chest hurts . . . fifteen . . . damned crampon, ripped pants . . . twenty! Air, air, air, air. Can't move, impossible. One, two . . . .

Barry: "Pete, I see black rock . . . gasp . . . could be . . . gasp . . . North Peak . . . gasp."

Me: "Jake, Barry . . . gasp . . . saw black rock . . . gasp."

Jake: "Groan . . . gasp . . . it's North Peak . . . gasp . . . fifteen hundred feet to go."

All: "Groan . . . ."

That's the only conversation I remember between nineteen thousand feet and the summit plateau, where we wobbled to a halt, too spent even to stop crisply. Barry asked Jake where the summit was, and Jake pointed his axe across the plateau to a white fin, which we knew rose eight hundred feet above us. The base of the fin was a half a mile from us. As far as I was concerned, we might have been in Anchorage. It was obvious to me that we weren't going to make it. It was just a matter of who was going to make the decision. I tried to eat some lunch and gagged. Because I couldn't spare the energy to vomit, I didn't eat. Bill said that he was feeling weak from hunger but, persuaded by the rest of us, didn't eat either.

Jake rose to his feet. I rose too and took one last look at the summit; it seemed to have receded. Jake stepped in front of me going in the wrong direction! He was headed across the plateau toward the summit. I wondered if he was disoriented but fell in behind him.

Crossing the plateau seemed worse than going up because there was no sense of progress with each step. We seemed to be marking time in place on a blindingly white plain arched over by a blue-black sky.

SOUTH PEAK OF DENALI
BC: Balcony Camp
T: Traverse
C: Cache
F: Camp Fatigue

Photograph by Bradford Washburn, courtesy of the Museum of Science, Boston, Massachusetts.

Finally, we started up, five steps at a time. About a hundred feet off the plateau, I looked back. Buckingham was lying face down in the middle of the plateau. Lucky Bill.

On the crest of the ridge, I looked down the north side, slowly turned left, and crept on up the ridge. We stopped. There was the bamboo pole placed on the summit by Bradford Washburn in 1947. I stood blankly, tears running down my face. Barry grabbed my hand to shake it. I confessed, in a casual tone, that I was crying. Jake said, "What do you think I'm doing?" And Barry, "My goggles are half full."

After pictures and a tape recording that consisted mainly of gasps, we wondered about Bill. I moved below the summit to wait for him, while Jake and Barry continued on down to check on him. The fun of making the summit would be gone if he didn't make it. In a few minutes Bill appeared, chugging his way along the ridge at an amazing clip. The gods may not always be just, but they're not completely crazy. Bill had stopped to eat and it worked. He sat by the bamboo pole and talked to me in a normal voice while every heartbeat slammed blood against the inside of my skull. "Do you realize what we four hackers have done?" I didn't, and didn't care to at the moment.

I had to get down to a lower altitude; my headache was past enduring. The scene from the top? I don't remember. I do remember that Barry said, "I've never been with any people who have put out so much effort, who pushed so hard."

We entered the clouds from above, at the top of the rib. There was no wind; the snow piled up quickly. Visibility was less than half a rope length. It was fortunate that we got to our ridge before the clouds reached us. We weren't in a storm, but the odds of surviving two days in the open at that height and that far north were not favorable. Even with the fixed rope we had retrieved after crossing the bumps below and had placed above Balcony Camp, it took an hour to descend the pitch above camp. The handholds and footholds had disappeared. The snow stuck to minute rugosities, piled upon itself, and gave the appearance of a rock projection where there was nothing but fluff. I rolled, slithered, lurched, and slumped down the pitch most unstylishly, but it eventually woke me up. I couldn't remember much of the descent until we got back to the ridge. They told me that I hadn't been completely conscious, that I had been able to make the descent as if I knew what I was doing, but that I didn't speak when spoken to. They had herded me down the mountain using the climbing rope as a tether.

It had been nine hundred vertical feet from Paradise to Fatigue. From Fatigue to Balcony was about double that. From Balcony to the summit we doubled our distance again, climbing thirty-eight hundred feet on the summit day and descending the same distance. This is not a recommended regimen for acclimatization. But given the delay at Concentration Camp and the pursuing clouds, this was the mountain's price for getting there. Now the problem was to get down.

It was still snowing when we woke up the next morning. Barry took on the unpleasant task, as usual, and retrieved the ropes that had been left on the first pitch above camp. He was not cheerful when he returned. More handholds and footholds had disappeared. Loose snow poured in at every opening in his clothes. He was surprised that he found the task so irritating. The demon that demanded of Barry efforts beyond those of his fellows had been placated on the summit push. He had not needed the extra work retrieving the ropes.

The foot of new snow had so transformed the mountain that it was as if we had been transported in our sleep to another place entirely. Before, there had been mountain after mountain, sky so deep it looked like ocean, cloud formations, flats, rivers, glaciers, all the colors of the spectrum, sunlight and shadow, and vast prospects. Now there was a gray-white hemisphere with a one-hundred-yard radius, sometimes contracting to six feet. Here and there the white was punctuated by the black of diminishing rock. It was a world devoid of color, form, or interest, except of course the interest in staying in it. The only sound not our own was the hush of falling snow. Strangest of all was the experience of knowing how high off the glacier we were but feeling like we were in the bottom of a pit.

All we could think about was the cache. Could we find it in the snow? Coming up, there had been one distinct ridge. Now there appeared to be dozens. Every little spur of thirty or forty feet looked like it might be the ridge. We soon lost track of how far we had descended from Balcony Camp, and our memory of how far the cache was below Balcony Camp had not been distinct to begin with. Jake was certain that he had planted the spare axe upright beside the cache—or almost certain. Weaving back and forth and then doggedly up and down the ridge, we pursued the cache. Every minute that passed made it less likely that it would be found, for the snow had accumulated to nearly two feet. A wind was stirring and soon there would be drifts. Finally we stopped to take stock at the place we all remembered, the spot where the traverse to the West Buttress would begin. The cache was "just" below. Barry and Jake went methodically down the ridge for one last try. Bill and I stayed so that the snow wouldn't swallow this place too. We maintained contact by shouting. Barry and Jake's voices got fainter and fainter until they could no longer be distinguished from the wind. Then I could hear only wind, whispering snow, and Bill munching on logan bread. Again, voices. I was unable to wait until they arrived to know. I yelled, "Did you find it?" "Yes," drifted softly up the ridge. Only the head of the axe had shown. The cache itself had not made so much as a bump in the snow.

We were young, strong, and proud of our resourcefulness. We probably wouldn't have perished without the cache. We later found part of another cache at Landing Camp. But Landing Camp was eight thousand feet below us, over terrain we hadn't seen, most of it glacier which had to be negotiated without snowshoes, and the first part of it unexplored by anyone. The traverse to the West Buttress in a whiteout promised to be excitement enough without the threat of starvation.

As we began the traverse, I felt as light as a pixie and wanted to run. Since I often couldn't see twenty feet, I confined my cavorting activities to an occasional hitch in my gait. It was like trying to skip while wearing hip boots and carrying a hod of bricks. After a bit it dawned on me that Barry, Bill, and Jake regarded this traverse as a nontrivial mountaineering problem.

When, three days earlier, we first looked at the traverse off the rib, we were delighted at how straightforward it was. To the left, that is, on the downslope side, there was a steep icefall. Above it, just about on our contour, there was a ramp which led through a crevassed area to the West Buttress Route. The mountain delivered everything that the photographs had promised.

In the whiteout, more blinding than fog or a ground blizzard, nothing was as we thought we remembered it. We moved in a darkness of white. In fog, ground or water provides contrast. In a ground blizzard, the wind is as reliable as a compass needle, and its pressure gives substance to your struggle. We were knee deep in powder snow lighter than the breezes that came from several directions. One would think that nothing could be easier than maintaining a course perpendicular to the fall line. But within our thirty-foot horizon, a bump would reverse the slope. Sometimes we didn't know which way was down.

Jake chastised himself for not remembering to bring a compass. No one ever used a compass in the Tetons. We recalled the famous tendency of lost people to circle, but we couldn't recall which way. We agreed that it was the same way as the Coriolis effect. One irony of our situation was that the leader saw least of all. It was one of the eeriest experiences I've had. To the left were crevasses. To the right were miles of imperceptibly sloping glacier. I was never sure whether I was carelessly thrashing about inches from a bottomless crevasse or gingerly tiptoeing across a solid snow plain the size of the Boeing parking lot.

Barry said that when he led each step felt like "a step into infinity." By mutual consent, we put Buckingham in front and kept him there. Once, while crossing a section between two small ridges running parallel across the glacier, we became convinced that both leader and belayer were between the lips of a huge crevasse. Bill later reported that he had never felt so alone and afraid. But he got us across. When we had about decided to stop where we were until we could see where that was, the whiteout thinned enough for us to catch a glimpse of the West Buttress. We scurried for it as the whiteout closed in again. When we reached the rock of the buttress we turned left and plunged down the glacier toward Windy Corner.

We found wands placed by an earlier party and we followed them until we descended out of the cloud. We could not depend entirely on the wands, for the glacier had changed since they had been placed. The glacier leveled out, comparatively, several hundred feet above Windy Corner; at the same place we came out of the bottom of the cloud we had been in for twenty-four hours. We took normal precautions against crevasses. In the warmth of sun this perhaps became routine: the rope was a little slack when Jake fell in a crevasse. He fell fifteen feet and hung from his waist loop, with forty pounds on his back. He hurt so bad that he thought he might have to let go of his pack or pass out. We needed all the gear in every pack. We managed to get a loop to him quickly, and Jake got out with only the loss of a parka and four rolls of film. In the next two hours, other bridges collapsed or were stepped through, but we did not let the rope get slack again. We had been reminded that we could become angels as easily in sunshine as in storm.

Windy Corner is a transition point. Above it you are on the mountain, below it you are not yet on or off the mountain, depending on which way you are heading. It was littered with expedition junk. Still, it was fun to go through the junk looking for relief from our now completely boring diet. I ate with relish C-ration jam I had refused to eat in the army.

We slept late the next morning then moved fast down to the broad snow plains of the main body of the Kahiltna. We had come to regard the fine weather as rightfully ours and the three days of snow as the only price we ought to pay for it. We were pleased, but not surprised, that we could move so easily on the glacier without our snowshoes. We had this mountain right where we wanted it. As we rolled on down the glacier, Jake suggested that Don Sheldon might take a scout-

MT. MCKINLEY (DENALI) FROM SOUTH
B: Base Camp
WC: Windy Corner
BD: Bogged Down

Photograph by Bradford Washburn, courtesy of the Museum of Science, Boston, Massachusetts.

ing flight to see where we were, and then, if he didn't see us, he would return on the appointed day a week hence. We convinced ourselves that Jake was right and that the next day, Monday the twenty-second, Sheldon would be out looking for us. I have forgotten how we made this fantasy plausible. I think the theory was that Sheldon would have flown out all his weekend sports and would just be dawdling around on Monday looking for something to do. We thought this in spite of the well-known fact that until November, Sheldon rested by napping while flying and while sitting on the toilet.

Ten miles down the Kahiltna from Windy Corner, we bogged down completely. We forgot that good weather meant melting snow.

I was leading in snow that got heavier and heavier until, suddenly, there was no resistance at all and I was in up to my shoulders. I was sure I was in a crevasse and was about to yell for tension on the rope when I felt solid snow under my forearm. I struggled onto it, thinking that I was being very cool. I marveled at Barry's rope handling: I hadn't felt a tug. While looking for a belay position, I went in again. Half crawling, half swimming, I struggled on, expecting to drop into the abyss.

Barry called, "Pete, have you got a tight rope!"

Did *I* have a tight rope? Who the hell was belaying whom! I looked back to see Barry going through the same antics I'd been going through. Jake and Bill were in danger of rupturing themselves with laughter.

We were there for the next three days. We found a hard part of the glacier big enough for our tents, but we had to belay each other out to take a crap. We did not inquire too closely about why this particular part of the glacier was hard. Someone had the bad manners to say that perhaps we were camped over a giant crevasse and cold air was circulating under us. All further speculation ceased.

The next day, we thought that we heard Sheldon fly over many times before we learned that some roars were from jets and some were from avalanches. The temperature stayed above freezing, so the falling snow penetrated our tents and dripped on our down bags.

On the morning of the twenty-fourth, I awoke to the sound of heavy snow flakes hitting the tent and water dropping on my sleeping bag. I was in the midst of a meditation about my warmth being robbed from me drop by drop when Barry called from the other tent to say that it looked like it would clear up. Bill and I were in the orange tent. In there, all light from outside looked like sunlight. We could imagine that it was clearing up any time we wanted to. But this time the dripping slowed, lightened, and then stopped. We both sighed with gratitude. If the sky would stay clear until midnight, the glacier would have a good chance of freezing.

By 2 A.M., although the glacier was not frozen, it was firmer, so we went. Conditions bettered gradually, and by 7 A.M., we had made our way to the pickup site.

It didn't take us long to find something else to worry about. We were low on food, lower on fuel. Without fuel we couldn't melt snow for water. A notion developed that because Sheldon hadn't materialized on the twenty-second, the day we had imagined he would arrive, it followed that he wouldn't materialize on the day he was supposed to arrive, the twenty-eighth. Jake spoke of what it would be like to travel forty miles down the Kahiltna to its snout. He used words like "five miles a day on a good day, if nobody got killed" and "ten crevasse rescues a day." Buckingham was impervious to such gloomy fantasies, and his good spirits never wavered. Most of the time I took Buckingham's view.

We were not seasoned expeditioners. When we had to contend with several days of enforced immobility, we survived, but not graciously. For example, two of my bosom buddies independently concluded that, regrettably, they would soon have to kill me because of the way I giggled over the book I was reading.

On the twenty-seventh we made an expedition across the glacier to the cache we had left two weeks earlier. The surface of the glacier had melted by an amazing thirty to forty feet. The part of the cache containing fuel had disappeared into a crevasse that had opened up under what we'd thought was solid moraine. The food, however, was intact.

Barry Corbet

MOUNTAINEERS BREITENBACH & SINCLAIR
To get away from tidal waves.

"The Great One"

"To the south face of Mount McKinley!"

With a clank of beer mugs, the four mountaineers tossed off a heady toast one night last summer and then sat down to plan their assault. They had picked a formidable foe: the continent's highest mountain, 20,320 ft. of rock, ice and swirling snow that Alaskan Indians call "the Great One." McKinley had been climbed 13 times since 1913, but never by the precipitous southern route, a feat considered the greatest pioneering climb remaining in North America.

Leader of the four was blond, slight Jake Breitenbach, 24, a guide at Wyoming's Petzoldt-Exum School of American Mountaineering. Like Jake, the others

TIME MAGAZINE, JULY 13, 1959

were young, but experienced beyond their years in their perilous art: Ski Instructors Pete Sinclair, 23, and Barry Corbet, 22; Math Teacher Bill Buckingham, 22, a member of the American Alpine Club.

Built-In Disposal. Last month, landed by a bush pilot on a glacier at 7,000 ft., the four began their long push—the kind of adventure that pales a plains dweller. At 12,500 ft., they labored nine hours to hack a 7-by-7-ft. platform from a 45° ice slope, wryly called it Concentration Camp, complete, as one climber noted, "with a handy garbage disposal —a 1,600-ft. drop." Ahead lay two deadly perils: a pair of giant, swelling domes of blue ice that left them as exposed to the fickle Alaskan weather as flies on a wall. Some 1,700 ft. of rope hammered into the ice took them across in safety. Then came Camp Paradise, the first piece of flat slope they had seen in several thousand feet; Camp Fatigue, when at 15,000 ft. the altitude started to hit them; Balcony Camp, up another 1,800 ft. and just big enough for their tent with a 7,000-ft. drop below. The weather started to worsen, and they decided on a gamble: a dash to the top, even though it was 3,500 ft. away.

Their dash made them look more like drunks in a conga line. In the thin air, no one could lurch more than 15 steps without rest. The final 400 ft. were up a near-vertical snow wall; somehow they made it, and there was the slender bamboo pole that had been planted on the summit in 1947 by Bradford Washburn, a mountain-climbing geographer. Three men burst into tears. "Do you realize," gasped Buckingham, "do you realize what we've done? Four hackers—we've made a great ascent, maybe the greatest outside of South America in the world."

Instinct Alone. It was not over. The weather, good for twelve days, burst with a snowstorm. All landmarks disappeared; at one point they were near panic at the thought of starvation when someone spotted the blade of an ice ax that Jake had whimsically stuck beside a food cache, a needle point of steel gleaming in an ocean of snow. On instinct alone, Buckingham found the snow corridor that threaded through a region splintered by crevasses. And finally back down to 7,000 ft., they were plucked from McKinley's flank by their pilot.

Why had they done it? Last week, resting in Anchorage, the four were almost too busy planning new assaults to answer. Said Sinclair: "We usually just joke, 'to get away from tidal waves.' You can't describe climbing to people. They don't have anything to compare it with."

The glacier hardened just before the morning sun hit it, giving us a paved strolling surface for our return to camp and allowing us to walk up to the edges of crevasses to peer into the blue/black depths. Several were huge, as much as a hundred yards from lip to lip. Of one, Buckingham remarked that an entire Teton glacier could drop into it and disappear from sight.

I was not sorry to see our emotional intensity dim in the evening of our expedition. We passed the time as we could. There was even a half-hearted attempt by Jake and Bill to climb a pile of rubble that rose to ten thousand feet. Not me, I didn't need an anticlimax.

All told, we spent one day out of three on the mountain in expectation of Sheldon. Years after the fact, from a safe distance of three thousand miles, I have wished that we had walked in and out.

Don arrived on the evening of the twenty-seventh and took Bill out first. Bill went first due in part to our tacit acknowledgement of his unwavering temperament and uniformly high level of performance. Barry was to go next in recognition of his position as the most powerful of us. Jake claimed last-to-go-out, as leader and because he had a love of being alone in the mountains that the rest of us didn't have. The last entry in my journal:

> TALKEETNA, SUNDAY, 28 JUNE 1959
> *The sweet sound of Sheldon's motor drifted over the glacier around 9* A.M. *I got a pleasant surprise when Sheldon said he wanted to take two of us. I crammed myself in back of the back seat and Barry climbed in front of me. We crowded what gear we could in and had an easy take-off. The weather was in the process of closing, so even if I had access to a window, I could not have seen anything. We landed to one of Mrs. Willett's famous breakfasts. Two and a half hours later, Jake came in and the expedition is officially a success. Right now we are enjoying the dreamed-of cigarettes and beer in the Fairview Hotel and listening to the fascinating conversation of Mr. Goro,* Life *photographer.*

CHAPTER 4
STAYING THERE

Fritz was in Alaska to photograph wildlife for an issue *Life* was doing to welcome Alaska to statehood. After meeting us, Fritz contacted Bill Smith, the *Time-Life* correspondent assigned to Alaska, and as a result, I got a job. Bill Smith interviewed us when we returned to Anchorage, did a story on us for the next issue of *Time,* and got Time, Inc., to develop our film. In addition to reporting, Bill was responsible for getting Fritz to where he needed to be to do his photographic essay on Alaskan wildlife. What Fritz needed was a guide, and he told Bill that he liked me. The standard pay was fifty dollars a day plus expenses while in the field. Would I be willing to do it for thirty-five dollars every day of the two months Fritz was to be in Alaska? That rate of pay was more than double the rate I'd been paid in the oil fields; I was willing.

Fritz was in his late fifties, regarded as somewhat demanding, was not an outdoorsman, was tough in the soul—we got along just fine. As we got to know each other while talking around campfires and in cafes, he told me about escaping from Nazi Germany in 1933. He had been an editor in Germany's second largest publishing house. He got out by first sending his family on a ski vacation to Switzerland and then, wearing ski clothes and carrying what portable wealth he could get together, boarding a midnight milk-run train that was not checked closely. He left Germany, his house, and his success as an editor forever.

In Paris, since he could no longer make a living as a craftsman of the German language, he learned to be a photographer. He learned quickly and was the second photographer to be hired by *Life.*

I also heard from Fritz that *Time* and *Life* photographers and writers learned to get stories past the desk of Henry Luce which would not have gotten past had Mr. Luce understood the full implications of their content. As an example he cited the picture in *Life* of a woman they called the Rat Lady. It was a photograph of a black woman who lived in the basement of a tenement, in Chicago, I believe. She was holding her child in her arms. I remembered the photograph. One of the baby's ears was disfigured. When Luce was shown the photo—he approved every photo that went into the magazine—his attention was not drawn to the child's ear, nor was he told that the disfigurement was the bite of a rat. That picture had a big influence on impending regulations of landlords. Fritz lived in a complicated world where he could best keep his integrity and express the truth by allowing his boss to deceive himself.

Fritz was demanding but his demands were not personal. They were imposed by the standard of his craftsmanship. "Photographers are not artists," he insisted, "but technicians." He was in more or less constant pain from bursitis. The pain made him sigh, but he only fretted about his equipment and his film. His procedures and routines were to be strictly followed, and I did my best because I guessed that by this apparent compulsiveness he kept his imagination unfettered by trivia, a good thing, I thought, even for technicians. Besides, Fritz was my elder.

From the time I was age six until I was age ten, the time of World War II, I had almost no contact with adult men. When I did have contact with my father and other males again, I paid close attention to how they thought and, when there was opportunity, to how they worked.

When I was fifteen years old, I worked for O'Connor Brothers, Contractors. They hired me to work with their uncle, George O'Connor, who was seventy-two years old. George had been selectman of the town for three decades. Knowing how to build and maintain roads was the vital qualification for that office. We did yard, farm, estate, and road work. I was hired mainly to humor him. As I soon discovered, the reason no one else wanted to work with Old George was that no one was accustomed to working as hard as he worked. George knew how to work with horses and hand tools. There were no more horses, so we worked with hand tools. George let me know that he wouldn't think much of me if I turned out to be stupid. He didn't like to repeat himself and reminded me if it was the second time he was telling me how to do a particular thing. I learned to become very attentive to both what he said and what he left unsaid. We got the jobs that were too insignificant for bulldozers, tractors, and steam shovels. George was a genius with block and tackle and levers—using small tools to do heavy work. If you did things George's way, the work was not easy but it was possible. I think he'd gotten cleverer as he grew older and his strength failed but his standards didn't. We worked an extra fifteen minutes every day. We did this because it took him eight hours and fifteen minutes at age seventy-two to do the work he did in eight hours at age fifty. Other boys my age got to drive dump trucks, tractors, and bulldozers. I didn't get to do that, but I learned another thing of importance.

At eight o'clock one morning, George drove us in his 1929 Ford pickup to a granite boulder three feet high and seven feet in diameter at the base. This rock had to be removed. The company bulldozer was broken. My heart sank when I saw how big the boulder was. I went to the back of the truck to get prying bars, picks, shovels, and sledgehammers. George chuckled. "You won't get it with those," he said. From the seat of the pickup he took a little canvas bag with pieces of iron in it. Then he selected two three-pound hammers from the tool box in the back of the truck. "Sit ye down a bit," George said, filling his pipe and pondering the rock. He took from his pocket a match and a piece of chalk. He lit his pipe with the match and, with the chalk, made several X's to mark spots for us to drill holes by hand with hammer and drill bit. After a coffee break, he filled his pipe again and directed me to drill one more hole while he put bits of iron, two wedges and a pin, in each of the holes we had drilled. Then we tapped each pin according to a certain sequence, and the boulder fell into pieces small enough to carry by hand. We stacked the pieces on a nearby stone wall and ate lunch at the site of the next job. I've been trying to recapture that experience ever since. Old guys know some surprising things, which, if you pay attention, they might teach you. I did not find Fritz's demands unreasonable.

Our first trip was to Mt. McKinley National Park for the census of the caribou migration by Dr. Adolph Murie. I had the impression that Ade would have preferred to pursue his work without us. It was here that Fritz began to downplay his credentials as a *Life* photographer and to put me forward as the young man who had just climbed a new route on Mt. McKinley. Mention of the climb was enough to start a conversation, and, once thawed, Ade Murie was a fascinating man to talk to. Later, Fritz told me that he had worked with other naturalists but had not met one who so completely dissolved his ego in his work. Ade seemed to have no personal agenda. He told us how he had lain on the tundra without a sleeping bag for thirty hours watching a wolf den because he unexpectedly got a chance to confirm his belief that female wolves will babysit for each other. It wasn't easy to get him to tell us about his work because he wanted us to talk about the world outside. Yards of bookshelves lined the walls of his cabin. Among the venerable old works glistened the dust covers of the latest books. He must have had a standing order for the nonfiction best-seller list.

Ade treated us as experts about the unnatural world, and we were embarrassed to find that our curiosity about either world did not match his. He was at odds with his employers, the National Park Service, because he was opposed to their effort to sell the wilderness as popular entertainment, which also may be why he did not like the presence of *Life* magazine. He was too good a man, however, to hold us responsible as individuals for forces he knew neither we nor he could stop.

I was not a great success during my first true test as a guide. We'd talked to Ade about what to do if we ran into a grizzly. He told us that grizzlies preferred, in general, to get away from humans but vied with moose for being the least predictable of animals. They were so timid that they easily felt threatened and forced to defend themselves, which, to a grizzly, meant attacking and driving away or destroying the intruder, whichever was handier. When he thought it prudent to quickly leave a grizzly alone, Ade always left behind something with his scent on it. He showed us a pack a grizzly had torn up. If we got out of sight, Ade told us, the bear would quickly lose interest in the attack. I should have asked for more information. In particular, I should have checked out what I thought I already knew about bears.

We drove through the park to look for Dall sheep and came upon a grizzly hunting for ground squirrels and roots near the road. There were people taking pictures of him; it looked like a scene from Yellowstone Park, so we continued on. We didn't have any luck with the sheep. In fact, we hadn't gotten a single good picture since we'd been in the park. When we got back to the grizzly, we decided to try for a good picture, even if it was a bear picture. The day was clear, our first, and Mt. McKinley was in the background. The bear had moved off from the road toward the mountain. The people were gone. He was in a shallow valley about a mile wide. If we got down low in the valley in the right position, we could get a shot of the bear, backdropped by the mountain, with Fritz's big telescopic lens. We wouldn't be very near the bear. The mountain in the background would be foreshortened so Denali would appear to rise up from a quarter of a mile behind the bear. The wind came from abeam of a line between us and the bear, and we could stay downwind until we got into position. Then, if the wind backed, we might get the shot and get out of there while the bear was deciding whether to eat us or just maul us. Or something. It seems such a dumb idea now that I can't remember what I had in mind, except to try to think like a person being paid thirty-five dollars a day and all expenses to be a guide in Alaska.

We loaded up with cameras and tripod and started out. There was nothing but low tundra between us and the bear. The wind moved aft of the beam not long after we started, not enough to bring our scent to him but enough to make me want to bear off. I moistened my palms and held them out to keep track of the wind. The bear appeared not to notice us. I had the notion that bears were shortsighted. He meandered toward the foothills on the other side of the valley, stopping now and then to root in the tundra. Although he didn't appear to be in a hurry, we had to trot from time to time to close on him. He reached the first hill, which was about two hundred feet high, and climbed up. This was perfect. If we could get to the top of the hill while he was still on the skyline, we'd get a good shot of the mountain. Maybe we'd only have to peek over the crest.

When we got to the plateau at the top of the hill, he wasn't there. To our left the hill sloped down gradually to a cliff band which fell into a stream bed. At the far end of the cliff a ravine cut back across our path at a right angle from the stream. There was a small grove of trees on the next hill beyond the ravine. If the bear had continued in the same direction he had been going, he'd be in the ravine. There went our shot of the mountain, but maybe we could catch him in the ravine and use a bush at our edge of the ravine as a blind. We were halfway across the crest of the plateau when the grizzly emerged across the ravine, turned in our direction, lay down, and stared at us.

There's a world of difference between looking at a nearsighted grizzly's retreating back and looking at the head and shoulders of a grizzly facing you. The bear was not surprised to see us. He'd not only seen us all along, he'd led us here. He lay in the sun swinging his head lackadaisically and glancing at us now and then.

Fritz, who had not been at all enthusiastic about chasing a bear across the tundra, was now very excited about the picture. He wanted to move up to the edge of the ravine. Nothing doing, I said. I was not taking one more step toward that ravine. You didn't have to be a bear expert to see that we were already on his property and that the ravine was his front door. Fritz would have to get his shot from where we were. He needed the tripod. I set a personal record in getting it out of the pack and set up. It seemed to me that Fritz was taking an eternity to get ready. Finally, he started shooting. The grizzly stood up. I didn't like that. The grizzly swung his head from side to side determinedly and then lifted his nose into the air to sniff. I liked that even less.

Fritz was making exclamations of delight. "Look at that! Vonderful! Vonderful!"

"Fritz," I said, "we've got to get out of here."

"Just a minute."

The bear moved toward the lip of the ravine.

"He's coming towards us, Fritz."

"Good, I'll focus on this edge of the ravine."

The man was absolutely fearless while looking through the viewfinder of a camera. The bear disappeared into the gully.

"Fritz, we're leaving!"

I pulled him away from the camera; we'd leave it for scent. Fritz resisted. It was at least a hundred yards to a place where we could get out of sight. I grabbed Fritz's Abercrombie and Fitch duckhunter's hat and threw it on the ground behind the camera in case the camera didn't have enough scent. That broke the spell the viewfinder had put Fritz under, and we started to run. I looked over my shoulder. The bear had already crossed the ravine. He was in the air when I last saw him.

"To the cliff band," I yelled at Fritz and then stretched my legs in an earnest effort to convince the bear that he had driven us away. The hairs above my collar alerted themselves to hot bear's breath. I was almost to the cliff band when Fritz called to me. I was terrified. Had the bear reached him? No, he was saying in a heavy German accent, "Dun vrun avay vrum me!"

I stopped, feeling both ashamed and angry.

"Come on! Run!" I yelled. He seemed to be out for a jog in Central Park. I reached into my pocket for my jackknife, feeling foolish as hell.

"Please, God, don't make me fight that bear!" There wasn't even a rock or a stick nearby. I knew I couldn't make myself go back and attack the bear. I also knew I ought to. The only thing I could think of was to try to draw the bear toward me instead of Fritz and beat it to the cliff band. With that thought, I found courage enough to look left toward the bear.

He was nowhere to be seen. I looked toward his grove of trees just in time to see him disappearing over the hill behind them. He could have caught us twice if he'd wanted to.

Fritz came up and said accusingly, "You ran away from me."

I wanted to say that I had run away from the bear, but I didn't. There was a chance that I could have gotten away from the bear but no chance that Fritz could have. He was in charge of taking pictures, and I was supposed to be in charge of the Alaskan wilds. It appeared that I was also in charge of being afraid. In the future we'd avoid situations where it would be dangerous for Fritz to go into his trance behind the camera.

When we got back to our car, there was another car and a couple waiting there.

"Were you the men looking at the bear?" they asked. "We took movies of you. The bear came toward you and then turned around and ran away from you as fast as he could go. It was funny to see you both running from each other in opposite directions. Probably it wasn't funny to you, but it was funny."

We laughed with them, "Heh, heh." Luckily, they only had an 8-mm camera.

When we saw Ade that evening, I said, "What's this about bears not being able to see very well? That bear must have seen us at least a mile away."

"Oh, they can see something moving as far as you can. It's not that they can't see, it's that they don't identify by sight but by smell. They don't know what they're seeing until they get the scent. He must have come over to see what you were and then ran when he got your scent."

Thank God for the obnoxious odor of man.

We shifted from Mt. McKinley National Park to the Chugach Range and from rented car to horse in order to search for sheep. By float plane we pursued trumpeter swans and moose on the Kenai Peninsula, arctic landscapes and tundra flowers on the north slope of the Brooks Range, and brown bear catching salmon on the McNeil River. Our last excursion was by fishing boat to Round Island in Bristol Bay, where we photographed basking bachelor walrus. However, wherever we went, one predator ruled the North Country, the merciless mosquito. On the North Slope, the mosquitoes landed on the camera lens in numbers such that Fritz had me brush my hat across the lens on three while he opened the shutter on four.

Summer didn't last long on the North Slope. The ice went off the lakes the week before we landed. We stayed there a week. The lakes froze again the following week. There were alpine flowers in bloom, spring and autumn flowers blooming at the same time. I wrote in my journal:

> JULY 22, BETTLES, ALASKA
> *At Shrader Lake we camped with a group from the Union and Ohio Oil Companies who were doing geological mapping. The oil prospectors are replacing the gold prospectors. History will assign both an important place in the development of this magnificent state.*

The gods grant in earnest what we ask for in jest. I thought the geologists were important because they brought money to the people who fed them and transported them, and I thought that was as good a way as any to use the tax relief the oil companies got. In Anchorage, I met Ray Smith, who was the head of oil exploration for Union Oil in Alaska. I remarked that we hadn't found any place in the Alaskan wilderness where there weren't oil company geologists. I asked him if Alaska was going to look like Oklahoma someday. He assured me not: "It would take a find as big as the Colorado fields for it to be worth it."

I wanted to stay in Alaska through the summer, so Bill and Fritz arranged for me to get a job interview with the U.S. Fish and Wildlife Service. When Fritz went back to New York, I went back to the Kenai as a game warden. I didn't catch anybody, but I tried. There was a way of doing the job that could get you killed and a way of doing it so that the local people would help you out now and then. It was important to know the difference between people who hunted for meat and what my supervisor called "Anchorage hunters." He did not suggest selective enforcement; if I caught a local red-handed, I'd have to take him in. The trick was to be in a position whereby a local, if caught, would know that I hadn't been after him, that he got caught because he'd done something stupid, and would blame himself and not me. The way to do this was to have a routine which the locals would know and strangers would not. The most effective thing I could do was to be seen a lot in all parts of my territory, an area of about one hundred by fifty miles. As I say, I didn't catch anybody.

One day, I met a man in Hope, Alaska, who recognized me from the pictures that had been in the Anchorage newspapers three months before. You have to look hard at a picture to do that. He was what I had come to think of as the typical Alaskan. He had a beautiful house which he had built himself over many years. He lived by doing a little fishing, hunting, farming, and working at whatever anybody was paying cash to have done. He was not identifiable by occupation or even by lifestyle but by a place and an attitude toward that place. He had a particular reason for talking to me. It wasn't to talk to a newspaper celebrity; he wanted to climb Denali. Would I guide him? He'd pay me a thousand dollars if I gave him a little time to raise it. Or would I tell him who would guide him? I was surprised. After I asked him why he wanted to climb the mountain, I realized that he was wondering how I, of all people, could ask such a dumb question. He turned to look over Cook Inlet, and said, "I've been looking at it for a long time." There, foreshortened and magnified in the clear, cold, subarctic autumn air, rising out of the Douglas fir, Alaska cedar, and Sitka spruce along the opposite shore, dominating land and sky, white with new snow, was Denali. I'd seen it in photographs; I'd seen the ice gully, Balcony Camp, and the summit. Now, in Hope, I saw the mountain as viewed by Alaskans for whom it was the image of that to which they aspire.

CHAPTER 5

SOUTH

When I got back to Jackson's Hole at the end of September, the climbing season had ended. At Jenny Lake, the guides and the climbing rangers were packing up. The big news of the season was that something new was entering the climbing world, unattached women. This was a welcome development but a troublesome one too. Semivoluntary celibacy had meant an absence of personal rivalries among climbers heated by the madness of love.

In the Tetons was a climber I had heard of but not met, Gary Hemming. Gary, a Californian, had been working in New York as a private detective and climbing in the Shawangunks. He was one of the first to create interest in each other between the top rock climbers of the East and the California rock climbers of Tahquitz and Yosemite.

Hemming had many close friends who loved him but no close friends, that I know of, who were entirely comfortable with him. Gary was big, rawboned tough, and light-haired and had uncannily blue eyes. His most arresting physical feature was his grin. It combined the innocence of a friendly, lively eight-year-old boy and the cynicism of an old satyr who has seen it all. He was reckless with his passions, had an insatiable appetite for what he (and I) called life, and an alarming capacity for suffering. He was an exhausting friend. When drunk or subjected to sustained periods of frustration, he could fall into a violent rage that was frightening even though he seemed always to not hurt but get hurt.

Gary and I didn't warm to each other for a couple of days, because, I think, he was a little embarrassed by his predicament. In New York, Gary had met and fallen in love with Judith. Then, as had many a man (and woman) before him, he had succumbed to the Pygmalion impulse. Gary felt that Judith, raised in the East, needed to experience life more intensely. By that he meant she should get to know climbers and their mountains. So he sent her west to the Tetons. He didn't come with her, which isn't as silly as it sounds. He had placed her in the care of Bill Briggs—another dropout climber from Dartmouth, a folksinger, and, he frequently complained, a celibate. He was not the only one. Once you became a serious climber, you would likely be celibate. Briggs had become a serious climber early. His celibacy was of interest to us because he was a year or two older and provided a measure of our probable term of abstinence. Gary didn't know about the influx that year of young women into the Tetons climbing scene, among them a woman who had straightened Briggs out before Judith arrived. Hemming, upon hearing disturbing rumors about Briggs's guardianship, arrived in Jackson a few days before me. The day before I arrived, the young woman, who had not given Briggs up to Judith happily, gave Hemming a detailed description of how dumb he was for having sent Judith west, finishing with a vivid account of Bill's prowess as a lover. Gary had a lot of things on his mind when we met.

Briggs and Bob Coltman, a folksinger from Dartmouth, had left the Tetons to travel around picking up folk songs. Judith had gone with them.

Still in the Tetons were Carlos Plummer, the first in several years of the serious Dartmouth climbers who had not dropped out, and Sterling Neale, who had been my main climbing partner when I first came to the Tetons. Sterling and Carlos were climbing partners at Dartmouth when I was there in the fall of 1958 and not only had got me back into the Dartmouth climbing scene after my hitch in the army but also had wined and dined me several times when I was living on the food I lifted from hospital trays. Carlos had grown up in Mexico and was going to visit his mother in Mexico City. Sterling was going with him, as was Chief Dunnigan, a climbing ranger. Briggs and company were to include a stop in Mexico City in their itinerary. This was a fact of great interest to Hemming. There was to be some climbing on Mexican volcanoes, which interested me. More interesting to me was the prospect of going south. Acapulco was a possible destination. I hadn't experienced a month without snow in a year, and there was a chunk of ice in the core of my soul which I felt only a week on a warm beach could melt. A snowstorm was brewing over the Tetons, over all the Rockies in fact, and when I considered that it would be nine months before it would be warm again in Jackson, I decided to blow the money I had saved in Alaska on a trip south.

So, Gary and I were included in the trek to Mexico. We began by going to Boulder, Colorado, just in time for the largest early snowstorm in memory. We were skiing in Colorado on October 4. We had two cars, Chief's small station wagon and Sterling's VW bus with two bunks in the back, and both ski equipment and climbing gear. When we left Boulder, we traveled around the clock until we got to El Paso.

Once we were in Mexico a good-natured squabble arose about the pace at which the expedition should proceed. Hemming and Chief wanted a leisurely pace, so they could "get to know the people." Carlos wanted to get to his home in Mexico City. Since it was hard for Carlos to make his case on other than personal grounds, Chief and Hemming won. Getting to know the people meant that we would arrive at a fairly large town like Ciudad Juarez, Torreon, or San Luis Potosi at about nine in the evening, locate a place to eat that tourists didn't frequent, find where people—again not tourists—were drinking, and find the red light district late in the evening. We weren't much interested in using the red light district, just in being there "with the people." We were like a bunch of college kids away from home for the first time, but it worked. We spent five to eight hours every night conversing with Mexicans who did not speak English. I had some Spanish vocabulary; Carlos knew more of course. (But upon crossing into Mexico, after giving us a lecture about how not to behave as American tourists, Carlos then announced that he was not perfectly fluent in Spanish. He had misspent his youth trying to not learn Spanish while growing up in Mexico.) In every town, we found at least one man who had worked in the U.S. as a migrant laborer and wanted to practice his English. His friends would be proud of him. As he said the English words, his friends watched his lips with half smiles on theirs. When we caught what he was saying and showed it by excitedly repeating it, bobbing our heads, the half smiles of his friends turned into proud grins.

Our efforts to learn the language must have been welcome because we were never the first ones to buy a drink. In San Luis Potosi we fell in with some miners, one of whom insisted on buying all of us drinks. I felt certain that two rounds cost him a day's pay in the mines and asked Carlos about it. He agreed. I asked if we shouldn't try harder to refuse. Carlos said no, it would be an insult because it would imply that the man was showing off rather than expressing friendship. The man was obviously pleased to have this opportunity, and we should enjoy it too. So, I put aside thoughts of starving wife and children and of my New England heritage, as much as I could, and worked on trilling my rr's as I yelled *arriba* in the requisite loud and long falsetto that had scared the wits out of me when I first heard it but which I now aspired to master.

Hemming was our chief asset. Carlos, Dunnigan, Sterling, and I still looked like college kids, but Hemming was obviously a Viking. His company was like gold—valuable, but a burden. He had an amazing ability to alter his appearance to suit his mood. One of his upper incisors was a partial plate. He removed it to leave a black hole in the front of his mouth, vowing not to restore it until he got Judith back. He had a tiny straw hat that he'd made more ridiculous by sticking an artificial flower in the brim. The hat and flower had some connection to Judith that he wouldn't reveal to us. I suspect that there are a half-dozen to a dozen women in the world who imagine that they understood him, and perhaps they did, but he was to us a complexity of forces: great strength and courage, great capacity for warmth and loyalty, great pride, great wrath, and great suffering.

Hemming became my assignment. He talked to me for hours about the pain of his love, of course, but we also talked about what we wanted from life or rather about what I wanted and Hemming was going to demand. We were more specific about what we were not going to do than about what we were going to do. We weren't going to go through life looking respectable and feeling lousy. We weren't going to work hard and obey orders with no purpose other than becoming an American consumer. We weren't going to be managed or managers. Our notion of hell was working for the Cosmodemonic Telegraph Company.[1] We wanted excitement, risk, and a big goal. For the present, that meant a tough route on a mountain.

Because I was Gary's confidant, it became my duty, for example, to tell him that he couldn't have a whore in San Luis Potosi. The night life district in San Luis Potosi was in a walled-off section of town, a kind of a fort, with one entrance and armed guards. As we entered, we were searched for weapons, and our pocketknives were taken from us. We decided that this was not a good place to get into trouble. We could get into trouble if Hemming had a girl because he could postpone ejaculation practically indefinitely, a heroic virtue in some contexts but to a girl who expects to earn her money in five minutes, exploitation. Hemming always stipulated that ejaculation had to occur or he would get his money back, and the girls always too confidently agreed. I wouldn't dream of telling Hemming what to do, but, in moments when he was willing to negotiate his

---

[1] I introduced Hemming to Henry Miller's *Tropic of Cancer* and *Tropic of Capricorn,* which were at that time banned in the United States. We bought pirated editions in Mexico City and smuggled them into the United States. Gary had just come from New York; he later, as did Miller, went to France.

mood, I was sometimes able to get him in an amused rather than aggrieved state of mind.

Carlos said more than once that Mexico was not a good place in which to get the attention of the authorities. One afternoon, we stopped at the square of a large village to stretch and exercise our legs. Soon after we started our stroll, a truck with half a dozen soldiers in back stopped a bit ahead of us on the other side of the street. They got out of the truck and picked people out of the passersby, apparently at random, and put them in the truck. We saw them take one man who had a young boy with him. The man didn't protest, but the boy did and was waved off by the soldiers. The boy continued along the street, just barely not crying.

When we later asked Carlos what was going on, he replied, "Who knows? It's election time."

"Can they just do that?" protested Dunnigan.

Carlos assured him that they could.

That same night, further south in the interesting part of Ciudad Torreon, my diplomacy with Hemming nearly got us into war.

Hemming was in a foul mood after the first beer in a small and very crowded bar. He refused to talk to me and seemed to enjoy being mad, so I went away and left him alone. After about an hour, he wore his warning smile, a wicked grin that, if it were words, would say, "This all seems very cheery to you now, I know, but I'm not having any fun and any minute now you won't be either." The rest of us held a conference. I was to rejoin Hemming and talk to him while Carlos persuaded the bartender to slip two seconal from our first-aid kit into his beer. It works in the movies.

I think Hemming saw the potions in his beer and pretended he didn't. He took a sip and whirled the glass like a discus thrower, spraying beer throughout the entire room, then smashed the glass into the wall and stomped out. For his next trick, he faced the crowd that followed him outside, held up three fingers, and yelled to the bartender, "Three! Any tres! You say them. I fight any three!" It was time for the phase of the plan which called for all four of us to throw a blanket over him, tie him up with a climbing rope, load him in the bus, and get out of there. We'd have to take our lumps when we let him go, but we'd avoid a riot.

We'd got the rope and blanket as Hemming challenged his grinning admirers. We jumped him and began noticing flaws in our plan. Hemming had the strength of three of us. He was being careful not to hurt us, I noticed, but he could easily change his mind. What had not been such a good idea to begin with began to look like an extremely bad idea when the very Mexicans Hemming wanted to fight started to side with him.

"Que pasa? You Amigo? Is not he your friend?" they asked.

"Si! Si! Es borracho! Es un poco loco!" I explained as I tried to pin Gary's right arm long enough for Chief to pass a hitch around it.

They kept saying, "What are you doing? Isn't he your friend?" A roomful of them were about to jump us when someone yelled, "Soldiers!" I looked down the block and saw what I imagined to be a platoon of soldiers in formation, on the double, with carbines at port arms. I yelled, "Soldiers, soldiers," into Hemming's ear, and he stopped struggling long enough for us to get him in the bus. Dunnigan, with wonderful timing, had a flat tire. We left anyway.

We stopped a couple of blocks away to fix the tire and discovered that Hemming had lost his hat in the fracas. Gary could not stand more than one trouble at a time. We had to get his hat. Sterling and Chief volunteered to go back for it, but when they got there, there were soldiers everywhere. Gary lost his fighting spirit and became despondent. We liked it better when he wanted to fight. Outside of the city, he leaped from the bus and ran into a cornfield. We could hear him crying in the night. He appeared the next morning smiling slightly sheepishly, and we continued on toward Mexico City and the anticipated rendezvous with Briggs and Judith.

Mrs. Plummer took us into her household without reservations. In spite of her full schedule as a dance teacher, she worked out an itinerary which introduced us to most of the major works of man in Mexico City—recent, historical, and prehistorical. It didn't take her long to sense that something was chewing at Gary and to find out about the impending confrontation. By keeping us busy and especially by engaging Gary's boyish curiosity in the wonders of Mexico City, she often rescued him from morbid concentration on his miseries. The first week went well.

Carlos was of the opinion that our main business in Mexico was to climb the volcanoes Ixtaccihuatl and Orizaba. However, I still had a cold spot down in my gut—which is pretty amazing when you think of everything that was going on down there—and Chief and Gary wanted to see more of Mexico. Acapulco seemed like the place to be. Gary, Chief, and I left for Acapulco a couple of days ahead of Sterling and Carlos to give the Plummer household some relief. After all, it wasn't Mrs. Plummer's idea that we all come to Mexico.

The descent to sea level from Mexico City brought us into terrain and atmosphere that were tropical. The air got hotter and more humid until, by the time we arrived in Acapulco, our breathing had become conscious. We slept near the beach the night we arrived and found a small hotel, really a rooming house, in the city the next day. It was in a tidy, lower middle-class, residential part of the city, and the hotelkeeper was a courteous, dignified gentleman, perhaps a retired civil servant. The warm water melted the cold spot in my soul and soon drained us of our northern busyness.

I livened up on one occasion. There had been a shark incident just before we arrived, which I knew about but didn't think much about until I cut myself while trying to land on a barnacle-encrusted rock in a three-foot swell. I sat on the rock thinking about sharks. The longer I sat bleeding, the more I thought. Chief and Gary helped me think. They said that, in all fairness, I should let them get to shore before I dove in and started trailing blood through the water. When they headed for shore, I waited as long as I could stand it. Then, upon noticing my blood running off the rock and into the water, attracting sharks all the way from the Galapagos I imagined, I dove into the water and made for shore with bad form but great energy.

As was our custom, we located the night life part of town. This was not easy because, when asked for directions, people thought we were trying to find the Acapulco Hilton and its pink jeeps. But we had developed a sense of how a Mexican town organizes itself and ferreted out the part of town we knew had to be there someplace. It was the liveliest such district we'd seen. It was, in fact, a little village within the town and maybe older than the town. During the course of our evening Spanish lessons, Gary became enamored of a girl who was somewhere between fourteen and seventeen years old and somewhere between six and eight months pregnant. He wanted to take her back to the hotel. She would go only if her two friends could come along. Hemming implored and Chief and I gave in, with the understanding that our girls would receive a reduced honorarium since it was to be for us a strictly social occasion. Chief and I would share one of our hotel rooms, and Gary would have the other to himself.

We entered the hotel and our rooms with stealth, suspecting that our landlord would not approve. The most entertaining part of the evening for Chief and I was watching the girls exclaim over the tiled bathroom and express delight at being offered a shower. Gary and friend retired early and got up late, which created for us a tactical problem. Chief and I got our guests out of the room before dawn. But not unobserved. The landlord lectured us sternly upon our return at 6 A.M. His was a respectable house, and we had not behaved like good guests. His tone couldn't have been better designed to smite our consciences. He was not angry with us, but saddened by the lack of respect we had shown him. We felt like the typical, crude, insensitive, American tourists we had been trying to avoid becoming. We apologized profusely and then went upstairs to figure out what to do about Gary and his girl. The landlord's chair on the front porch was by the front door, positioned so that he could see the street, the inside stairway, and the upstairs landing.

That effectively not only blocked the back entrance; it kept Gary and the girl pinned in their room across the hall from us.

At eight o'clock, the landlord still hadn't moved. Our room let onto balconies at both the front and the back of the house. Gary's room let onto the balcony only at the front of the house. The balcony in the front was not continuous but the railing was. There was a stretch of eight feet of blank wall between his balcony and ours, crossed by the iron balcony railing that continued along the wall between the two balconies. This stretch was directly overhead of the landlord, but if he stayed in his chair at the back of the porch, he would not see someone climbing along the railing. We had to try it. We just couldn't face the landlord again. So, pregnant and in high heels and crinolined dress, the girl made the traverse, Gary steadying her from behind, Chief and I reaching across to her. She crossed ten feet above the landlord, who at least pretended he didn't hear her. Now what? Lower the girl on a climbing rope from the back balcony. There were problems. A woman was doing her wash on the roof in back of us. When she finished, a man emerged onto the back balcony from the room behind Gary's room. He paced back and forth brooding. It seemed as if he'd never get his mind cleared. Once he went in only to reappear just as we were about to step onto the balcony. Finally the coast was clear, except for faces that appeared from time to time at windows in the neighborhood. When we got the girl to the ground, a dozen people appeared in windows and on rooftops up and down the alley and gave us a cheer. Later that day Ster and Carlos arrived. Once they got within the neighborhood of our house, they found us easily. "Oh, yes, the three North Americans with the girls! One block east and two blocks south."

On the way down to Acapulco, we had seen a huge waterfall halfway up a forested mountainside. On the way back to Mexico City, we decided to hike to it. To our surprise, once we entered the forest, we found it crisscrossed with well-worn trails. We came to a village of indeterminate size. Perhaps a hundred people, perhaps several hundred, lived dispersed among the trees in houses with gardens. There was no road leading to the village. Right in its center was a large church fallen into disrepair. We wondered how its great stones and timbers had been transported. One door, weighing five hundred pounds minimum, hung permanently open because the fastenings of the top hinge had loosened from the frame. But the church was obviously still used, though there probably had been no priest in the village since 1928. Communication with the villagers was difficult. The problem was in finding, not someone who spoke English, but someone who spoke Spanish. Most of the people spoke their aboriginal tongue. With the aid of sign language, we finally made someone understand that we were trying to find the waterfall. We understood from them that there was a man who was a guide to the waterfall. We were beginning to have to worry about money and tried to get a price estimate, but were not successful. The people kept shaking their heads. After a bit the guide appeared. He was somewhere between forty and sixty years old, shy, and intelligent looking. We felt that he wouldn't take us too badly and asked him to lead us to the waterfall. He led us up through the forest to a large gravel road that, he told us smilingly, began not at but near a town and led into the forest and stopped. There were no tracks on the road. It had been built by hand and might never see motorized, wheeled vehicles. Across the road we came to a graded and carefully maintained trail. In steeper parts of the trail, there were stone-paved steps. At every switchback there was a little station with an icon to the Virgin. Eventually, we understood that our guide had spent twenty years building this trail himself. It was his life's work. He did not work for the government; he received no pay; he worked "for the Virgin." At the top of the trail, there was an amphitheater overlooking the pool at the base of the waterfall. We were two hundred feet above the basin, but, even so, there was a fine spray in the air, with rainbows coming and going in the forest-filtered light. In front of the amphitheater was an altar. The altar and amphitheater were constructed of the trees felled to make the clearing for the amphitheater. It was an astonishing and humbling experience. Gary scarcely took his eyes off our guide. Me either. This was a man worth knowing about. We were in the presence of a saint, compound European Catholic, Aztec pyramid builder, and forest Indian. When we returned to the village and asked our guide about his fee, he was offended. He kept saying, "For the Virgin." Shamed again, rich gringos grasping their money. We finally got him to take some money by holding it out to him and repeating, "For the Virgin." Perhaps he could pay a priest to say a mass in his forest cathedral, perhaps he would buy a tool. He told us that before he died he wanted to pave the whole trail with stones. I hope to go back there some day.

Another reason for returning to Mexico would be for the bullfights. I had read *Death In The Afternoon* and was prepared to not find bullfighting repulsive. Watching the bullfights turned out to be also a religious experience, but a quite different one from the Saint of the Waterfall. There we had seen man's capacity for devotion, humility, a reverence for life growing out of worship of Mother Earth and the Mother of God. It is not reverence for life that the bullfight celebrates but a passion for life and a kind of pride in one's mortality. Death threatens, the force behind the searching horns a hundred times greater than the puny blow required to kill a man. The man dances and the cape swirls gracefully and death thunders past. The man fears the bull, but, if the bull is good and the man is good, they are mortally bound. The one dies certainly now, the other certainly later and perhaps now. The bull has over the man great strength, speed, and an implacable desire to kill. The man has sword, cape, a plan, and a fierce desire to live, to live beautifully and artfully before he dies. The one great advantage that the bullfighter has over the bull is that whereas the bull thinks only of the death of the bullfighter and does not consider his own, the bullfighter, by the ceremony of the bullfight, has in mind and tells with his body the story of the death of them both.

There were wonderfully beautiful women at the bullfights, and that seemed important. The icons of the Virgin at the waterfall, the beautiful women in their shawls at the bullfights, the mysterious Judith ever in our thoughts—were our adventures those of the male band off on a hunt or a patrol or were we a band of boys playing just out of sight of our distant but still watchful mothers?

Carlos's mother, with genteel discretion, checked in with Gary once in a while. Gary knew that Mrs. Plummer wished to help him if she could, and he responded with his best courtly manner. But with Gary it was more than company manners. I think women liked Gary less for his looks or the challenge than because he was genuinely interested in women, each one.

Finally, the big day: Bill, Judith, and Bob arrived. Hemming had a staged scene worked out. After Bill called asking for directions to the house, Gary assigned us positions in the entry hall and living room for their arrival. When the wave of hellos subsided, but with the trio still just inside the entryway, Gary emerged from the hallway leading from the back of the house. This was effective. Bill's doubletake was quite visible. Judith dropped her eyes and bent her head in the Madonna pose. Gary told me some years later that he always respected the way Briggs handled that scene. "He knew I could break him in half and that I might, yet he stood up to me." Then the negotiations began, and they seemed endless: Bill and Gary, Gary and Judith, Judith and Bill. Whenever Judith and Bill would go off to talk things over, Gary would torture himself with visions of them lying under a bush someplace. "I'd like to catch them both and impale them with an ice axe." I pointed out to Gary that we were near the center of Mexico City and it was miles to the nearest suitable bush. Then Gary began timing their absences.

It finally came down to an agreement that Judith would take a bus home, but she would first accompany us to the base of the climb of Orizaba. (We had already climbed Ixtaccihuatl shortly after returning from Acapulco.)

The Orizaba climb was an example of the results of the complex negotiations Gary and Bill had been working out. Gary, Sterling, and Carlos were the only ones to make the ascent. Briggs's bad hip was so bad that there was no chance that he could make the climb. He was to make an attempt but got only to the base camp, where he sent the climbers off with a hearty breakfast and awaited their return. I, because of an infection, wasn't even to make the hike. I was to stay at the hotel in town as guardian to Judith.

I also gathered that I was to get to know Judith so that Gary could talk to me about her and I might say something intelligent in return. Judith, however, was not dumb. She had no intention of being talked about by Gary and me on long winter evenings. After two days of being with her constantly, I knew no more about her heart and soul than I did five minutes after I met her. Judith had mastered the art of passivity to the point where it was a looming presence. She, like a rock at the entrance to a strait, held all eyes. Some voyagers, mesmerized by the danger, ventured close enough to be wrecked. By making no demands, she made every demand. By answering neither yes or no, she drew all questions, permitted any hope. She sat, stood, and walked in the Madonna pose: head not actually bowed but inclined slightly forward, eyes not downcast but slightly lidded, silent but seeming to be listening intently to everything—not listening so as to respond, listening from above.

When Gary had a chance to talk to me alone, he asked me eagerly what I thought of her. I had little to report. Gary was disappointed but not surprised and started once again his agonizing search for words that would explain her to me and to him. She remains in my memory one of the most puzzling women I've met. I have no idea what she was, Circe, Calypso, Penelope, Criseyde, or a scared girl trapped by madmen in a foreign country.

November was in its last days; it was time to head back. Dunnigan, Judith, Bob, and Briggs left before us. Carlos was staying home for a while. Gary, Sterling, and I headed north for Laredo and were arrested crossing the border.

A few miles before the border, I had developed a fierce headache. It felt like an altitude headache. Aspirin didn't help, so we dug into our climbing first-aid kits and got some codeine. A young Chicano border guard, his second day at the job, lingered on, suspicious, although his supervisor had already passed us through customs. He just knew we were doing something wrong because we just didn't look like American tourists. Maybe he was prescient and recognized us as the edge of the wave of hippies that was yet to come. He picked up the bottle of codeine tablets and asked us what it was. We told him. "Anything else?" We told him about the seconal and the morphine. The word morphine gave the border guard a real shot in the arm. There were interrogations and phone calls to Hanover, where Sterling had gotten the prescription from a doctor who was the advisor to the Dartmouth Mountaineering Club, and phone calls to the U.S. Attorney's office. What made them most suspicious of us was Gary's journal. In it, Gary vented his passion and rage in language and in detail that the customs official instinctively felt shouldn't be allowed to cross borders. Gary had four volumes of his journal with him, and I believe that the chief of customs read every word. After we were interrogated separately, after they satisfied themselves that we weren't narcotics smugglers, and after the U.S. Attorney decided not to prosecute us, the chief of customs called us to his office. He wanted to know who Judith was. Gary would not talk about her, so I said that Judith was a girl Gary was in love with. The chief of customs said that it didn't sound like he loved her. The customs chief wanted to warn Sterling in particular about associating with Gary. Sterling came from a good family, went to a good school, and ought to be careful about his friends. He didn't appear to be as worried about me. Perhaps Gary's journal revealed that I was a Henry Miller pusher.

No criminal charges were brought against us, but the bus was seized for transporting narcotics across the border. This was a civil proceeding that could not be waived by a prosecuting attorney. We could borrow the bus back from the people of the United States by posting a twenty-five-dollar bond until the civil procedure had ground its way through the federal bureaucracy. (Sterling's bus was not to be legally his for eleven months.) The process could not be set in motion that day, which meant that we had to stay in a hotel that night instead of in the bus. When we finally escaped from Laredo, we barely had money to buy enough gas to cross the state. We had to find jobs in Texas.

The first night after leaving Laredo, we stopped outside of a little town to eat our porridge, without milk or sugar, and to sleep. We weren't there for an hour when the sheriff pulled up, talked to us a while, and offered us the jail for the night. He was friendly, but we had the impression that it was an offer we ought not refuse. He told us that it was for our own protection. If there were any crimes committed in that area that night, we would not be blamed.

The ceiling of the cell was covered with images, religious scenes and naked women. We at first thought that they had been done in charcoal. Closer inspection revealed that they had been done in smoke. The area covered was about forty square feet. Some prisoner, for some unimaginable number of hours, had lit a match and held it to the ceiling. Then he had lit another match . . . .

We went to Brownsville to see if we could get a job on a ship. We were told that it had been two years since anyone without seaman's papers had shipped out of Brownsville.

We turned back north, checking the want ads whenever we found a discarded newspaper. We thought we'd try to get jobs as private investigators. Yvon Chouinard's brother had an agency in Southern California and often gave climbers temporary jobs. Gary had worked there and had also worked as a private eye in New York. The lady in charge of an agency was willing to hire us but warned us that we wouldn't like it. All she had available was undercover work. As an example, she said we'd be working on a loading dock until we discovered who was pilfering from the shipments. She didn't think we were the type, and we agreed. She seemed to have a higher estimate of our characters than did the chief of customs.

Out of money, with nothing to eat but porridge, on our last tank of gas, and nearly out of ideas, we needed some luck. We passed a hitchhiker.

"Hey!" I said.

"Shall we pick him up and see if he's got gas money?" said Sterling.

"Yes!" I yelled excitedly, "I know that guy. That's Charlie." He approached the bus and looked in.

"Charlie, do you remember me? I worked with you in Big Piney."

"Yeah, I forgot your name, but I remember that I owe you five bucks."

We cheered. I'd forgotten that.

"Boy is that lucky, Charlie. We're broke and on our last tank of gas."

It was lucky, but not because of the five dollars. Charlie didn't have any money either. What he did have was experience.

When Charlie discovered how poorly we were doing, he decided to help us out. It puzzled him that we, who had been to college and had climbed great mountains, had not learned how to survive. He said, "I've never been to the big cities in the East but you could drop me right in the middle of one of those cities and I would not miss a meal and I'd have a place to sleep every night. I'd have smokes too."

Charlie told us this as we passed through a town in search of a pipeline construction site he'd been trying to find. At a corner where there were men standing around, Charlie told us to stop the car.

Charlie sidled up to one wall-leaner. They talked for a while. Then the man gave him a cigarette. They talked some more. Then the man gave Charlie another cigarette. Charlie returned to the car and gave the second cigarette to me. He'd found where the hiring for the pipeline was being done, too. He had presented his credentials.

We arrived at the town nearest the end of the pipeline too late in the day to see about jobs. Charlie would have none of our porridge; we had to get real food. Our first attempt was to go into the biggest cafe in town and offer to leave Sterling's typewriter as security for our tab. The owner and all the people in the cafe were white Texans. She said, no, she already had two typewriters and didn't need a third. "Why don't you try the Mex restaurant across the street?"

Charlie thanked the owner as if she had made a helpful suggestion. When the Mexican waitress across the street told us that the owner was off on a hunting trip and wouldn't be back for a couple of days and that she couldn't take a typewriter for security in his absence, Sterling and I disconsolately returned the typewriter to the bus. But we couldn't give up. Charlie said we should not miss a meal, and Charlie knew what he was talking about. However, we had to do something to help ourselves. Charlie was already going to go out on a limb to get us a job; we couldn't expect him to feed us too. So while Charlie and Gary remained in the cafe talking to the waitress, Sterling and I decided to go to a little cafe around the corner and ask if we could wash dishes for a meal. That was one of the greatest psychological efforts of my life.

Behind my trepidation was my father's depression talk: "Even in the worst of the depression, when your mother and I were eating only one meal a day so you kids could eat three, I never begged anybody for anything, I never accepted charity, and I never went on the dole. The worst I did was to work for the government, and I got out of that as soon as I could."

The cafe was perhaps fifteen by thirty feet including the back kitchen. There were eight stools and four booths. A man was sweeping the floor and a woman was wiping up behind the counter. There'd be no dishes to wash; they were about to close. My heart sank. "Oh Lord, they're probably glad to see us, glad they delayed closing, thinking they might make an extra dollar which might make twenty dollars for the day." There was no escape. I was in the door and had to account for my presence.

"We're just closing. Would you like some coffee?"

"Well, uh, we came in to see if we could wash dishes for a meal. We're trying to get a job on the pipeline. But since you're closing . . . ."

"Sit down. How about a hamburger and a cup of coffee? We can cook you a hamburger. No trouble."

"Yeah, that would be great." So the woman cooked us hamburgers, and I ate one, too ashamed to ask for catsup and too ashamed to accept it when it was offered.

When we thanked them and left, I felt wonderful, not at escaping humiliation, but because I'd done it! I'd begged for a meal, I'd accepted charity, and I didn't feel like committing suicide!

We looked for Charlie and Gary, feeling bad because we'd eaten and they hadn't. We needn't have. We found them still in the "Mex cafe" seated at a table in the middle of dinner. They saw us peering through the window and came and got us. The waitress had offered to buy all our meals herself until we got a paycheck. I couldn't believe it.

"If you need help down here," Charlie said, "ask a Mexican. They'll always help you."

The waitress was middle-aged, not as pretty as she had obviously once been, but she seemed to me then, and I still remember her as, one of the loveliest women I've ever met. When we left, I gave her a beautiful black lace mantilla which I had bought in Mexico to give to a woman in Jackson, the woman who is now my wife.

Charlie got a job driving a piece of equipment and got us jobs too. He was a little apologetic. It was the worst job on the pipeline, "chopping dope." We were to replace four Mexicans who had quit. We gathered that they had quit because nobody lasts very long at that job. "Dope" is a tar-like substance which is melted in tar pots and spread over the pipe as it is laid. The dope comes in fifty-five-gallon drums and, before it goes in the pots to be melted, has to be chopped into chunks with axes. This is easy if the temperature is below fifty degrees because the dope is brittle and splits, but when the sun warms the dope, the axe embeds itself and sticks. For this reason, chopping dope starts at 4 A.M. We were worried about the three of us trying to replace four Mexicans, but the foreman thought that three big, strong climbers ought to be able to accomplish as much as four 5'4" Mexicans. The foreman was wrong. We worked hard for three days and got farther behind until we were holding up the pipeline.

We had been warned to stay out of the smoke because it would burn our skin. And burn it did. It was worst when you took a shower to wash it off. Cold water felt like it was boiling. Our faces and hands were one solid red, and by the third day, the smoke permeated our clothes. Red blotches appeared on our skin. We were overjoyed when the foreman told us that he had to fire us.

Charlie quit his job. He decided that he wanted to see New York. He'd also like to stop at home in Oklahoma. There was a minor problem associated with this: we couldn't enter his county in daylight. The sheriff in Charlie's county had an old grievance with Charlie which Charlie thought the sheriff might not have forgotten. It was past midnight when we got to the little farm where Charlie's folks lived. While he talked to his family, we napped in the car. We left in time to get across the county line before sunrise.

We stopped for a day in Missouri to visit Chief, spent an afternoon at Stephens College where Sterling's sister was going to school, and then went on to Cleveland in time for Sterling to spend Thanksgiving with his parents. Sterling's uncle is the T in TRW, so Charlie and Hemming got to meet people from regions of American society they had not visited before. They made a big hit. Sterling's dad lent Charlie a tuxedo and outfitted Gary and me so that we were at least presentable. We watched George Szell conduct the Cleveland Symphony from the family's box. Sterling's lovely cousin introduced Charlie and Hemming to some of her friends, and debutantes proved to be not immune to the Hemming magic. Charlie, who was about six feet four, blonde, and well muscled, looked very good in Mr. Neale's tux and seemed to be in constant conversation with a fascinated young lovely as well. The fact that the tuxedo was a little small in the arms and shoulders did not spoil the effect. Charlie himself was amazed at what the tuxedo did for him. He told me that he was going to get him one the first chance he got.

After Thanksgiving, Sterling drove Gary, Charlie, and me to New York and returned to Cleveland for the Christmas holidays. Charlie and Gary were going to poke around New York for a while then head for Florida to see if they could get work on the shrimp boats.

The first thing we did when we got to New York was to follow Hemming into the basement of an abandoned building in search of some Puerto Ricans Gary knew who had some marijuana. Gary had discovered the incipient growth of the pot culture while working in New York as a private detective. The Korean veterans I'd met in the army had told me about the importance of pot to that war. I'd once smelled it in the latrine of a Fort Dix barracks but I'd never seen it. Ex-sergeant PFC Kendrick, a black soldier from Denver who had taken me under his wing, told me what the peculiar smell was. He called it "tea" and said that it had been smoked incessantly during those interminable weeks in the bunkers while they waited for the Chinese attacks. He said that the soldiers were often so stupefied that the only way the sergeants could get the soldiers out of the bunkers to defend their positions was to shout that the Chinese were coming to get their tea. The connection was strong between soldiers in their bunkers during those Korean winters and the Puerto Ricans holed up in the basement of a ruined building in New York in December.

All they'd sell to Gary was a couple of cigarettes. Gary lit one as soon as we got on the street and insisted that we try it. My heart wasn't in it. I thought that a New York street was the most public place on earth.

It was near dark but not quite dark. It was cold. There were lots of people, but they were thinly dispersed. I could not see anyone's face. Where we were, most of the store fronts were empty and unlit, as were the doorways. There were people in the neighborhood, but few appeared to live there. It was inconceivable that anybody could live well there.

Gary somehow knew that smoking marijuana was to become popular and insisted that we have this experience. I took two drags, reported that it had no effect, and refused to take more.

I went to Grand Central Station to catch the train for Connecticut. It was about ten when I got there, and the train was not to leave until after one. I strolled around the cathedral-like main concourse watching the holiday crowds, happy to be in the light. When the time came, I descended to the dark tracks tunneled beneath the station and got on a train.

In the same car was a former fraternity brother from Dartmouth. He had been a senior when I was a sophomore. He was handsome, witty, unconventional, intellectually tough, but very personable and gentle in manner. He wrote short stories that we admired. He was in love with a girl who I thought was just about perfect. She had class and somehow managed to look both soft and athletic. Her smile had gotten stuck in my memory. They were ardent lovers. I remember one warm spring day in Hanover, a Green Key weekend. We were moderately drunk. She was sitting on a car hood in back of the fraternity house, surrounded by old trees and new leaves. As if it were the most natural thing in the world, like taking her hand, he leaned toward her, parted her legs and kissed her on the inside of her thigh. She chastised him gently, but I blushed more than she did. He was the sort to whom such a gesture was permitted.

Now he was heavier. His tie was loosened from his collar, and his collar showed the dirt accumulated from sixteen hours of New York air. It had been almost a day since he had shaved. He was nearly sober and asked about Jake Breitenbach and Barry Corbet, who had also belonged to our fraternity, and we talked of them for a while.

What was I doing on the train?

Going home for Christmas.

From Wyoming?

No.

From Alaska?

No, from Mexico.

And he? He worked in the city for an ad firm whose name I'd heard, and he lived in Connecticut. He and his beloved were now married, and there were children. This evening he had been to a party after work and had been delayed by a woman, how exactly wasn't clear. He spoke of his wife with slightly shame-faced affection. She "understood." I wondered what it was she understood—the hour, his having drunk too much, or the woman—but didn't ask.

He had thought about me, Jake, and Barry a lot. There we were, all three of us dropouts, and we had already made *Time* magazine. He thought he might make *Time* someday, but he'd never know because he would accomplish just enough in his life, as he saw it then, to make the obituary column.

Outside was one of those New England nights for which I was never homesick. Not quite raining, cold without the temperature being particularly low, no snow on the ground, it was a familiar New England scene but one you never see on calendars. We were not uncomfortable with each other and were both delighted at the chance meeting. But we didn't have as much in common as we needed to overcome the shabbiness of the time, place, and occasion. This same train, Monday morning, would fill up with ambitious, energetic men. In the evening, the train would bring them back from the city, tired in many different ways. We were on it long after even the tiredest had reached home. When he left the train at the station, I traveled on, feeling uneasy. I didn't feel sorry for him but for us. He was still both sharp and warm, as I'd remembered him. He was feeling a little down, but that was most certainly the result of "postalcoholic depression," as Jake used to call Sunday afternoon at the fraternity house. What saddened me was the mention of the obituary in *Time* magazine. I thought about how your fingers were always gray after reading *Time.*

I was vindicated in dropping out of college and eschewing a successful career in whatever it was at which I might have been a success, vindicated by the very document which recorded success and consigned failure to oblivion, *Time* magazine. My friend had acknowledged my "success" and had also at least alluded to the possibility of his own failure, something both of us would have considered unthinkable four years earlier. It had been a wonderful year for me, perfect, but as the year and the decade ended, all the way into Hartford I found myself involuntarily moving my thumb across my fingers as if to rub off the gray.

I was the figure in the picture in *Time,* holding the axe straight up in the sky. We were laughing at ourselves with that picture, the notion of conquest having become absurd. But it was that photo that *Time* picked out of many hundreds. Was that it, I wondered, my achievement? What I was not sophisticated enough to be able to articulate, but did understand as I rode through the night alone, is that there is an important distinction between celebrity and fame. Celebrity comes with luck. Fame has to be deserved. The other thing I knew was that whatever I deserved would be earned in the West.

CHAPTER 6

WEST

We have precious times when we glimpse the trajectory of our lives, when we are free enough from the nudge of things done and the tug of things to do to have a gravity-free movement of lucidity about what we are up to. One such moment for me came during a pause in grooming a ski trail near the top of Snow King.

I planted my shovel next to my skis and loosened the top of my Jackson Hole Ski Patrol jacket. Wooly warm air escaped to mix with the cool scents of pine, fir, spruce, and lichen, pulled sweet and soft into my lungs. It was January, 1960. I had my job on the ski patrol back, which was fortunate because, although I had earned good money working on the oil rig, I spent it on the Denali expedition. The even better money *Life* paid me I spent going from Alaska to Mexico and crossing the continent west to east and back west.

Having decided to get a certain amount of money and gotten it was proof that I could take care of myself. I had been dependent on my parents, the navy scholarship, the army, and, until he taught me to ski well enough to get a job on the patrol, Barry. Just as important, I had gotten money when I needed it at jobs that were themselves adventures. I called that taking very good care of myself. Below and before me was one of the world's great landscapes, the landscape of the West, whose most important promise is not gold or a second Eden but simply that you do not have to go back to where you came from. You can forget what you want and are able to. Maybe that is Eden. There was no reason why I should not live the years to come just exactly as I had lived the past year: winter air, mountain forest, warm wool, ski edges biting the snow, laughing voices in otherwise quiet air, a little shoveling, a lot of skiing, being lofted up the hill by the chairlift, enough to eat, all foods tasting good, deep sleep, quick waking, and, at the moment, no woman making me heartsick. I turned back to my work knowing that I might be the world's freest man.

As we know, the gods are concerned that we dwell not too long in such states of mind. That afternoon the loudspeaker called me to the lift office. At sunset the next day, I was skirting the Red Desert on a Greyhound bus eastbound to New York. It was a relief to be among strangers. I hadn't learned how a person waits for their mother to die. I guessed I would learn that, faking it when I had to say something. Maybe not. Maybe she would be okay. Don't kid yourself. Get ready. Four days to the East Coast, plenty of time to compose thoughts. I assumed I was leaving Jackson for good. Either the operation would work or my mother would die. To allow myself to hope that she might recover and I could resume my life where I left it the morning before seemed disloyal, refusing to face what she could not but face. The only morally safe course is to assume the worst.

Not far east of Rock Springs, as distances go in Wyoming, the highway crosses the Continental Divide and flanks the southern edge of the Red Desert. The terrain is high but not mountainous. In places I could see South Pass, sixty miles north, where the Oregon Trail crossed the Wind Rivers. I watched the Wind Rivers over my shoulder until others in the bus began peering out their windows to find what I was looking at. Looking back that way gave me a sensation that I was sitting still and the land was moving, that the West was slipping from me. I sat back in my seat. One hundred miles over the northern horizon, but present in my thoughts, was the place where I had first slept under the Wyoming sky.

After I was discharged from the army in August 1958, I hitchhiked west. At Rawlins I decided to head north to Muddy Gap and then west to Lander and Dubois in order to enter Jackson's Hole by Togwotee Pass instead of taking the Rock Springs-Pinedale route. I could see on the map that the rides would be harder to come by if I went this way—there were only two large towns in two hundred miles—but I had been so struck by the high spaciousness of the Laramie Basin that I wanted to be afoot in this Wyoming country for a few hours.

I had no trouble getting to Lander. There I stopped to buy a cowboy hat, feeling like an imposter as I tried to suppress my New England accent. I got a ride out of Lander from a rancher, who, noting my climbing rope, asked if I was a cowhand. From the way he smiled as he asked, I guessed that he had also noted the newness of my hat. When he learned that I had come west to climb, he was interested. I showed him the rest of my equipment and explained how it was used. Near Burris, he dropped me off at the driveway to his ranch; his driveway was forty miles long. He warned me that I might have a tough time getting a ride and invited me to his ranch. He was going into Dubois the following day, and I would have a better chance of catching a ride from there. I assured him that I had a tent, sleeping bag, and food. He said he'd look for me tomorrow.

In the next five hours only two local cars passed. About two dozen from out of state came by, but I had already learned that tourists do not give you rides in spectacular country. They're afraid you'll ask them where they're from. I decided I'd better walk the two or three miles to Burris to get water. I filled a canteen in Burris and bought some cheese and a can of spaghetti and decided to make for a place further on toward Dubois where the map showed Dinwoody Creek crossing the highway. By the time I arrived at Dinwoody Creek, the sun was behind the mountains.

There was a gas station-store on the other side of the road, and people were watching me. They did not appear standoffish, but I didn't want to talk to them. I slipped as unobtrusively as I could into the grove of cottonwoods and aspens lining the creek. I wanted, without feeling that I was camping in somebody's backyard, to think about where I'd walked that day.

The automobile had shrunk the desert, but to a man on foot, the townless highway had looked as if it couldn't hold out long against sandstone and sagebrush. I knew that the pioneers had not passed here. At the other end of the Wind Rivers, they had gone right through the Red Desert to South Pass, a much more serious country. I tried to imagine the wild hopes or desperate pasts that had kept them going. I imagined them plodding through the dry sagebrush toward the forest green and snow white of the mountains for days instead of hours. I did not imagine, as I hiked, that I was in a survival situation. I could see the bluffs above the Wind River; I would not become a sun-bleached skeleton. Nevertheless, Dinwoody Creek was the only oasis I'd ever had a chance to visit. It was all only a bit of make-believe, make-believe I'd paid for with two years of living in army barracks. So, I pretended that the gas station-store and its citizenry didn't exist, that there were only the cottonwoods, creek, bluffs, plain, mountains, clouds, and sky.

I pitched my tent on a grassy knoll that the spring runoff had left marooned in dry white sand. From my island no human habitation was visible. To the north was a garden of geologic marvels: buttes, canyons, and river cuts with aeons of geologic time layered in rock like annual rings in a tree. Overhead, the puffy white afternoon clouds were dissipating, dissolving in an evening sky of metallic blue.

I gathered wood for a fire and cooked supper. It was dark by the time I washed my pot, and as the fire dimmed, the sky deepened. The stars brightened until the night sky became three dimensional, and I had to try to comprehend not the distance to the stars but the distance from planet to near star to further star to furthest star to unseen stars beyond. There is no sensation of vertigo on a mountain wall comparable to briefly imagining yourself perched on a planet falling into the sky. I pulled my vision back to the tree tops, remembered the Wind

Rivers as I had seen them in the sun that day, and crawled into my tent and into my sleeping bag.

I awoke at sunrise, and then went back to sleep until the heat drove me from the tent. I was packed up and hitchhiking by eight. By eleven, I was wondering whether I could walk to Dubois before dark. Then five cars passed and stopped together down the road. A dark-skinned man I took to be an Indian waved. This was the Wind River Indian Reservation. Though I had seen few Indians, those I had seen had driven slowly and somewhat erratically down the highway, talking and laughing and looking around. Wyoming Indians seemed not to take the ownership and operation of an automobile very seriously. I was not eager to ride with one, not because there seemed to be any danger, but what if they just lost interest when I was fifty miles from the next store?

One of the five cars, a '56 Chevy, was being towed, and the man that had waved to me was in the tow car. Upon finding out where I was headed, he told me to put my pack in the Chevy and to get into his car. The whole party consisted of four men and two women. There was a family resemblance between three of the men. The women resembled each other but not the three men or the fourth man. From close up, I wasn't so sure they were Indians. They looked more like the Portuguese fishermen I had known in Rhode Island as a child.

We stopped in Dubois for gas. There the man who picked me up and who seemed to be the leader asked me if I had a driver's license. When I said yes, he asked me to drive the Chevy over the pass. I was positioned in the middle of the fleet and told to stay there. It appeared that during the short ride to Dubois they had fathomed enough about me to trust me a little, but not completely. Or perhaps it wasn't me they had doubts about but the woman that would have had to ride with me to assure that I didn't run off with the car if I were allowed to go ahead or drop behind. Or perhaps it wasn't me or the woman that the leader had to worry about but the imagination of whichever man was the husband or lover or suitor of the woman that would have had to ride with me. I saw that being the leader of this group might be a complicated job.

They claimed they had bought these cars in Iowa and Nebraska and were taking them to Oregon to sell. I wondered if they were stolen but decided they weren't. The fanciest car of the five was a '57 Dodge with a dented fender. I didn't reckon car thieves would bother with these cars.

For the first twenty miles out of Dubois the highway tends west-northwest up the valley of the Wind River through sage-brush hills. Where the sagebrush ends and the forest begins, the valley narrows to a canyon. It came to me that I was about to cross both a large mountain range and the Continental Divide for the first time. All the water I had ever seen either flowed to the Atlantic or was the Atlantic. Within the hour I would enter the domain of the greatest ocean of all, the Pacific. I was approaching the rim of the larger part of the world.

I expected the pass to be a col, to have some kind of edge to tip over. Instead, at the summit, the highway leveled onto mountain meadows with gentle streams. There seemed to be more wildflowers in view than all the flowers I had ever seen.

We descended for some time, me uncertain that we were on the Pacific side, when, dramatically, the road came out of the forest into a meadow, swung over to the lip of a canyon, and there, twenty-five miles across a valley, were the Tetons.

I knew that the earth had done something about mountains here she hadn't done before. Because I came to climb them, they scared me a little, the steepness of them some, but mostly their perfection as mountains. Had I earned the right, climbing cliff bands in New Hampshire, to approach these summits? That worry passed and was replaced by a feeling that whatever and wherever it was that I had been trying to get to, I had arrived.

When we pulled over to look at the view, emboldened, as if we were now on my turf, I ventured to quiz the leader: "You're not Indians, are you?"

"No, we are Gypsies."

Wonderful! In a caravan of Gypsies, driving a white and green '56 Chevy, I rolled into Jackson's Hole, Wyoming.

A memory of an experience like that helps in a bus trip across Nebraska.

Back home in Norfolk, Connecticut, I entered the emotional twilight of the family visited by cancer. I guarded against my thoughts. I wrote a letter to my climbing friends in which I described the situation, discussed the possibility that I might have to leave the mountains, and claimed to be facing my lot bravely. These impulses of self-pity which came upon me from time to time made me sick of myself. Few succeed in being completely sensible in these circumstances.

The operation was performed and declared a probable success. A cure could not be claimed until five years had passed. Now what? Wait five years? I decided to go to New York City. New York wasn't an unseemly distance from home, and I'd always felt that I ought to know New York better than I did. New York was where my father went when he left home.

I knew the place where I wanted to enter the life of the city—Dylan Thomas's tavern, the Whitehorse. Standing at the bar beside me was J. Bruce Crabtree, professor of mathematics at Stevens Institute of Technology across the river in Hoboken. When Crabtree discovered that I wanted to get to know the city, he thought that we might begin right then. That was Friday night. At five Sunday morning, the lesson ended with me falling asleep on the couch at Crabtree's. He was still listening to music. It would have been okay with me if my introduction to the city had ended at five Saturday morning, after we'd done the Fulton Street Market, but Crabtree kept remembering new places that had to be seen. I had attempted a nap at two Saturday morning, leaning my head against the wall in an Irish tavern, but Crabtree shook my shoulder and said, "Say, they don't like you to do that here." "Oh," I said, "sorry," and supported myself by gripping my glass with both hands.

Looking for work in New York was a sobering experience. By using Al Lowenstein as a reference, I got a job with a clothing manufacturer in the garment district through an employment agency. My title was assistant to the buyer. My duties were to match buttons to the material used to make men's suits and to shuffle orders and invoices. About once every three days I had to make a decision. It sometimes happened that the materials for a coat and liner were combined in a way that wasn't on my list. I then got to pick the type and color of buttons to be used. I never did figure out how that assisted the buyer.

Within a very short time, I knew I had to get back out to the mountains. I had a new sense of how difficult it was to find a place and feel at home in America. I was beginning to take this problem seriously. I quit my employers without giving notice and without picking up three days' pay that was owed me. When I walked out of the building on the third Friday, I stopped, turned around, and looked at the door in an agitated state. I could not enter that building again. I considered writing a note or calling somebody, but the problem with that was that I still owed the employment agency money. I intended to just disappear. Fritz Goro had invited me out to his house for the weekend. I called him to let him know that I wouldn't be there. Crabtree and I went over to the Village for one more evening. I was taking the bus to Wyoming on Sunday morning, so Saturday I packed up, checked my bag at the bus station, and went uptown to visit Al Lowenstein.

At that age, I happened occasionally upon someone with whom there was nothing to be done but have an all-night conversation of the utmost earnestness, in pursuit of a new purpose or a new thought. Hemming and I had these conversations. Another person with whom I used to have them was Anne Koedt, a friend in Jackson. Lowenstein was the third. All three of these people were critics of my thinking and my purposes. All three chastised me for being uncommitted. Hemming felt that I was not emancipated enough. Anne charged me with being socially uncommitted, with having no social conscience. Al charged me with being politically uncommitted. These three became people in my life who were important out of proportion to the amount of time spent with them. They are examples of the power of earnestness. I didn't do the things any of them thought I should do, but they nonetheless influenced the course of my life. Many lives have gone into the shaping of my own, including many who were more important, but Al, Anne, and Gary were voices in my head.

As it happened, Al was too busy to talk to me much that evening, but he introduced me to a friend of his, Libby. Poor Libby. She had to stand in for all the people I wanted to say things to. I talked through the afternoon, on through the evening, and into the night. We went for a walk across town to the Hudson River. Finally, at dawn, I stopped. That girl was a saint. This may not be credible of one who is writing an autobiography, but I didn't often talk about myself. This was one time when I had to take stock out loud. I headed west again with a new sense of purpose, although, beyond wanting to be once again on a snow-covered mountainside with or without a shovel in hand, my sense of purpose had no specific content.

The army, my mother's cancer, and my stint at the clothing manufacturer had awakened in me a consciousness of my mortality, of at least three ways in which the world could regard me as expendable. I had no marketable education or skill and had served no apprenticeship. I didn't need much, but the world appeared to be constructed to have me use all my time and energy just to survive. Having to struggle to survive was not an unattractive prospect in itself. In the context of climbing mountains or of settling the last frontier in Alaska, surviving was purpose enough. But the Territory of Alaska no longer existed, and living only to climb didn't quiet the voices in my mind. I had some kind of responsibility to other people on the one hand, and on the other, the kind of purposes I had seen in many of my peers at Dartmouth didn't seem to be mine. I remembered one case in particular, that of a classmate who had studied business. Business as a poker game on a larger scale seemed okay to me. I could understand why somebody might want to do that. This classmate had two job opportunities upon graduation. One was an offer to manage a new branch of a small but expanding company; the other was a job as a very junior executive with a large corporation. He took the job with the corporation, not because there were bigger fish to fry, but because it "has a better retirement plan." My consciousness of my mortality didn't work that way.

Sterling Neale also arrived in Jackson, also broke. Lynn and Gary Wright gave us a place to sleep. We got temporary jobs with the town, building the boardwalk around the town square. After paying our debts, we each had thirty dollars left. Unfortunately, a blister on Sterling's hand had gotten infected. He went to the doctor's office while I waited for him in a bar. To pass the time and to supplement our funds, I bet on the clock, a simple gambling device in the bars of Jackson at that time. The odds were six to one against me. At the end of two hours Sterling had given all his money to the doctor, and the bartender had all but two silver dollars of mine. We decided to have a beer with those. With our fortunes as with the boardwalk, we ended where we started.

Sterling's plan for the summer was to apprentice as a guide. I thought I might do that too. The way it was done was to build a reputation as a climber and fill in when there was too much work for the regular guides. My prospects for work that season wouldn't be good, but I could begin to catch up to my peers in climbing ability, making up the two years I had lost in the army.

The season was just getting underway in June when some of my friends among the guides suggested that I apply for a position as a ranger with the park. There was no opening for a climbing ranger at Jenny Lake, but accidents had been increasing in recent years and both Doug McLaren, the district ranger, and Russ Dickenson, the chief ranger, wanted to hire climbers for as many of the park's seasonal positions as they could. Barry said that this rescue team was the best in the country, and with Dick Emerson not returning, the team had to be rebuilt. They had two good rock climbers, Tim Bond and Dave Dornan, as climbing rangers at the Jenny Lake Ranger Station, and they were looking for others.

I was sure I was meant to get that job. I'd be climbing for pay as part of my duties. What greater redeeming social value could climbing have than saving lives? I thought of the flat-brimmed hat and forgot that I hated uniforms. I'd be a professional hero.

I had performed my first rescue when I was nine years old, near the end of the Second World War. My father was in the Pacific, after having served in the Atlantic, and had been gone so long we could not remember what he looked like. We lived in a navy housing project in Middletown, Rhode Island, just outside of Newport. Between the project and the sea was the navy base. Our house was next to the tall chain link fence, capped by barbed wire, that surrounded the base. On the landward side of the project, toward the interior of the island, was a countryside of farmland, mainly dairy farms. The meadows, groves, brooks, and ponds stretching for miles in three directions were where we went in the summer to learn about cows, manure, bugs, snakes, eels, fish, polywogs, trees, dogs, running, jumping, climbing, talking, and resting idly in the sun.

One day in early spring we dragged our sleds to a hill not far from the project. It was not a cold day, but there was some snow left. My brother Ernie was eighteen months younger than me; my brother David, four years. With us were two sisters from across the street. At the bottom of the hill was a cow pond. Acting big brotherly, I said we should be careful because the ice on the pond might not be safe. Acting little brotherly, David flopped on his sled, slid down the hill and out onto the pond. When he reached the middle, the ice collapsed. Until that moment, David did not know how to swim. He didn't seem particularly afraid, which perhaps is why I did nothing at first. I also did not know how to swim, which is also perhaps why I did nothing at first.

The two little girls were screaming and laughing, nervously, at the same time. Somehow Ernie got me moving. I think he started moving down the hill. Then I was on the ice yelling encouragement to David who was swimming energetically on his back. David, unlike the rest of us, knew what he had to do.

I was a few feet from David when the ice broke under me. I'd been hoping that would not happen. My foot touched something solid, David's sled. The water was just under my chin. I grabbed David and pushed him onto the ice. It broke. I pushed him further. It broke again. Once more and Ernie was able to reach him with a sled. I held onto the unbroken ice on the side of the channel we made and extended the channel shoreward until I touched the bottom.

Were we happy! Gibbering and shivering, we sloshed home. In talking about the incident, a notion formed that I had done something brave. My mother concurred. "You did a brave thing," she said. I had to admit that what I had done, a hero would certainly have done, so I could see how the notion that I had done a brave thing had come up, but I didn't believe it. I had hesitated, which, whether it was from fear or stupidity, was not heroic. I hadn't thought out any action, which a hero would have done in an instant, and I had refused to consider the possibility that I might be killed, which a hero would have considered and laughed to scorn. If I hadn't actually felt terribly frightened, that was because the girls started screaming first, being as always a little sharper than us boys, and because I didn't have any thoughts at all until I was in the water with David. I was glad that my mother thought I had done a brave thing, and I wouldn't argue with her. My private conclusion was that few young boys have a chance at being a hero; I did have the chance to be a hero, and I had missed it.

I knew about young heroes because I read about them in comic books. Many comic books had a one-page story about a boy scout who saved someone. The scout always seemed to be in uniform when he was needed, and he often wore a flat-brimmed hat.

I did get the job as a ranger and as a member of the rescue team, but I had to work at the entrance station at Moose. Russ Dickenson said that they were hoping to expand the operation at Jenny Lake and eventually I'd get a job there, certainly by the following season if I wanted to continue.

When you work at an entrance station, you really have the feeling that you are paying your dues. About once every five hundred questions someone asks, "Don't you get tired of answering the same questions all the time?" When that becomes one of the questions you're tired of answering, you've learned the last thing there is to learn about working at an entrance station.

Finally, three weeks after I had begun working, the rescue team was called out. The day before, a man had hiked the eleven miles up to Lake Solitude and had not returned. A man that might have been him had been seen above the lake, toward the divide, but that wasn't certain. It was midafternoon when the decision to search was made. He had been given as much time as possible to get out by himself and leave us still enough light to start a search. It is difficult to get lost for long in the Tetons and impossible for an experienced hiker. The man who was missing was a London doctor who seemed quite fit and experienced. Still, he was sixty-four years old.

Ron Trussell, the backcountry ranger in Cascade Canyon, had made a preliminary search up to the snowline below the divide. Paintbrush Divide is at the head of three canyons. The trail, which wouldn't be free of snow until later in the season, goes up Cascade Canyon to the lake, over the divide, and down Paintbrush Canyon. Since there is thick brush and no trail in Leigh, the third canyon, it's a mistake soon discovered if you get into it. The subdistrict ranger, Jim Langford, and Dave Dornan would go up Paintbrush Canyon. I would join Ron Trussell in Cascade Canyon, and we would all meet at the divide. Tim Bond, the ranger-in-charge at Jenny Lake, would await word and organize more searchers if we were unsuccessful or organize an evacuation team if needed. We met at the divide at 6 P.M. without having seen a sign of Doctor Lowey.

There were two likely possibilities. Either Doctor Lowey was injured some place off the trail in Paintbrush Canyon or he was bushwhacking out of Leigh Canyon. We decided that Ron should search with Jim in Paintbrush Canyon as far as Holly Lake and that Dave and I should follow some tracks that led toward Grizzly Bear Lake in Leigh Canyon. We would bivouac at our respective lakes that night, continuing down our canyons at daylight. Tim Bond and another park climber, Fritz Ermath, would start up Leigh Canyon at 5 A.M.

That, my first bivouac in the mountains, remains my favorite. We had lost the tracks by the time we got to Grizzly Bear Lake, and Dave and I prepared for the night. This was the first time we had been in the mountains together and our first chance to get to know each other. Dave, like Buckingham, was born in Jackson's Hole. He was younger than Bill, and Bill had gone off to college before Dave had started climbing seriously. So they, the only two native Jackson's Hole climbers, didn't know each other well. Norfolk, Connecticut, was the same size as Jackson, Wyoming, was while Bill and Dave were growing up. Both were towns with "summer people." I knew what it was like to be a young man with a different plan than my schoolmates in such a town.

Dave was majoring in philosophy at the University of Colorado in Boulder. He was about my size and build, even thinner and wirier than I, and just looked intellectual. He had the philosopher's manner of speaking only when he had something interesting to say or when he had an interesting way of saying something ordinary. I envied that manner. Were I that way, I would have been spared much embarrassment in my life. As night came on, I began to have thoughts about getting through it. I had a down jacket but was not otherwise prepared for a bivouac.

"We'll build a white man's fire," said Dave.

On the hillside above the lake, Dave located a tree that had fallen from the top of a twelve-foot outcrop. The bark could be separated from the tree in long segments, and the tree trunk formed a sloping ridgepole against which we leaned the bark strips to make a lean-to. Then we gathered wood from three to eight inches in diameter and of random lengths and made a stack that was taller than we. We watched the sunset and the stars and burned our stack of wood. We didn't sleep much, but we weren't cold for an instant and only felt a tiny bit wicked about our extravagant expenditure of wood. We were out here to save lives; we were allowed.

After dawn we started beating our way down through the brush, zigzagging back and forth across the canyon. We found more tracks leading down the canyon. Then we found tracks going back up the canyon. What now? He couldn't have passed us in the night, not with our fire lighting up the entire head of the canyon. Had he been avoiding us? Were those his tracks at all? At three that afternoon, word came by radio that he had climbed back out of the canyon, crossed the divide, and had returned down Cascade Canyon. He was a tough sixty-four year old. He must have gone by us just after dawn. It had cost the taxpayers some money, but it had been fun, much better than the entrance station to which I returned for the rest of July.

Then, on the afternoon of August 4, 1960, I found myself on the trail headed for the south side of Nez Perce with seven other park people and two volunteers that we had recruited. The park people were Jim, Dave, and Ron, Greg Engstrom, Dennis Wik, George Kelly, and Jack Dodd. The volunteers were Art Gran and Leigh Ortenburger—Art for his technical skill and Leigh because he knew that area and every other area of the Tetons better than anyone in the world. The other two members of the team, Tim and Fritz, weren't with us. Fritz we presumed to be at the site of the accident. Tim was who we were going to get.

What we knew was that Tim had been climbing on the south side of Nez Perce with Sally, his bride of a few weeks. He fell, was injured, and was suspended in the rope somewhere below Sally. We knew that Sally had talked to Tim after the fall. If Fritz and his younger brother Mike, who had heard Sally's shouts, had gotten there in time, we didn't know.

We pushed ourselves. How close had Fritz been when he heard the shouts? Maybe Tim had fixed Sally in her belay position so that she could tie off the belay rope and help him somehow? But Tim was an eastern climber; that was Yosemite stuff we were just starting to learn. She couldn't lift him—none of us could have without rigging mechanical aids. Did Sally know how to do that? Maybe there was a ledge she could lower him to.

Sweat poured from our heads and ran down our chests and down the small of our backs. Our packs creaked with the heavy loads. Our necks ached. Our thigh and calf muscles strained and knotted. Then, we stopped. Sally was approaching, with Mike Ermath.

Her eyes were still swollen, but she wasn't crying anymore. She wasn't seeing anything, at least not anything there on the trail.

"He fell and hit his head.

"I tried to pull, but he was so heavy.

"I couldn't tie the rope.

"I got it around a boulder.

"I yelled and yelled and yelled.

"Finally they came.

"He climbed down the rope to Tim.

"And Tim.

"And Tim.

"Was dead."

This she recited slowly as if she were trying to be heard long distance over a bad connection. At the last word she turned and paced down the trail. Because she seemed to be out of her mind, I was relieved. The people below us on the trail melted out of her path. Because she had nowhere in particular she wanted to go, was perhaps not eager to leave these mountains nor eager to face what awaited her in the valley, she moved slowly. Hiking traffic was backed up on the trail above us. No one would pass her. One hiker hung back until Sally was out of hearing and then jumped into the brush below the trail and scrambled down the mountain to come out ahead of her on the next switchback. As I watched this, the distance between humans seemed as the distance between stars. Sally had lost her husband. The hiker had a table reserved at Moore's. I had my own thoughts.

Tim had fallen about twenty feet to the ledge Sally was belaying him from, landing on the edge. He hit his head in the fall and slipped off the ledge to hang in his waist loop five feet below the lip. Semidelirious, with his waist loop cutting into his body, he called for Sally to lower him. She did, about another twenty feet, until she realized that there was nothing below Tim for several hundred feet, no place to lower him to. The rope slowly cut off circulation, and, later, Sally was tied to a rope which had the corpse of her husband tied to the other end.

This was the image we tried to keep off our minds as we continued up, her memory our future. Not right away, but after a switchback or two, we slowed to an easy pace that we could go at for hours. There was no need to hurry to where she had been. When we got there, we didn't want to be exhausted. Our shadows lengthened as the rays from the westing sun came parallel to the slope of the mountain. The shadows stretched head first toward the valley. When passing uphill of a tree, my shadow popped up from lying across the meadow to stand vertically beside me on the trunk of the tree and then fell back down the meadow. I refused to think ahead of the next footfall. Alpenglow and the evening quiet came and left and we kept moving up.

Cold air from Teepe's Snowfield and the Middle Teton Glacier washed over us as if it had been kept dammed up by the sun, bowing balsamroot and Indian paintbrush as it rushed valleyward. Bearing the day's snowmelt, the stream draining Garnet Canyon crowded through the boulder fields, nudging huge boulders imperceptibly downward. The stream dropped from the mouth of the canyon and plummeted ecstatically toward Cottonwood Creek, then into the Snake River, down the valley and out, across southern Idaho to the Columbia, finally to salty silence and insignificance in the soundless whirl of the deep Pacific currents that have nothing to do with snow and sand and grasses and flowers or rocks, boulders, valleys, canyons, deserts, and mountain ranges: currents that dance only to global winds and the swing of the earth, moon, and sun through their orbits. Sand, pebbles, glaciers, and the mountain itself followed in a more dignified, but no less determined, geologic flow. Still we went up, breasting all the downward-beckoning signs.

Then it was dark. People are not nocturnal animals. The last time I had been in the mountains at night and not sat before a fire, as awake people are meant to do at night in the mountains, was with Barry, Jake, and Bill when we did the second complete ascent of Mt. Moran via the South Buttress Route. That was the climb out of which grew the climb of the Southwest Rib of the South Face of Denali. When we got to the top of the buttress, we bivouacked until the moon came up. Then we climbed all night to reach the summit at dawn. It was fun to climb at night, not seeing exposure we knew was there. We chose our route according to the angle of the moon, moving in a pool of moonlight as if God held a lantern for us.

This night, the low, waning moon didn't reach down to us. The indifference of the mountains towards things human became animus. Fritz was somewhere above us, alone on the ledge in the midst of the debris of climbing gear. A rope ran taut up to a piton and then down again to the lip of the ledge and into darkness into which Fritz would not peer. Up high, the wind was soughing across the summits but not down in the canyon where we were.

The wind aloft quieted and we yodeled to Fritz. That was a mistake. The walls above us converted the sound into a hideous laugh, echoing and re-echoing in the canyon. We decided that Fritz couldn't hear us and didn't yodel again. Our head lamps cast a wan light which allowed us to place our feet but didn't help in route-finding because the lamps destroyed night vision. That made the dark darker. I turned mine off and always after that in the mountains at night did without a head lamp as much as possible. We tried to move silently because of what the night did to sounds. "This is not fun; this is awful," I kept thinking to myself. Through the night, we kept moving up; the pain from our heavy loads was familiar, constant, and, as a rein to our imagination, a comfort.

We reached a place where we could no longer climb unroped safely and stopped to rope up. We were close now. Fritz had talked to us, but we couldn't make out what he said because he kept to the back of the ledge and his voice passed over us out into the canyon. Art led a pitch and brought me up. The others carried on a shouting conversation with Fritz, trying to find where we'd gotten to and ought to go. We finally understood that we were in the wrong couloir. Art prepared to descend.

Fritz heard Art and me below him and came to the lip of the ledge. In a normal voice he spoke down to us, "He's right above you."

"Uhn!" I forced myself to contract the muscles in the back of my neck to turn my face up. The first light was in the east, but mercifully it was still too dark to see. Art continued on down to go with Leigh to pick out the route, and I stayed at the top of the pitch in case we should decide to climb up from there.

Then it wasn't too dark. He was swinging, one arm extended, legs askew and stiffly crooked. He rotated around just off the wall until a boot hit, THUMP, and back around, THUMP again. When I saw, I realized that the thumps had been happening for some time but I hadn't heard them. They were why Fritz had stayed at the back of the ledge, where sometimes he could not hear them.

Down the large ledge which we had climbed to reach the couloir was a ramp leading up to Fritz's ledge. I chose to be one of the ones to go up to the site of the fall. Partly I wanted to be doing something; mainly I wanted to be lowering the body, not receiving it. I did not want to put the corpse in the body bag.

Using Tim's rope and our own and a third, we lowered the body. The ropes didn't quite reach. Art climbed up to receive the body and continued the lowering from there. We did not hurry down from where we were; nevertheless, we arrived in time for the bagging of the body.

"Well, I guess I might as well get it all," I said to myself.

Tim had bared his teeth in his final moment, trying to lock in his last groan and keep it from Sally. The rope wouldn't come free of its groove in his body. We tugged gently and then just cut the rope rather than have to yank on it. There's a limit. His eyes were not closed. Tim had been tall, his body was long. It had to be bent a little to be fitted into the litter. That's when the last groan escaped.

"Stomach gas," said three of us at once. We must have all read the same war novel.

There was no water up there. We'd been without water since shortly after midnight. The canyon we were in had no trail. It was obvious that even if we were fresh it would be dark before we could reach the valley. In our fatigued state, it would take an entire day. We asked for help. Phil Martin, Bob Hall, Bill Lewis, and Jim Huidekoper, another volunteer, set out to bring us water, food, and their muscles. The park decided to try a helicopter. There appeared to be a level place down in the cirque between Nez Perce and Cleaver Peak. We would make for that.

Slowed by fatigue and thirst, we worked the litter between, over, and under the boulders in a boulder field. Then we thrashed and tugged and stumbled through brush. We had stopped thinking of the body as Tim. He hadn't looked like Tim out of the bag; in the bag he was just weight. Someone had looked up his weight on the registration sheet before setting out. That was one of the little rituals which helped to separate us from what we had to do: so many pounds, to be lowered so many rope lengths, to be carried so many hours, by so many people, to be paid so many hours of overtime.

At midday, the support team arrived with water and food. We sat beside the litter to rest. When I noticed that my elbow was resting on the body, I started slightly, then left it where it was.

It didn't look as if the helicopter could reach us. The wind was fifteen to thirty in gusts. The flat place we had to use as a landing pad was right up against the wall of Cleaver Peak. The only helicopter available had a maximum safe altitude of 10,000 feet. The top of the wall was 10,200, and over the top of the wall was the only possible approach. A helicopter in air is like a boat in water. If there's no wind, then it's like canoeing on a glassy lake. If there is wind, then it's like a tidal or river current. If the wind is pouring over mountain peaks and saddles and funneling down canyons, it's like rapids, cataracts, and waterfalls. Flying in a canyon, we could be thrown horizontally, dropped down, or lifted up. Two out of the three ways we could be pushed were not good.

At 3:30 we were within forty-five minutes of the cirque. We could see that the landing place was a good one, and we imagined that the wind had eased a little.

The helicopter pilot agreed to look. Doug McLaren was with him, and though there was no hurry about Tim, Doug knew that we were spent. The pilot didn't like the looks of things. Doug urged him to try. The pilot agreed, and then Doug had reason to regret his urging. As the chopper came over the ridge near the summit, it got caught in a downdraft and dropped a thousand feet. The pilot checked its descent just a hundred feet above the litter, hovered, and landed.

Five minutes later, I sat with Dave Dornan, watching the burdened chopper skim over the tree tops down the canyon and then swing out over the Snake River. I would be joining Dave at the Jenny Lake Ranger Station to take Tim's place. It was also Dave's first year. He had gone up to the ledge for the same reasons I had, with the same results; we were spared none of it. We lingered a few minutes longer, watching the play of sun and shadow on mountains and valley. We laughed at our fears of the night before. During the next couple of rescue seasons, he and I were to have a lot of such moments as that brief respite sitting on a boulder together in a high mountain canyon. Eventually Dave would quit rescuing. He would encourage me to do the same. We were together on that boulder as few men are ever privileged to be, but in spite of our similarities, we had arrived there by different routes and so would depart. He would become a climber again. For seven seasons beyond that one, I would continue rescuing, which, as I would eventually learn, is not pure climbing.

CHAPTER 7
OUT THERE

If anybody had noticed how lucky I was to have just walked into park headquarters, asked for a job and a position on the rescue team, and been hired immediately, I would have explained that I was perfect for the job. In fact, I was really hired because backcountry and mountaineering activities had doubled in a year. The park was ill-prepared for a doubling of accidents, if that should happen as well. It did happen. Toward the end of my first season, there was a week where we spent only one day in the ranger station and spent four days in the backcountry evacuating injured climbers and, as we said in our reports, a "fatality." From that year, 1960, hence, mountain rescue has been the main work of the Jenny Lake rangers.

I returned season after season, and more and more climbers came. I got better at the job, but doubts also grew as to my perfectness for the work.

As with other work of this sort, a degree of emotional numbness was inevitable and welcome. It had to be a selective numbness. Staying alive required attention, all perceptions—sight, hearing, smell, touch, taste—functioning well. Therefore, it was also inevitable that some unwelcome images and scenes slipped past the guard to lurk in the darkened theater of my memory.

At times I cannot foresee, I glimpse a girl lying still at the bottom of a hundred-foot cliff. Her face is calm and beautiful, half of it.

There is this conversation at the base of another cliff:

"What is *this*?"

"It looks like part of his brain."

"I can't get it back into his head."

"Maybe we should bury it."

"Something will eat it. I'll just put it in the body bag."

"No, not loose! Here, I've got a sandwich bag. Put it in that first."

There are other kinds of moments, too, odd moments of peace. The end of summer, when climbers crowd themselves to fulfill the expectations of spring, is the prime accident season. My birthday is August 25. It became traditional with us to expect a rescue on my birthday.

Because the accident was a long way off and we got the word late in the day, Dave and I went out in advance carrying only first-aid stuff in order to reach the victim before dark. The rest of the team was to carry in the equipment during the night; we'd take her out at dawn. Dave and I added a bottle of wine to our light load for my birthday.

The girl had been lucky. She had taken a tumbling fall of two hundred feet and had not hit her head. Both legs were broken at the ankle, but it wasn't until sometime after the fall that she remembered that she was a dance student.

"I started falling. At first I thought I could stop myself. When I realized that I was going to fall a long way, I remembered that you are supposed to relax. I said, 'You'd better relax.' Do you know what I worried about? My fingernails. I've been trying to get my fingernails to grow back. I used to chew on them. I finally had these nice long fingernails and all I could think about while I was falling was 'Oh, my beautiful fingernails are going to break.'"

She was a pretty, high-spirited girl who bore her pain better than anyone we had seen. We built a fire and she, Dave, and I watched the sunset, the fire, and the headlamps of the rescue team winding slowly up the mountainside while we sipped on the bottle of wine.

The young people who had summer jobs with the Grand Teton Lodge Company had more accidents than any other group we could identify. A few of these employees felt that since they sort of worked for the park, the sign-out procedures ought not to apply to them.

One such young man—I'll call him Thomas—had been something of a smartass when he checked out at the ranger station for a climb. He then went off with his partner and started up a climb other than the one they signed out to do, a climb we told them was above their abilities.

It was mainly a coincidence that Dave and I were on the trail below when they retreated from the climb, which they found they could not do. It was not a coincidence that we stayed to watch their descent. We radioed headquarters that we were going to watch them for a bit because it looked as if they were headed for worse trouble. Even so, I was not fully prepared to see in the binoculars Thomas fall sixty feet down a chimney to a ledge. I lowered the binoculars from my eyes, stunned but also feeling that this was not the first time I'd seen that image in binoculars.

Memorial Day, 1957, Fort Sill, Oklahoma. There was a demonstration of a combined infantry and artillery assault on a series of hills. Officers, wives, officers from other nations, and we, OCS candidates, were in a grandstand observing. The artillery bombarded the top of the near hill while the infantry ran crouched to its base. The artillery bombardment moved ahead a hundred yards and the infantry moved up the hill a hundred yards. The artillery ceased and the infantry charged the summit of the hill. The artillery changed its target to the second row of hills. Two battalions of howitzers and mortars fired at the second row of hills—minus one battery. That battery forgot to change the settings on its guns. Four rounds landed in the infantry platoon which had "taken" the top of the hill. While I watched through my binoculars, one soldier was blown up in the air, end over end, and fell back to earth. The assault on the second hill continued, while the announcer paused and then continued his narration, saying nothing at all about what we were looking at. In a few minutes, helicopters came to drop troops at the base of the second hill and pick up the dead and wounded from the first hill on the way back.

When the first hill was cleared, a candidate remarked, "I think that's going too far to make it realistic."

The ledge Thomas fell to was only one pitch above the scree slope. We reached the base of the pitch from the trail in less than five minutes and appeared on the ledge, in uniform, in another ten minutes. Thomas was alive, another shock for us.

I had seen him bounced from wall to wall in the chimney and had assumed he was being smashed to a bloody pulp. He was bloody, but as a mountain goat deliberately bounces from wall to wall in a controlled fall when it descends, the same procedure, though involuntary, had worked for Thomas. His partner, who had somehow gotten down to the ledge while we approached, was huddled at the back of the ledge, as far from the edge, and as far from Thomas, as he could get.

Thomas was lying on his back, moaning and gibbering, when two uniformed rangers stepped into his field of vision. He was beside himself. "God, you guys are fast, how did you . . . ?"

"It's our job," we told him. "Also, you weren't on the climb you signed out for."

He got in a confessional mood.

"I'll never do that again. I've gone on a lot of climbs without signing out; I'll never do it again."

Then he got in a devotional mood.

"Oh, God, just get me out of this and I'll never go climbing again."

He saw Dave and me grin at each other.

"I'm not really religious," he said, "just when I get into a tight spot."

We burst into laughter. God must have been amused too. Thomas suffered only bruises and a cut knee, and when he went climbing again a month later, he came back unharmed.

There were times when I wondered if the numbing was not going too far, whether I wasn't becoming an aesthete of gore.

A climber we knew well fell and cut his head badly. He was unconscious when his partner left him to come for us. Peter Koedt and I went ahead to find him while the rescue team geared up. The description we had been given of his location wasn't very precise, but we knew he was about a thousand feet up the drainage of a stream which fed the main creek in the canyon.

Five hundred feet up the side drainage, we came across drops of blood. His partner hadn't been cut, so we knew that our friend had regained consciousness and was wandering around on the mountainside. The trail of blood disappeared into chest-high brush. If he stumbled, the brush would cushion his fall, but the brush concealed many small cliff bands. Also, if he reached the creek, which was full of snowmelt, and attempted to cross it, he'd be lost.

We called, but carefully. It's not unusual for even an uninjured person to become terrified of the shouts of searchers and break into a panicked run. Peter scrambled onto an outcrop and spotted a hand waving above the brush. But for his wave, we might not have found him in time. Because he was wearing dark clothing and his face and hands were black with dried blood, he was so effectively camouflaged that we couldn't see him until we got within three steps of him.

We tried for a while to keep the flies from swarming over the blood on his face but gave it up. He thrashed around, as is usual with a head injury, until some corner of his mind told him that the matter was out of his hands, that his job was to preserve the dimming spark of life in him, and he became still again. Peter and I rested ourselves on either side to wait for the rest of the team. The hikers passed along the trail below us. No one looked up to see our two dark forms crouched over one inert form until we were joined by the rest of the team.

By the time we got the litter across the flooded creek, with fancy ropework of the sort we did in rescue practice but seldom used, a crowd had gathered on the trail above the creek. I found myself anticipating the crowd's response to our lord of the flies when they got a close look at him. We might have scrubbed his face and hands at the creek but didn't.

Our audience opened up as we reached the trail and then closed in to sneak a quick look. Some were unable to suppress a gasp. It went like that all the way down the trail. We'd approach, they'd step off the trail, we'd pass, they'd stretch their necks for a look, I'd smile following the audible gasp.

The day was clear and comfortably cool. The work hadn't been excessive. There was a responsive audience. The bad part was that our friend wasn't completely comatose. He was suffering badly from thirst. We gave him a sip at a time, which barely wet his lips before he passed out. Then, in a bit, he'd begin moaning for water again. If we had stopped every time he moaned, it would have taken all day to get him to the hospital.

At one point he stayed conscious for a few minutes. He called me to him. He couldn't open his eyes; he was afraid that he was blind. I washed his eyelashes to loosen the encrusted blood. He looked at me.

"Don't be sadistic," he groaned. Then, as if not certain he had the right word, "Don't be masochistic." He kept it up, "Don be stistic, don be maskist." It spoiled what had otherwise been a good day's work.

There were times when I feared for my character.

Three of us returned to the site of what had been a long, more than ordinarily dangerous rescue to retrieve equipment we had left behind. We would also retrieve what we could of the stuff left behind by the party we rescued. There was more than we could carry of their stuff, so we had to choose. Some of their climbing gear was better than we could afford for ourselves, and there was reason to believe that the party we'd rescued had no further use for the gear. When one of us selected gear to carry down to keep for himself, I kept an uncomfortable silence.

As leader, I had a strong influence on decisions but not dictatorial powers. We were too dependent on each other for that. Whatever the task prescribed by the United States government, once we were roped up, the main thing was to get up and back down alive. For that, everybody had equal responsibility.

That's looting, I thought, staying a distance from him on the trail. He is looting and I am not going to do anything about it. If I said he shouldn't do that, he would ask why not. I wouldn't know what to say.

There were times when I had to admit that I was not completely sane.

"I wonder what it sounded like?" I mused half aloud to Rick Horn.

"What what sounded like?" he said sharply, a touch of panic in the tone. I looked at him; he had grown suspicious of me of late. That morning he had called me crazy.

We had learned of the accident the afternoon of the previous day. Rick and I hiked in to camp at a lake in the meadow at the base of the mountain. I had decided that I would not carry both a five-pound sleeping bag and a ten-pound body bag. I told Rick that the bag had been thoroughly cleaned since it was last used, and anyway, since we had several in the rescue cache, nobody knew exactly when it had been last used. I didn't sleep well, for physical not psychological reasons. The thick rubberized canvas was too hot to sleep in; the night was too cold to sleep without it. I tried sleeping thirty minutes at a time in the bag and thirty minutes on top. That didn't work because my clothes got wet from sweating when I was in the bag, and then I'd be instantly cold on top of the bag. Finally, I fell asleep for about three hours with the bag unzipped all the way. I woke up in a pool of sweat. When dawn came, I complained about the night to Rick as we packed up. He looked at me with that same look, said I was crazy, and headed off up to the face. Rick's reward for dashing ahead was to be the first to reach the body.

"His head," I replied. "I wonder what his head sounded like when it hit."

"God, Sinclair!" he said.

The usual candidates had come to me, eggs, watermelons, coconuts, the click of billiard balls. The curious thing to me was that the head was not badly misshapen. It was approximately the right shape. But so much skull bone had shattered that none of the curves were fair curves, like the heads of clay we used to sculpt in kindergarten.

Our talking was loud in the windless silence of the canyon. It was probably the silence of the place that had made me wonder what sound had been there yesterday. Did he yell? Probably not. He was certainly killed instantly. The death odor was very faint, so faint I couldn't be sure it was there yet. There was the ferruginous odor of dried blood, like unrefrigerated meat, marinated in sweat. Even bloody victims who are alive have that odor. Fatigue leaves a kind of iron taste in the mouth, too. Fatigue, dried blood, and death were flavors or odors I thought of as a family; the first whiff of death is an odor of honeyed iron. That odor had not yet come.

What probably bothered Rick about my question was that I could notice the skull at all. For me it was a minor triumph of self-control. The most noticeable thing in the landscape, which included four mountain ranges, the Wind Rivers, the Gros Ventres, the Absarokas, and the Tetons, was the victim's eye. When he hit, the eyeball had popped so that the optic muscle had extruded two inches from the socket, with the eyeball still attached to it. The body lay on a sloping ledge, face up and oriented valleyward. The eye stared periscope fashion across his forehead into the lake and meadow in the canyon. The other eye was gone completely; I had been searching for that eye when I'd asked Rick about the sound.

Rick stared at my hands. They were scratching around in the scree absently. I realized that at any moment they might find the eye. I stopped.

As we loaded the body into the bag, it occurred to me that the victim wouldn't have to worry about sweat. That thought

I kept to myself. We had a lot to do yet. I didn't want Rick looking at me that way as we belayed the body and each other down the mountain.

Whenever I went into the mountains, I watched the ravens soaring back and forth across the cliffbands. It seemed to me that there was always one nearby when I was struggling up a difficult pitch. I became afraid of them. I glowered at them in the distance and yelled obscenities at them when they were near. I feared someday arriving at the site of an accident and finding one feeding on the victim. I'd heard that they begin with the eyes.

I made such a fuss about my phobia that my friends laughingly called me "The Crow."

When I quit rescuing, the phobia went away.

The raven has to make his living too.

Photograph by Leigh Ortenburger, courtesy of the family and estate of Leigh Ortenburger.

EAST FACE OF GRAND TETON
L: Ledge Where Main Party Stopped
TB: Turn Back Point of Joyce and Blade

CHAPTER 8
EAST AND WEST

he back room of the Jenny Lake ranger station had a stove because in the winter it was used as a patrol cabin. On stormy days or on rest days it was a good place to make tea and to talk. Leigh Ortenburger spent much of his research time there when he was in the valley, and since he was our historian, the back room became one of the two storytelling places in the valley. The Climbers' Campground was the other one.

Late in July, 1962, there was a storytelling session going on with Leigh Ortenburger and Dave Dornan in the group. On a couple of occasions while climbing with Leigh, I had surpassed myself and had managed to do the crux moves of new routes we put up. This prompted Leigh to remark, "It really isn't safe to go into the mountains with Sinclair; he's a madman." Dave looked at me and said, "You can do this stuff; you ought to." What he meant by "this stuff" was his current project, raising himself to Yosemite standards. He had accepted the Yosemite challenge. That is, he did not expect to become as good as Chouinard or Robbins but he wanted to be good enough to carry on a conversation with them.

Dave wanted me to work on No Escape Buttress with him. Mt. Moran's south buttresses presented Teton climbers with a chance to do something that resembled Yosemite wall climbing. The easternmost of these buttresses, No Escape Buttress, was the last and most difficult of these problems. This did not sound like the climb for a person who climbs well only to escape, but because Dornan wanted this climb, I had to try.

There were encouraging signs in the heavens as we rowed across Leigh Lake in a rotting plywood skiff, one rowing, one bailing. The clouds looming up on the Idaho side of the range were massive and black. Such clouds in the morning indicated that this was not to be an ordinary storm; we were sure to be stormed off the climb. The prospect pleased me. We'd do a couple of pitches and then go home. Maybe I'd be more ready next time.

Dornan was near the top of the first lead when the storm hit. He rappelled off and we ran for the lake. Crossing the lake in that storm was one of the dumbest things we'd done. Fortunately, the energy of the storm was released in impulses rather than as a sustained force. The wind and rain combined to beat the surface of the lake down instead of lifting it into breaking whitecaps, or we would have been swamped. Dave, chortling because he was no longer a rescuer, remarked that if there was anybody in the mountains, my day was not over. I wasn't much worried. This storm was severe enough that the most desperate vacationing climber, with one day left on his vacation and fifty weeks of being chained to a desk facing him, could not pretend that this was a passing summer shower. It was cold as well as violent. There was a smell of the Gulf of Alaska about it.

As Dave and I headed back to Jenny Lake, I looked forward to a few quiet days in the ranger station. The climbers would be out of the mountains, and the campers would be heading for motels or the desert. The back of the ranger station would be warm, full of climbers drinking tea. The guides would be in, looking at our photographs of the peaks, planning one more climb, swapping stories.

When we got back to the ranger station, things were less peaceful than I'd hoped. The big news was that Lyn, Sterling's wife, had rolled their Volkswagen bus. She wasn't hurt badly, but she and Ster had a good fright. A minor piece of news was that the other ranger on duty had been sent out to check on an overdue party of ten from the Appalachian Mountain Club. This was an annoyance but couldn't be thought of as serious. Ten people can't just vanish in a range as small as the Tetons.

People frequently get benighted in the Tetons in circumstances like those attending this climb: a large party composed of people of varying experience, climbing a route that is reputed to be easy but is seldom climbed. Those circumstances are practically guaranteed to produce a bivouac. Normally we at the ranger station would give the party plenty of time to extricate itself from the route and get back before we went looking for them. Often there would be another party in the same general area who had spotted the late party. From when and where they were seen, we could make a reasonable estimate of how long it would take them to get back. We'd set things in motion if the missing party exceeded our estimated time of return as well as their own. Even then we wouldn't scramble a full-scale search. Our first action would be to send out a ranger, two if there was to be technical climbing, and, if possible, combine the search with some other activity such as a patrol. We would also pass the word around to one or two key rescue types that a party was overdue. What that meant to them was that they'd be where they could be easily reached and maybe pass up the second beer until the word went about that everybody was out of the mountains.

Sometimes a worried family or concerned friends who were waiting in the valley would take exception to this stalling for time. But there was no other way to do it. If we did a full-scale search and rescue operation every time a party was overdue, the expense would have been enormous. In addition, that increased pressure on the party to get back in the time estimated might well result in more injuries and deaths.

In this case, we did not stall as long as we normally would have before sending someone out. There were more than one hundred people in the Appalachian Mountain Club encampment, with little else to do but worry about their overdue party. Also, the storm increased the possibility that the party could be stuck for some time, and the party was not well equipped for cold weather. Thus, very soon after we were notified, Ranger George Kelly was on his way into the mountains on a patrol. He would begin by organizing a search party from the Appalachian Mountain Club encampment.

It's not that we didn't worry. We were paid to worry. There are people who do it for nothing. It was not difficult to imagine the worst, even after one hundred repetitions of our imaginings turning out to be worse than the fact, but we had learned an orderly procedure to follow in these cases and kept our imaginings for entertainment. It happened that in this one case, the event was much worse than we had imagined.

The leader of the party, Ellis Blade, was himself not an Appie but a hired expedition leader. He was in his fifties and had years of mountaineering experience.

The rest of the party varied greatly in experience. Steven Smith, quite young but a good rock climber, was the assistant leader. The other good rock climber was sixty-five-year-old Lester Germer. Charles Joyce was a good recreational rock climber, respectful of the western mountains because his experience had been mainly on the cliff bands of the East. Janet Buckingham was experienced mainly as a hiker. Lydia and Griffith June, Charles Kellogg, and John Fenniman were in various stages of beginning to learn to rock climb. Mary Blade, Ellis's wife, was also along and was an experienced mountaineer. The route they were to climb was known as the Otterbody Route after the shape of a snowfield in the middle of the east face of the Grand Teton.

The party got off as planned at 4 A.M. Thursday morning, a good sign. There had only been a couple of minor problems for Ellis Blade in the days prior to setting out. He hadn't been able to generate much enthusiasm for conditioning climbs. The time to get the party into condition had been scheduled, but things hadn't quite worked out. Going into the wilderness to set up a new society is an American passion, but it takes a lot of energy just to eat, sleep, and talk in a situation like that. There are new people to meet and hierarchies, liaisons, and enmities to be established before the group can truly focus on its stated purpose.

The problem, other than the lack of conditioning, that Blade might have had on his mind that Thursday morning was that Smith, the young assistant leader, was suffering from an attack of nonconfidence. Smith did not like the looks of the weather. He had vomited the evening before. Blade was fifty-four and Steven Smith was twenty-one. Smith had not approached Blade directly about his worries and nausea but had confided them to Joyce, who did talk to Blade. If Blade's employers considered part of his responsibilities to be training the next generation of leaders, then it would have been up to Blade to establish a rapport with his young assistant. ("Lack of communication" was just coming into vogue as a new sin—to which persons in positions of authority are particularly prone—so it is astonishing how much communication and its lack became a theme in postevent analyses of these events. In retrospect, the whole sequence of events seems another case of the gods using tragedy for parody.) Blade did not establish a rapport with his young assistant. He had all he could do just to get his party up and off the mountain. It is also true that mountaineering in America was undergoing a growth in rock-climbing skills; hundreds of good young climbers were, within three years, learning to do moves on rock routes that older climbers had thought only feasible on campground boulders. Blade would be an unusual man if he did not feel his authority somewhat undercut by this new generation.[1]

As for Smith, it's possible that he had a touch of the flu or had picked up a bug from the water. One or the other happened to me at least once a season in the Tetons and to all the guides and climbing rangers I knew, which may only be saying that we all have our moments of discouragement. The bugs were always there. They determined the kind of sickness we would get, not when we would get it.

---

[1] For the events I did not witness, events in the AMC camp before the climb, and Charles Joyce's story, I am indebted to the work of James Lipscomb, the results of which appeared in two issues of *Sports Illustrated*, June 1965, "72 Hours of Terror," June 14, and "Night of the One-Eyed Devils," June 21.

Whatever caused Smith's lack of confidence, the events of the rest of the first day conspired to keep him low. The early start was the last thing to go well.

Four and a half hours later, at 8:30, they started up Teepe's Snowfield, two and a half hours behind according to Blade's schedule. Making such schedules is the curse of being the party leader.

As the snowfield got steeper, Janet Buckingham broke out of her steps in the snow, and although Smith held her easily, Janet's feet ineffectively flailed away at the snow. Anybody who has taught beginning climbers is familiar with the scene. The student or client literally loses contact with his or her feet and thrashes away hoping that a miracle will occur and one of them will stick. Perhaps Smith didn't know how to deal with the situation; perhaps he hadn't the chance. It was Blade, leaving his own rope, who talked her back into confidence in her steps again.

There is something else about beginners on snow which Blade may have been thinking about while restoring Janet to her feet. To a beginner, going up is four times easier than going down. Ascending, the snow is right there in front of your face and you can touch it with your hands. You go up by slamming your foot directly into the slope. Descending, there's only empty space in front of your hands and eyes. You go down, not by shifting your weight from one firmly planted foot to the other, as in going up, but by stepping off a firmly planted foot into air. Every step going up is reversible at any point in the move. Every downward step is irreversible, a nervous-making succession of total commitments. What would it be like to try to descend this snowfield with people having these difficulties ascending? The incident with Janet might have been soon forgotten by all involved except that disturbing incidents began to accumulate.

The lead rope of five made it to the top of the snowfield half an hour before noon. The second rope, Smith's, didn't join the lead rope at the top. They stopped on an outcropping about three rope lengths below for their lunch. This area was scarred by debris fallen from the cliff band and two snowfields above.

This detail did not go unnoticed by Joyce, and he was the one who spotted the ice falling from above and gave a warning yell. One block carried away Fenniman's ice axe. Another glanced off Kellogg's foot. Joyce had two blocks to dodge and only managed to dodge one. He was hit hard and knocked into the air. Though briefly stunned, he was uninjured.

To this point, Joyce, though he was Smith's confidant, had been maintaining neutrality on the question of whether the climb was advisable or not. After being hit, he still wasn't as shaken as Smith, whose hands were trembling, but he was now of Smith's opinion that this was an ill-fated climb and they ought to go down.

While they were getting underway, Joyce said to Smith, "Let's get out of here." Smith, who told Joyce that his alertness had saved their lives, said, "He'll kill us all," again the kind of tossed-off remark that usually doesn't survive the moment.

As the entire party joined at the top of the snowfield, a storm hit. It was noon. This was not the familiar late afternoon thunderstorm but the first impulse of the big storm that drove Dave and me out of the mountains. The party took refuge in the moat between the top of the snowfield and the rock. Smith finally confronted Blade directly with his desire to retreat. Blade responded that the snowfield was hardening and had become dangerous. As the heavy rainfall and hail from the first huge cumulus cloud passed and the rain moderated, Blade gave the word for everyone to put on their packs and start moving up. Joyce sought out Smith.

"What's he doing? Is he nuts? We've got to go down. You're a leader. Tell him we've got to go down." Smith could not. Eventually it would be Joyce himself who would take command and make the decision to go down, but that was to be two days hence.

The party traversed the top of the snowfield to the base of a rock couloir. Blade sent Germer ahead to scout the route, asking him to report "how will it go." In the aftermath, every turn of phrase appears significant. If Blade's real question was Ought we attempt it? he asked it the wrong way. Germer did not interpret Blade's question as a request for advice but as a request for a technical report.

This couloir, carved in the seam of the East Face and the East Ridge of the Grand, joins the Otterbody Snowfield to Teepe's Snowfield. It is rather alarmingly free of the debris which packs the bottom of most Teton couloirs. It is too steep and too water, ice, and rock washed to hold anything in it. Obviously the rock is not particularly sound, which is why a couloir developed. Griffith June saw the couloir first as a bowling alley and then found in his mind the inscription from the Inferno, "Abandon hope, all ye who enter here." Wet, cold, late, tired, with weather threatening and tension in the party growing, it could not have been a cheerful party who geared themselves up for rock climbing.

Germer returned with his report, which he recalled thus: "I told him it looked easy. I know now he was asking for advice, and I gave him a rock-climbing opinion. It was easy rock climbing. I was not considering the safety of the party. The camp had chosen Blade as a leader, but I should have said something."

Possibly there was something else at work here. The opening sentence in the description of the Otterbody Route in Ortenburger's *Climbers Guide to the Teton Range* (1956 edition) says this of the first ascent, "Petzoldt ranks this as one of the easiest routes on the Grand Teton." Twenty-seven years after the first ascent, an eastern cliff climber of Germer's stature would be reluctant to rate this climb as more technically difficult than the first ascent party found it to be, unless Blade had reason to think that he was seriously off route. What Germer was acknowledging with his "I should have said something" was that of those who did say something or might have spoken, he was the only one whose view Blade would have had to seriously consider.

When Smith once again said that they ought to go down, Ellis Blade retorted, "I've been on that glacier before in weather like this. It's as hard as ice. If we go down, someone will get killed."

Smith pressed the point, "We can't climb the mountain now."

Blade's response was "You keep your mouth shut."

"Well, I'm assistant leader of this group," said Smith, "and I think my opinion should be considered."

"Well, don't you forget that I am the leader and I know it is safer to go up."

In the hours that followed, they all got soaked, Lydia June got a shock from a lightning strike, Smith avoided a rock avalanche only by leaping across the couloir into the arms of Griffith June, and Kellogg was hit by a rock that drove his crampons through his pack and into his back. Griffith June thought of leading a splinter group back, a serious responsibility. He had the authority within the AMC organization but not as a mountaineer, and they were very much in the mountains now. He did urge Blade to lead them back, but Blade replied that they were committed.

Blade climbed quickly and well then, getting the party three-fourths of the way up the couloir. Griffith June found a huge boulder two pitches from the top, big enough for them all to sit on. Joyce secured them with pitons, and all bivouacked there except Blade, who had reached the wide ledges and easy slabs at the top of the couloir. There was to be no reconsideration of Blade's decision. There were some complaints, perhaps fewer than there might have been had Mary Blade not been part of the group. A decision to go down would have been a decision to abandon Blade on the mountain.

Three inches of wet snow fell during the night. They had no down garments or dry clothes, some had no wool clothes, and they had run out of food. In the morning, Germer asked Smith what he thought. Germer didn't like the rotten rock and had been weakened by the bivouac. Smith replied that he didn't know the route. Once almost out of the gully, even Smith seems to have lost interest in going down.

It took all of the next day, Friday, to get the party up the remaining two pitches to the top of the couloir. Joyce and Fenniman climbed up to Blade. June slipped on the ice just below the point where the angle of the couloir eased. He tried repeatedly. He cut steps up, almost made it, and fell again, this time further and over an overhang. There was danger of his being strangled by the rope. Smith muscled him over to the bivouac pillar, where June collapsed exhausted.

Germer then went up and set up an intermediate belay position, where he stayed until all six remaining climbers were up the couloir. (This was during the time when Dornan and I were being driven from No Escape Buttress a few miles to the north.) Though fit enough, Germer was in his sixties and the effort was too much; he had used all reserves. His hands were claws; he clutched a piton in each and made it up the ice. Blade moved on but was called back. Germer announced he was dying.

Blade assessed the situation and came up with a new plan but not a new direction. He was like a man possessed of an ultimate truth. There can be an infinite number of situations, tactics, and explanations, but there can only be one conclusion. He, Joyce, and Smith would go up. They might find climbers at the top. If not, they'd go down the Owen Spalding Route and get help. There was twice as much more snow above them than they had climbed on Teepe's Snowfield. There was a cliff band to climb between the Otterbody Snowfield and the East Face Snowfield. There was the descent from the summit, which, in icy conditions, is no easy matter. Ellis Blade knew about all this but appears to have forgotten it. He appears to have been in that state of mind where it's impossible to think beyond the next move. Every plan he had made, all preparations for the future, had been thwarted by unforeseen circumstances. It's happened to most of us.

When George Kelly got to the Appalachian Mountain Club camp at the Petzoldt Caves, there was no word of the missing party. By the time he radioed this news down, we were back in the ranger station and instructed him to organize a search. We were getting a little nervous. The search was, to a certain extent, window dressing. Any place the AMC people could be allowed to search would be a place the missing party could get out of by themselves. What they could do was look at the mountain and listen. They did, and what they saw was three members of the party up on the Otterbody Snowfield.

The need for a plausible explanation for what was happening with that party was increasing by the moment, while the prospects for getting such an explanation were decreasing. At their rate, it would be two days before they got to the top. We were at first inclined to believe that these three could not be from the party we were seeking, but there wasn't anybody else on the east side of the mountain. They had to be three of the ten. There was no way to make sense of it. It was hard to believe that, if there had been an injury or a fatality, someone couldn't have gotten out to tell us. If there had been some kind of horrible disaster and these were the only survivors, it would explain why we hadn't heard from them but not why they were going up. Only one thing was clear, we had to get serious about finding out what was going on.

There had been a short rescue the evening before involving a client of the guide service. The guide service had provided most of the manpower for the rescue. Barry Corbet was one of those on the rescue. He had been scheduled to take a party up the Grand on Saturday, so another guide had taken Barry's party up to the high camp at the Lower Saddle Friday morning while Barry slept late. Barry was on his way up to join his party when he met George Kelly and was pressed into service. As they followed the track of the party up the snowfield and into the couloir, the storm renewed itself. Barry was equipped and George wasn't. (They had gotten, as we later determined, within four hundred feet of Blade's group when they turned back.) Barry joined his party; George came back down.

Doug McLaren, district ranger and member of the rescue team when it was originally organized a decade earlier, was our supervisor. He organized and coordinated rescue activities. Doug ordered a pack team to move as much equipment as we could reasonably muster up to Garnet Canyon. Garnet Canyon is the cirque which is rimmed counterclockwise from north to south by Disappointment Peak, the Grand Teton, the Middle Teton, the South Teton, and Nez Perce. Doug, Sterling, Jim Greig, and I left in the advance party at 7 P.M. Rick Horn and Mike Ermath, the remaining strong climbers on the park team, were to follow with more equipment. All the available Exum guides and some friends had volunteered: Al Read, Fred Wright, Pete Lev, Jake Breitenbach, Dr. Roland Fleck, Bill Briggs, Dave Dornan, and Peter Koedt. These guides and volunteers would come up in the morning. Another guide, Herb Swedlund, was holding at the Petzoldt Caves, awaiting developments. A majority of the professional mountaineers in America were to carry out this operation.

The four of us got a little sleep at the end of the horse trail, about an hour below the encampment at the caves, and started up around 4 A.M. We arrived at the top of the snowfield at about 10:30. Here I made a mistake in route finding. The party had to be either on the cliff band between Teepe's Snowfield and the Otterbody Snowfield or at the top of the Otterbody just above the point where the three climbers had been spotted. There were two obvious routes up the cliff band. One was the couloir to the right of the cliff band, dark, wet, rotten; and the other was a nice sunlit rock line straight up from where we were.

I'd never been there before, but I'd been near there six weeks earlier looking at it from a col four hundred yards to our left at the southern edge of the snowfield. I had come to take a look because the climbing pressure on the standard routes was becoming such that I was interested in finding another easy route to the summit that we could recommend to those climbers who mainly just wanted to get to the top of the mountain. What I had seen in June was far from being the easiest route on the mountain. The sun reflected off the snow into the couloir to reveal a mass of contorted ice. Debris, both ice and rock, cascaded out of it. It seemed the picture of unpredictability. The mountain seemed to be saying, "Here I keep no pacts." At the same time, I noted the comparative warmth and orderliness of a sunlit route up an open chimney just to the south of the icy corner. I decided that the sunny route was the route Petzoldt had gone up. Though it may have been easy for him, it didn't appear easy enough for the type of climber I had in mind. I descended from the col without bothering to traverse the snowfield to take a closer look.

Now the ice was gone and water poured down the couloir. My comrades were of the opinion that the route went up the couloir. I said that was impossible, anybody could see that was no place to be. My memory of my first look at the couloir was influencing my present perception of it. Thus, I persuaded them to follow me up the route I had seen to the south (which is in fact not the Otterbody Route but, ironically, the Smith Route).

Though my view prevailed, the discussion had planted enough doubt in my mind that I wanted to make sure the climbing went as easily as I had claimed it would. I strained to find the easiest possible line. I almost frantically scanned the rock for holds, while trying to climb with as nonchalant a motion as I could. The climbing, while easy, was not trivial, and at the point that the guidebook account of the Smith Route describes as "the difficult overhanging portion," the climbing became seriously nontrivial.

As we paused to deal with this appearance of fifth-class climbing on what was supposed to be a third- and fourth-class route, we heard voices coming unmistakably from the top of the couloir. We spent the next hour rappeling back down to the top of the snowfield.

We decided that only two of us would go up to investigate, partly because of the rockfall danger and partly because the voices we heard seemed to be singing! Sterling and I had traveled together, worked together, and climbed together. I wanted him to stay at the bottom with Doug because it looked like that was going to have to be the organization point. I could not imagine what the tremendous barrier was between where we were and where they were, but there must be something keeping them from descending. Sterling could practically read my mind, and I wanted him where he would be in a position to do something if things got complicated. Also, Jim was bigger and stronger than either of us, and there were at least seven of them up there someplace.

Angry because of my mistake, I climbed carelessly and managed to break my hammer soon after we got underway. I remember the climbing as being more difficult than does Jim. The last two pitches, bypassing the overhang and crossing the ice, could easily intimidate a party not in good form. It was not any one thing; it was an accumulation of aggravations.

Once the overhang was passed, the route went up the right-hand, or east, side of the ice at the top of the couloir. The party was across the ice on the slabs at the "tail" of the Otterbody, about thirty feet above and half a rope length in distance. There were seven inches of snow on the ice, just heavy and wet enough to adhere to the ice while bearing our weight. We weren't able to protect the pitch in a manner which could stop a fall short of the overhang. We had neither ice pitons nor crampons. A rope from them above would be just the thing.

For the first time, we turned our attention fully to the party we'd come to rescue. They seemed calm. Did they have a climbing rope? They did. Would they toss us an end? They would. The young man, Fenniman, stiffly approached the lip of the ledge with a rope. He seemed a bit perplexed. We instructed him to give the coil a healthy swing and toss it down to us. He swung the coil back and then forward but failed to release it. He did the same thing again. And then again. And again. He was not swinging the coil to build up momentum but was swinging indecisively, almost as if he weren't sure he wanted us to cross over to them and disturb the calm which reigned there. The swinging motion became mechanical. He'd forgotten that he was not only to swing the coil but also release it. We hadn't told him that he had to do both, swing and release. We told him. The coil, released in the middle of the swing instead of at the end of it, dropped in front of his feet. Jim and I exchanged glances. Perhaps if he climbed down the slab to the next ledge toward us?

"I won't! I won't!" He spoke not directly to us but first to the air at our left and then to the rock at his feet.

"Stay where you are!" we said in one voice we just managed to keep from rising. We were in for it, no doubt about that; we'd really gotten into something very strange.

Jim "went for it," and we made it across and joined them on their ledge. They undoubtedly had been badly frightened and were probably making an effort to recover their wits. Possibly they were embarrassed. It seemed to be an effort for most of them to acknowledge our presence. There was a polite smile, a curious, almost disinterested gaze, the sort of thing I'd experienced in New York subways. Mary Blade seemed positively cheerful. They'd been singing, she told us. She also told us that Lester had been having a difficult time. Lester wanted to know if we'd brought any strawberry jam. We hadn't. We should have. According to Lester that's what we were supposed to do, bring strawberry jam and tea. He was a little put out with us and seemed to doubt that we knew our business.

I was offended. My first thought was, "Jesus Christ, Lester, if I knew what we were going to find up here, I would have brought the Tenth Mountain Division!" Lester's intimation that we didn't know what we were doing was not far off. What were we going to do?

I signaled to Jim. Under the pretext of moving to a better radio transmission site, we climbed up to the next ledge and walked behind a boulder to talk.

"What in hell are we going to do?" asked Jim.

Jim later told me that I calmly lit a cigarette and replied, "We're all going to die, that's what we're going to do."

I guess I had to say it to get it out of the way. I'm glad I did. Life doesn't provide many opportunities to deliver a line like that. Anyway, the notion that we might be there forever was not that farfetched. The radio would not work, and we had managed to get off without taking an extra battery. I restrained myself from throwing the radio down the mountain and satisfied myself with shouting into it, cursing, and shaking it.

Eventually, by moving about from rock to ledge to chimney and bouncing our voices off the walls on the East Ridge, we found a place where we could shout out of the couloir and have some words heard and, we hoped, understood by Ster and Doug. All we could tell them was to stay out of the couloir. What we wished to have been able to tell them was that we would be setting things up, up here, while they organized the equipment and men coming up from below. At some convenient moment, we would freeze all motion in the couloir while they set up belaying and lowering positions below us. Then we would have a bucket brigade of various techniques, fixed ropes, maybe a litter or two, rappels, belay, and so forth, depending on the terrain and the condition of each person being lowered. It was an elegant picture I had of how it should go, but it was not to be. Jim and I would just have to start moving the party down the mountain any way we could until we were back in communication with our teammates or until they could see what was needed, we could see that they could see what was needed, and we all could do what was needed.

We started. There was a ledge big enough for the whole party below us, but it was further than the two short pitches Jim and I could manage with the equipment available. Could Fenniman, the only one of the party who was reasonably ambulatory, help us? He'd have to. The fact that we had to use Fenniman in the shape he was in made us feel absurd. We played existentialist.

"Do you think this boulder will hold?"

"If it falls off we can go down the mountain and roll it back up."

The system we decided on was for Jim to lower one to me, me to lower that one to Fenniman, and he to belay them to the ledge. I anchored Fenniman to a slab about thirty feet above the big ledge and gave him precise instructions, which I repeated several times. While doing so, my sense that things were absurd became a feeling that things were desperate. The entire operation had to funnel to and through this youngster just out of high school who was headed for Dartmouth. I'd once been a kid just out of high school headed for Dartmouth and couldn't imagine what I'd have been able to do if I had been in the position he was in. He had been here, crawling around in this couloir, for two nights and now nearly three days. We put him in what must have appeared to him as the most precarious position he'd been in during the entire nightmare. He was securely anchored, but he had only my word for that. It would not be surprising if he had come to doubt the word of people who claimed to know better than he the position he was in.

I felt that I wasn't talking to Fenniman but to a messenger the whole Fenniman had sent to hear me out. The messenger seemed reliable, even heroic. I felt that Fenniman would get the job done but had the odd thought in the midst of talking to him that I'd like to meet him some day. I thought he might untie himself from the anchor and step off the mountain. That had happened a few years before to a guide with a head injury on this same mountain, three ridges to the south. I moved the knot tying him to the mountain around behind him where it couldn't be reached accidentally as he tied and untied the people we sent down. I made my instructions simple, precise, and routine while attempting at the same time to speak to him as a peer. This stuff I'm telling you to do, this situation you're in, it's just routine for mountaineers like you and me.

It worked. He did it exactly as I instructed him, exactly the same way every time. It may be that when he swung that coil mechanically back and forth when we asked for the upper belay, some part of my mind had registered the potential in his precise movements and had seen that his "I won't! I won't!" could be made "I will! I will!" But in the end, it all came down to the fact that Fenniman was the only person who stood up when we arrived.

We first assumed that they could provide their own motive power and set their own pace of descent while we belayed them along a fixed rope. The least experienced of them would not have found the first pitch at all troublesome under normal circumstances, but they fell down on flat ledges, fell into a stream two feet wide and three inches deep, and spent thirty seconds trying to figure out how to step over an eight-inch rock. Sometimes you see this in a beginning rock climbing class when the client is really frightened. There are ways to deal with it. But these people did not look frightened. What we were seeing on their faces and hearing in their voices wasn't fear but confusion, as if the problems of balance and motion were complicated math problems. We gave up trying to talk them through the moves. We were becoming exasperated at the ineffectiveness of our explanations and instructions and knew that our exasperation would only make things worse.

Tactfully at first, and then less so, we relieved them of their autonomy. Staggering, slithering, stumbling, as long as they kept moving, they could pick their own way down. If they stopped too long, a segment of time which became shorter as the sun got lower, a tug or a nudge and finally a steady, unrelenting pressure kept them moving.

After the first of them had gone down the snow-covered ice, it wasn't snow covered. All pretense of down climbing could be abandoned. They got soaked sliding down the ice and water, and I shivered for them. The wetter they got, the slower they moved. The wetter they got, the greater the need for speed.

Fenniman caught on. I overheard someone ask Fenniman to wait because he had lost a foothold. To which Fenniman replied insistently, "They say you have to keep moving."

Speed under these circumstances was relative. We, who were trying to imagine that we were in control of things, were tying, untying, handling the rope with one hand, gesticulating with the other, and talking and thinking at a furious rate. Those who were being controlled were rudely precipitated off a pitch, tied to an anchor, and then left to a shivering wait of a half hour or more before it was their turn to move again.

Once down to the big ledge, things seemed better. Perhaps the ledge above on which they had spent so many uncomfortable but relatively safe hours had been difficult to abandon. The feeling of us and them lessened. There was some conversation. We found out what we could about what had happened. I began to learn their names and to take account of them as separate people. I noted that the Junes seemed to be holding together. That does not always happen to couples under stress in the mountains. I wondered if Germer was recalling warm summer days rock climbing in the Shawangunks. Janet was the wettest, coldest, seemed most out of place, but I was impressed by her endurance. I wondered if Mary Blade were worrying about Ellis and, if she were, would she be most worried about his safety or the repercussions that seemed obviously destined to come to him. Kellogg seemed to be not too badly off but looked haggard, like a nice young man just recently embarked on a course of dissipation.

There was little time for these thoughts. Above all was the fact that we could make a mistake and kill one of them or not make a mistake and still have one of them die. Lester Germer was the obvious candidate, the one everybody was worried about, but there were others. And what of the missing three? We had to take Mary's word that they were in pretty good climbing shape, but what did "pretty good" mean? The best we could do was to hope that they would be spotted by Barry, who was on the summit that day. The trouble was, Barry should be down by now. Perhaps Doug and Ster already had news?

I chafed at our slow pace. My mistake cost us about two hours, and that was going to make the difference between day and night in this gully, between warm sun and thirty-two-degree granite, between wet pitches and ice pitches, between a snow you could heel down and snow as hard as ice. My mistake might end up meaning the difference between life or death for one or more of these people. Once you parade yourself in the world as a rescuer and once you take charge of the party, everything that happens after that is on your head.

I tried not to let myself think about the fear, pain, and suffering of the victims, except as objective facts which had to be entered into the calculations along with everything else that had a bearing on getting off the mountain by the quickest, safest means available. A sympathetic understanding of their plight could help little. Whether the pain and fear was tolerable or intolerable, being dealt with well or ill, there was still only one solution, getting down. But in this case, the sheer numbers of suffering people made it difficult to maintain that attitude. Jim appeared to accept the slow pace better than I, but he too had his troubles holding off their suffering.

We made another effort to talk to Doug and Ster. Our message was that we did indeed need everything they had, but they had to stay out of the gully. It was frustrating for them, and for the guides that had arrived too, to watch the shadow of the Grand move out over the valley while we appeared not to be moving at all. The rockfall we were setting off was fairly convincing. The main thing we wanted to be happening down there was to have the snowfield all set up for lowering so that as each of the party arrived at the top of the snowfield, they could be lowered quickly from anchor to anchor.

Just before dark, Jim called down to me the news that two of the missing three were coming down from above. The significance of the fact that there were two, not three, took hold slowly. I could not imagine how the third could be rescued. If we stopped everything to bring a litter and eight climbers up through us, I was sure somebody would die of exposure, there would be rockfall both above and below, and there'd be nobody left to help us get these seven down. I also found myself fervently hoping that I wouldn't have to go back up the mountain.

When Blade got down to me, I interrogated him fairly fiercely about the condition of the third. It was Smith and he was dead. I was in danger of feeling relieved, and that made me ruder. Also, it was difficult to believe. "Are you sure he's dead, because if you're not sure somebody has to go up. How did you check? How long did you wait before leaving him?" Blade told me that the body had started to get stiff. That soon? Well anyway, whether he was dead when they left him or not, he was certainly dead by now. Still, I'd given a man up for dead on secondhand information. I sized up Joyce. He was in better shape than anyone else. It was surprising to see a normal person who was apparently unaffected by this place. I asked him. "Yeah, he's gone."

I had taken Blade aside to question him. I could imagine what the impact of the news that this strong young man had died of exposure might do to the will to survive of the rest. Furthermore, if someone else was going to die it was unlikely that they'd do it quickly and allow us to go on. I had an image of being immobilized there in that gully helplessly watching a slow chain reaction of dying. I told Blade not to talk about it.

He moved across the ledge and gathered everybody there around and made a little speech about how we were trying to help them and they'd have to cooperate with us. I found that astonishing and a little amusing. Astonishing that he still was functioning as a leader and amusing as I tried to imagine how they could not cooperate with us. Then I had an awful insight. What, from their point of view, would we be doing differently from what we were doing if we were not trying to save them but trying to kill them? They were back in the dreaded couloir, were wet again, rocks were falling around them, there was no tea and jam. Whatever his mistakes, Blade was one of them and not one of their tormentors.

I was ashamed of my tough talk to Blade. I had my own mistakes to worry about.

Janet got soaked again. She lost her footing while being lowered, swung into a waterfall and was too stiff and cold to roll out of it without help. I began to feel that she might not make it, and I had to do something personally to give her heart. The barrier the rescuer maintains between himself and the victims makes stepping across it a more effective gesture.

I made her squeeze in behind a flake which would protect her a little from the cold evening westerly pouring down on us from the snowfields above. I made her take off her Levis, lectured her about the fact that denim was the worst possible material to wear in the mountains, and wrung the water out of them a much as I could. They were new and stiff. I imagined that she'd bought them down in Jackson, in honor of her visit to the West. I gave her some food I'd been saving for someone to whom it might make the difference, me, for example. Then I took my favorite sweater out of my pack and made her put it on. I tried levity. I told her that it was a twenty-five-dollar sweater and she'd better not get it dirty! She thought I was serious—so much for levity.

There were shouts from below. They were coming up, and we were to be careful about rocks. It was worth being a climber to feel what I felt then. For the feeling I had, you have to learn to do something which is dangerous, has a code, and requires performance to a certain standard. Then you have to get in a jam and have "your mates," as Hemming would have said, get you out of it only because you are one of them.

First to arrive were Pete Lev and Al Read. Lev was the picture of earnest strength. Read was the picture of a man in command of himself. Witty, quick to perceive the ludicrous as the ironic, he is a natural leader and an unobtrusive one. Lev is very compassionate and was taken aback by what he saw, including me and Jim. Pete and Al were looking at us as if we needed a cab to get us home. Suddenly it seemed possible that most of us might escape from this place. Suddenly the mountain seemed covered with people who knew what they were doing.

Swedlund was down there, Swedlund who would joke with the Devil. I couldn't wait to get down to hear him say something like, "Sinclair, you're quaking like a dog passing peach pits." Horn was down there, probably performing great feats of strength and daring while screaming, "The world is contrived to drive us insane."

The next pitch below ended in the middle of a slab which bulged out from the base of the couloir. Every rock that came down the couloir had to hit that slab. Jake was at that anchor. When I got to him, I was afraid for him, a fear that was familiar. Then I recalled the boulder that seemed to pursue us in the great ice gully on McKinley. He, however, was ebullient. For him, this was what it was all about. He remarked, "How often do you get to have fun like this, up here in an interesting part of the mountain with practically all your climbing buddies?" He was good for the people we were rescuing, too. He told them, as he prepared to send them down the vertical slab below, "We always arrange to have these rescues at night so you won't know what you're stepping off of." He picked them up and kept them going. For one or more of them, it is likely that Jake made the difference.

The one I was most eagerly waiting to get to was Sterling because once I got to him and passed below, he would take my place.

I asked Pete and Al if they had set up the snowfield. They hadn't. It turned out that the guides Jake Breitenbach, Al Read, Pete Lev, Fred Wright, Dave Dornan, and Herb Swedlund; Mike Ermath and Rick Horn of the rescue team; and Dr. Walker from Jackson had arrived at the base of the couloir just minutes after Jim and I reached its top. Even if the radio had worked, the word that we needed masses of gear would have gone out too late. Again, the critical two hours I had lost. There went my hopes that things would soon speed up. It had taken Jim and me five hours to get the party down five pitches. It was to be another seven hours, 2 A.M., before the last victim would be lowered to the top of the snowfield. Just two more ropes would have cut that seven hours in half.

Al and Pete tactfully suggested that Jim and I go on down to the snowfield; they could handle matters up there. They received no heroic protests from us.

My last image of the gully is of Horn working on the pitch exiting the couloir. I was rappeling down a steep slab and Horn came racing up by me, foot over hand it seemed, to help someone who'd gotten hung up on a ledge. He was muttering to himself and lunged to the ledge just as I realized that he was climbing unroped. I asked him if he thought that was wise. He didn't, but there weren't any more ropes.

At the top of the snowfield, a huge platform was being cut, large enough to hold all the rescued and some of the rescuers. After telling him he looked good enough to kiss, I described the situation above as best I could to Sterling. I told him that it wasn't at all clear that they all were going to make it. Lester had expressed a wish to be left alone to die. I'd been tempted to let him and was glad it was out of my hands. Actually, the fact that Germer had the whole party dedicated to keeping him alive gave them a badly needed focus for survival. Lester Germer was, I believe, in some degree conscious of this because, as we later found out, he had spotted the rescue team coming up Teepe's Snowfield and had said nothing to his companions. Not knowing that help was near, they'd kept some sense that they alone were responsible for their survival.

Jim and I stood around on the snow platform until the first victim arrived. The system was in place. There was some debate about whether to set up a series of anchors down the snowfield a rope length apart or establish fewer super anchors to which we would just add ropes. I tried to join in the discussion and realized that I couldn't think very well and that it was no longer our show. Jim and I headed down.

We were without ice axes and crampons. The surface was so hard that we couldn't kick steps deeper than half an inch. The pitons we held in our hands to stop a slip weren't convincing. I couldn't judge the surface either by sight or touch. I had difficulty keeping my body balanced over the pitiful footholds we were kicking because there was no elasticity left in my legs. At any time I could have moved from a marginal hold to a place where I quickly needed a good hold and found that I was on water ice, and that would have been it. I'd be rocketing down the snowfield at fifty miles an hour, slowing only as I hit chunks of ice. And I said we wouldn't need crampons.

We paid little attention to the commotion above us except to remark that we hoped our mates didn't bomb us with one of the victims.

What was going on up there was a battle of life and death which was literal but which had become for Fenniman an allegorical battle of good and evil. We had placed Fenniman in an ambiguous position by enlisting his help in the rescue. From his position in-between he could see that there were two sides in this struggle, those being done to and those doing it to them. He had been trapped into complicity in inflicting suffering on his comrades. In his suffering and exhaustion it was difficult to see that his life was being saved, and he could undoubtedly sense that Jim and I were not certain that we weren't killing them. After helping us with the second pitch, he rejoined the ranks of those being done to. It had been twelve hours since we first started them down the couloir. Progress to safety at that rate was imperceptible. Toward the end, the mountainside was filled with shadowy beings with one eye (the head lamps we wore), pushing and pummeling, binding and unbinding them, forcing them into one terrifying experience after another. Finally, Fenniman's great heart rebelled. He decided that we were one-eyed demons trying to drag them into hell and the only way he could escape was to kill us. He was one of five tied into one rope, the entire rope to be lowered at once. He endured one lowering down to where Pete Lev had established the second anchor. He untied himself from his waist loop and went after Peter's axe, announcing his intention to kill "them." Peter was twice as strong as Fenniman, but Fenniman had the superhuman strength of the mad and wasn't worried about falling. Rick Horn tied off a fixed rope and swung down to help. Fenniman then went for Horn. Rick ducked a round-house swing, grabbed Fenniman from behind, and tied him into the rope and moved off. Fenniman then went for the party on the big ledge. Sterling pushed him down the glacier. He came again. Rick shouted at him, trying to explain that they were trying to help him. Fenniman reiterated that he was going to kill all the devils.

When he reached the ledge, Rick gave him a tremendous kick to the head, which failed to improve communication between them. Fenniman went down and started to come out of his waist loop. Rick lowered himself to Fenniman to tighten the loop, fearing that he had killed him. He began slapping him to bring him around, which worked but probably didn't do much to disabuse Fenniman of his interpretation of what the one-eyed devils were about. From then on, Fenniman was Rick's personal responsibility. When Fenniman saw that he wasn't going to be able to kill the devils, he fought passively, digging in his heels and refusing to be lowered. Rick finally sat on him, knocking him out when Rick couldn't take the punishment. Rick was soon gasping from exhaustion, retching, and moaning, and the rescuers began to wonder if he was going to make it. Sterling and Rick together wrestled, rolled, and fought Fenniman to the bottom of the glacier. It took practically the entire rescue team to get him out of his wet clothes, into a sleeping bag, and bound into a litter. When he got warm, he woke up and calmly told them about the strange dream he had been having. Who was the bravest? Joyce, who never lost his self-possession, or Fenniman in his great-hearted madness? Odysseus or Achilles?

Jim and I slowly returned to the mouth of Garnet Canyon. We stopped to doze on a flat rock in the boulder field below the snowfield until the cold pushed us on. We slept at the cache of equipment until we heard the helicopter come in to pick up Fenniman and Germer. The rest of the party stayed further up the canyon, at the AMC camp, to recover, which they all did fully and quickly, except Germer, who'd suffered frostbite. The job of getting all the gear off the mountain would now begin, but I was relieved of that duty because something had to be done about Smith.

Throughout the day, Sunday, Jim and I wandered leisurely out of the mountains to spend one night in a bed before going up for Smith. We didn't want to bring the body down. The chief ranger, Russ Dickenson, and the superintendent contacted Smith's parents and asked for permission to bury him on the mountain. I don't know how they found the words to ask them, and I don't know how the Smiths found the words to grant it, but they did. I felt awful about it, as if we were violating the code that Achilles violated in refusing to allow Priam to give Hector a proper burial. Achilles relented, we didn't.

On Monday, Rick, Jim, and I were transported to the Lower Saddle by helicopter. The weather looked lousy. Soon it started to snow. We stayed in the guide's hut, enjoying the luxury of lounging on several layers of sleeping pads and drinking tea. Rick told us about his adventures with Fenniman. He still hadn't quite recovered from that experience and didn't relish the task at hand. Our plan was to go up the Owen-Spalding Route, cross over the top of the mountain just south of the summit and descend the snowfield to the shoulder of the Otterbody where Smith's body lay, bury him, and descend on down the evacuation route. The snowstorm was not an auspicious beginning. This was turning out to be one of the worst climbing seasons in memory. Jake used to say that Owen-Spalding is both the easiest and the most difficult route he had climbed on the Grand. When it snows, the lesser angle of this route allows more ice to stick to the rock than a steeper route would hold. That worried me some, but that wasn't what was worrying Rick, much the strongest climber. Every hour or so Rick would inquire as discreetly as possible as to what we thought he would look like when we got to him. It dawned on Jim and me that this was to be Rick's first corpse, and we laid it on a little. We weren't unsympathetic, but we knew that nobody can help you through that experience. The best you can do is to gain what distance you can by finding what humor you can, not laughing at the death, but laughing at what your imagination is doing to you.

It snowed throughout Monday night and for much of Tuesday and then began to clear. We would leave for the summit before dawn on Wednesday. It was not an unpleasant prospect. We were well rested, we were in good physical condition, and we'd spent most of the past five days high in the mountains. Compared to what might have been had we been setting out to carry the body down the mountain, we were lucky.

The Owen-Spalding Route is on the shaded side of the mountain. It was bitterly cold Wednesday morning for midsummer, and the whole upper part of the mountain was completely iced over. It might have been November. Jim and I climbed slowly and cautiously, protecting every high-angle pitch, but Rick found that maddening. He very much wanted to get to the summit ridge, out of the cold, and into the sun. We could not prevail upon him to be careful, so we just let him go. He shot up the seven hundred feet of roped climbing below the summit ridge at the same rate he would have if there had been no ice. Yet Jim and I felt little danger. Rick was inspired; he didn't hesitate, and he slipped slightly only a couple of times. It happens sometimes when climbing that you know that everything you know is at your command and no wayward doubt or fear is going to intrude to break your concentration. It is inconceivable that you could fall. Rick had it at that time, and we let him go, insisting only that he had good protection when he belayed us up behind him.

Over the crest of the ridge we found a beautiful summer day in the mountains. Not hot of course because we were in fresh snow above thirteen thousand feet, but the sun opened our jackets and loosened our overtensed muscles. We called a halt for an early lunch. Rick was outraged; he wanted to get on with it.

"Come on, Rick," said Jim, "relax. It's beautiful here." And it was. The partially mown hay fields made squares of light green between the darker green willows along the Snake and Gros Ventre rivers and the greenish-grey and light brown sagebrush flats of the valley. The snow was clean and too bright for unprotected eyes. We had passed from winter to summer in the space of a few moments and a few yards.

Rick agreed to stop but not to eat. We stripped off our clanking gear and lay back in the sun, Jim and I chatting idly, musing over the events of the past few days, beginning to formulate them into shreds of the story of our lives. Rick was silent and then said, "I can smell him." We roared with laughter. "Rick, he's a thousand feet below us and frozen stiff!" In the face of our laughter, Rick's imagination relented and he smiled a little. We, in turn, agreed to get going and get it over with.

We moved at normal pace, picking out a route with caution in the couloirs we had to cross to reach the snowfield, and then descended with an occasional belay down the East Face Snowfield to the rock band which separates it from the Otterbody Snowfield. The body was on a ledge in the middle of the band. Some scrambling and a short rappel got us down to it. Near it was an empty matchbook; the matches lay scattered about. Each one had been tried; none had lit. We tried to imagine what it had been like there but weren't to find out until three years later when Jim Lipscomb published the account he had gotten from Joyce:

> *Joyce, recalling what followed, remembers looking into Smith's dazed eyes, realizing that he was far gone and saying, "Steve will never be able to climb."*
>
> *"Of course he will," said Blade. "We have got to get him moving." So Joyce reached deep into his pack and pulled out a can of pineapple, one he had hidden there before the climb began. The*

three shared the fruit. Smith could not move his fingers to hold the pineapple pieces. He opened his mouth and Joyce dropped them in, chunk by chunk. Then they drank the juice.

Again, Blade started to climb. Smith's eyes were blank, his skin colorless. Air rasped in his throat. Joyce, recognizing the symptoms of shock, called after Blade, "Smith can't climb."

"Let's not talk about it," Blade said. Blade moved very slowly. Joyce, standing behind Smith and belaying Blade with one hand, reached down with the other to put his arm around Smith. But Smith threw his arms over his head to push Joyce off. Joyce tried again. Smith threw up his arms again, hitting Joyce in the face.

A glove fell off Smith's hand, dropping 10 feet down the slope. Joyce retrieved it and tried to get it back on, but Smith's hand was stiffened into a claw and Joyce could not get the glove on it. Joyce called up to Blade, "I think he's dying."

"Don't talk like that," said Blade. "I don't want you to say anything like that again."

Joyce watched. Blade was still climbing very slowly above them. Finally he called down, "All right, come on up."

Joyce answered, "Smith's dead."

Blade climbed down. "This is terrible," he said. He forced Smith's mouth open and blew air into his lungs.

"He's not coming back to life," Joyce said.

The two tied Smith's body in its bright-red parka to the ledge. They began climbing upward again. "It was the first time," recalls Joyce, "that we really moved fast." A hundred feet of progress brought them to the top of the couloir. They now faced the East Ridge snowfield, still 1,000 feet below the summit. A foot of new snow rested on top of the old crust.

"This snow won't hold," said Blade.

"Let's traverse, then," said Joyce, "over to those rocks."

"The route is to the right," Blade said.

"Well, don't just stand there, what do you want to do?" said Joyce. Blade cast about, unable to decide. Turn back now? What could that mean to Ellis Blade, the leader who had insisted

> *that going up was the only safe way for the party to get down? Blade turned to Joyce, looking past him to the valley below.*
>
> *Then Joyce took Blade by the shoulder. "We are going down, down, down!" Joyce said. "And this time we are going all the way." And the two men started down.*
>
> *For three days Blade had led all the pitches, taking the most exposed and dangerous positions. In descending, the first man down a slope can be protected from above and normally the more experienced climber would take the second position. But Blade, no leader now, was moving down first, with Joyce belaying him.*[2]

We took what personal effects we thought his family might like to have, tied a rope to the body, and maneuvered the body over the moat between the base of the cliff and the Otterbody Snowfield. Jim and I relented in our education of Rick and handled the body while Rick handled the ropes. Getting the body adequately protected was a problem. We selected a place near at hand where the snowpack was thickest and seemed least likely to bare the rock in a dry year. Rick was anchoring the body. From a stance a few feet above the body, I guided the rope to a position where the body would drop directly down a small chimney to the debris at the base of the cliff. Jim straddled the rope at the body with his knife out.

I had forgotten to bring a Bible. Jim said, "Well, so long, Buddy," made the sign of the cross over Steve Smith, and cut the rope. We covered the body first with small rocks, in case there were any carnivorous rodents up there, and then with larger rocks to keep it safe not only from rodents and insects but from the motions of the mountain itself as the snow waxed and waned and as the granite flesh of the mountain checked, cracked, and sloughed off in its slow journey toward the valley.

---

[2] *Sports Illustrated,* June 21, 1965, pp. 67, 68.

We descended the Otterbody to the ledge where we'd found the party. Then we descended the gully. Scattered all down the gully was evidence of the drama that had taken place there four days before, runners, torn clothing, abandoned packs. I was surprised to see color in the couloir, patches of green lichen and many more shades of color in the rock than I recalled. In the early afternoon sun it was not an unpleasant place to be. No inimical spirits lurked there. At the time Smith died, noon Saturday, Ster, Doug, Jim, and I had been here three or four hundred feet below him. To Steve Smith, who had lost all hope of leaving the mountain, the ledge where he was, out of the cold wet gully, may have seemed a good place and the moment a good time.

There was a lawyer in Jackson who was designated to handle the misdemeanors cited in the park. If the park had been a town, he would have been called the justice of the peace. This particular attorney had a broad interpretation of his responsibilities. He called a kind of inquest at which the park officials, the Appalachian Mountain Club leaders, and a few of the rescuers were asked to appear. (The head of the AMC had flown out from the East to offer to reimburse the park for the expense of the rescue.)

It was an odd proceeding. At the outset, the head of the AMC remarked to the attorney that it appeared that he was acting as judge, prosecutor, and grand jury. The attorney replied that he was "just looking into the matter." I was called to testify. The first questions were about the sign-out procedure. Then came a series of questions which called for an hour-by-hour account of the entire rescue. I became uncomfortable. After every much publicized rescue, there are people who write to the newspapers demanding that the government take steps to keep climbers from needing to be rescued. There were sentiments like that even in Jackson's Hole, "the last of the Old West." There are people who think that risking one's life in anything but combat is immoral.

Russ Dickenson put an end to the questioning. He said, "We have no action we wish to take against the AMC," called me from the stand, and we left. There would be no frontier justice while he was chief ranger.

Ellis and Mary visited me at the ranger station. We went outside to stand in the sun. We had talked a few times in the weeks they had been in the park before the AMC encampment arrived. If I had known him better, I could have simply asked him, "Ellis, what happened?" But I didn't know him that well. I thought he might take the question as coming from an official instead of another climber. Had I been wiser or even just older, I might have had the thought that Ellis came to me with the hope that I could help him answer that question. But I didn't have that thought.

Climbing rangers and guides held their own informal inquest as we chanced to meet one another. Most of us wanted to find a way to let Ellis off the hook and to blame the Appies. Their huge encampments and their quasi-military hierarchies made a visit by the Appies seem to us like the incursion of a foreign army. Also, distrusting easterners is the sign that you are a westerner.

Ellis and Mary talked about Steve's death. They said that Steve had refused to cuddle with the others, both on Thursday night when he'd been with the main group and Ellis had been above, alone, and on Friday night when the three of them had bivouacked at the top of the Otterbody Snowfield. Mary thought that Steve was prudish, that he might have thought that huddling together for warmth was a sexual act. That sort of post-Freudian explanation is difficult to refute, but I have never believed it.

There was another phobic explanation in the air. It was said that Ellis had a bad experience on Teepe's Snowfield. This was a more plausible explanation of Ellis's part in the story because Ellis himself gave some evidence for it. In his report to the park he said, "My strong feelings on this matter (not going down the snowfield) go back several years to a previous experience getting a party down this very same Teepe's Glacier when in a hardened condition; also to other difficult experiences on hard and steep Teton snow; and finally, to the long list of this year's snow accidents including a fatality." It is possible to make out of this a phobic response specific to Teepe's Snowfield. It is not a good explanation of why he went there with his group in the first place and stayed there.

At the time of our last conversation, I knew nothing about how isolated Ellis became from his party. Nor did I know that another leader, Walter Herman, was originally scheduled to help Ellis but stayed behind with an infected foot. Nothing in my conversations with Ellis led me to think of him as an autocratic leader or, to speak psychologically, an authoritarian personality.

I still don't have an account which fits all the facts, but there are some points I think about.

The party was too large for one man to lead.

The party had some bad luck; how much is hard to judge.

Smith's physical isolation from the party was an image of Blade's psychological separation from the party.

We, the rescuers, experienced similar feelings of separateness when we took command of the party.

The party consisted of four individuals and three teams of two—the Blades, the Junes, and the friends Smith and Joyce—made one by the presence of an hired climbing leader.

Ellis Blade's authority to lead was not as absolute as subsequent events may suggest. He was designated leader, Germer was the rock expert, Smith was the strongest climber but inexperienced as a leader, Mary Blade was designated leader when Ellis was gone and Germer was down, Griffith June had status in the AMC organization but none as a climber, Charlie Joyce emerged as the one who could make the decision to go down.

The direction to go if you're leading a climb is up; in a rescue you go down. Leading a rescue party is not less difficult than leading a climb.

After the incidents on Teepe's Snowfield, the base of the couloir seemed a better place. Once there, climbing up the rock with a group whose only experience was on rock seemed better than climbing snow. When benighted in the couloir, getting to the top of the couloir seemed better than staying in it. When

Germer's strength gave out and it was impossible to think of leading the whole party out, it was still possible to think of leading out a party of three. The climb up then could be also thought of as part of a rescue effort, as going for help, as Jake, Barry, Bill, and I escaped from Denali by going over the top.

Take your choice. Smith with a sexual phobia, Blade with a snowfield phobia combined with an authoritarian personality, or too many strangers in an indifferent place at a bad time, for not good enough reason, led by Blade who wasn't sure where he'd gotten to but knew he was neither with the people he was with nor on his own.

CHAPTER 9
IN THE VALLEY

I worked as ranger in charge of the Jenny Lake Ranger Station for eight summers, 1960 through 1967. Though the work was seasonal, I considered it a career, as a commercial fisherman thinks of his seasonal work. During the rest of the year I was a student, a husband, and a father. With encouragement, in the form of an unsolicited loan from Crabtree, who visited us every summer after 1960, when we met in the Whitehorse Tavern in the West Village, and also thinking to make myself a more respectable husband and father, I decided to finish my B.A. I enrolled at the University of Wyoming in Laramie in the winter of 1962 to study philosophy and literature. During my last semester at Wyoming I decided to go on for a doctorate in English literature at the University of Washington in Seattle.

There were moments when I had to admit that it appeared that I was on my way to becoming a college professor, but I continued to think of myself as a park ranger who happened to be interested in the academic study of literature. The traditional alternative, seasonal work in the summer, unemployment in the winter, is harder for a Yankee to do with a clear conscience than getting a Ph.D. (There are a few other possibilities of course; the last time I was in Jackson I heard a disk jockey say on the radio, "Jackson, where all the men are boys, and all the women have two jobs.") Given the turmoil in the profession of college teaching and on campus at the time and given that I was not an inactive participant in the turmoil, it was far from a foregone conclusion that I would enter the academy. Many of my friends who were professionals in the sixties still are. There are a lot of gray-haired summer mountain guides and winter ski professionals or trekking leaders around Jackson—Bill Briggs, Pete Lev, Dean Moore, Rod Newcomb, Chuck Pratt, Al Read, Herb Swedlund, Jack Turner—and I've heard that even Yvon Chouinard will turn his hand to guiding for special occasions. These guys invented the notion of making a career of it and included the notion of lifetime tenure in the invention. But for me it really came down to a choice of the Park Service or the academy.

Russ Dickenson and Doug McLaren and other people like them who had made the Park Service their career were why I thought of the service as my career. I had never seen people who worked as hard or as willingly as did they. I had never seen people as willingly bound by a code of conduct or as rigorous in adhering to their code. Russ Dickenson was particularly good in teaching me about the badge.

Park rangers as law enforcement officers are more like English bobbies in manner than they are like highway patrolmen, whom they resemble in uniform. We had guns but seldom wore them—never in the years when Russ was chief ranger. Donning a uniform and a badge does something to you: it's expected to. In uniform, you find that when you chance to meet a stranger, his first thought is that it isn't a chance meeting. The thing that a ranger has to learn to remember is that the aspect he has donned gives him a public and not personal authority. It can happen that the ranger will remember that his authority is not personal but the visitor will not. At such times, the inexperienced ranger can turn a chance meeting into a showdown.

Late in my first season, in September, 1960, I had one such meeting. There had been a week of rainy weather which had cleared out the campground. I took a walk from the ranger station along the road to the boat dock a quarter of a mile away. Where there had been for most of the season exhaust fumes and the odor of hot asphalt, there was the fragrance of wet lodgepole pine needles and a promise in the air of mushrooms brewing out of the compost. Through the trees on the lakeward side of the road, the summits of Teewinot and Mt. Owen lay upsidedown on the calm lake, their angularity set quivering here and there by trout poking the surface. The insects they were taking were invisible to me, so it looked as if they were nibbling the air. I had survived my first season of rescuing and my first season of answering the same five questions several times an hour, and I was still sane. This tranquil stroll was no more than I had earned.

On the bridge across the outlet, to which the boat dock was anchored, stood a man fishing. I told him that fishing was not allowed on the dock, bridge, or along the shore to the water tower by the ranger station. Since he had rested his kit bag against the NO FISHING sign, it is possible that there was a touch of weariness in my tone. He wanted to know why there was no fishing there. There were several reasons, and I did not stint him. It turned out that he was not interested in why other people could not fish there; he wanted to know why I would not let him fish there. My abundant reasons did not constitute a good argument because they presumed the usual circumstance of there being several hundred people in the area. His argument was that no one would see. Furthermore, his tone gave me to know that, whatever the lot of those unimaginative souls who went through life reading signs and obeying them, he was accustomed to exceptional treatment. I chose to stick with abundance as my rhetorical strategy and recited my reasons again, making no effort to sound interested in his reasons. After hearing my account the second time, he was no happier and kept after me. Later in my career, I learned that the third time through an explanation seldom fails, but I didn't know that then and allowed myself to be drawn into trying to find other ways of saying what I had just said.

He understood that I would not give in, and as my expression got more wooden and my voice colder, he got madder. He called me a liar. It was true in a way. The reason he had to stop fishing was because I was there to forbid his fishing, and I didn't say that. There is a nonobnoxious way of saying that: you just laugh and say, "You can't fish here because you got caught." I didn't know the trick then. I knew that I was being called a liar by a man I hadn't known existed ten minutes earlier. I was astonished. Then I was furious.

When I told him that if he didn't leave the bridge immediately I would forcibly remove him from it, his fury turned to astonishment. He might have thought that I was going to put a come-along hold on him and trot him off the bridge. The idea I had in mind was to pitch him headfirst into the creek.

He left, but I knew I had really lost the conflict. I felt rotten. The Park Service has a term for my action, badge heavy. I drove immediately to headquarters and confessed to Russ. First he told me that there is no conceivable situation where a man wearing a badge has a right to get angry. Then he told me a story.

It happened in the years when Russ had worked on the gate for five years, in a desert park, in a five-by-eight kiosk without air conditioning. It didn't seem to him that his career was going anywhere. A man drove up to the entrance station and refused to pay the entrance fee. Russ patiently insisted. The man became abusive. Something in Russ gave way. He reached into the cash drawer, pulled out a .45 automatic, leaned out of the kiosk, pointed the .45 at the middle of the man's head, and told him that he had by God better get the hell out of there or he would have his head blown off. Russ was trembling still the day after the incident because he wasn't certain that he wouldn't have pulled the trigger had the man cussed him out again. Since then, Russ had never lost nor found it hard to keep his temper while on duty. He ended his career as director of the National Park Service.

There were two things about my talk with Russ that won him my allegiance. The first was that he had given me an absolute rule of conduct which I understood. The second was that he had told me a story which I had to know in order to do what I had contracted to do, without considering how the story might alter his image in my eyes. I had the feeling that the Park Service might be my place.

My job, ranger in charge at the Jenny Lake Ranger Station, was a privileged position in the Park Service. The station, a small cabin made from roughcut board-and-batten lumber painted brown, was located on the east shore of the south end of Jenny Lake, near the outlet. Jenny Lake was in the middle of Grand Teton National Park and was the hub of the activities for which the park was originally intended.

There were historical reasons for Jenny Lake's importance. The early entrepreneurs of tourism in the valley of Jackson's Hole established themselves there. The history of the subsequent development of the area was the history of the Park Service's efforts to distribute visitor use more widely about the park, away from Jenny Lake. The signs pointing the way to Jenny Lake were not prominent. The new roads in the park led away from the lake or skirted it. This tactic worked for those visitors who saw the park only while driving to or from Jackson and Yellowstone. Visitors who wanted to actually visit the park found their way to Jenny Lake and knew they'd found the place everybody who told them about the park remembered.

The pioneers of the tourist industry did not settle at Jenny Lake by accident. It wasn't game trails or Indian trails or cattle trails which brought them to the lake; it was geology. The major peaks for climbing and viewing are between Mt. Moran, 6.2 miles north of Jenny Lake, and Buck Mountain, 6.6 miles south of Jenny Lake. A line projected from the summit of Mt. Moran west by south would pass within a half a compass point of Mt. Owen, the Grand Teton, Middle Teton, South Teton, Cloudveil Dome, and Mt. Wister and through the summit of Buck Mountain. A line one mile east of that line with exactly the same bearing would line up Rockchuck, Mt. St. John, Teewinot, Disappointment, Nez Perce, and Shadow Peak. No peak looks very much like any other peak; each peak is a distinct sculpture. The variety of mountain views is what you see from the valley floor. The symmetry of the range as a whole you see from a distance, as in my first view of the Tetons from Togwotee

Pass, or by getting yet closer and climbing to one of the summits. The reason for the north-south symmetry of the range is that the peaks were carved from a single fault block which rose up concurrently with the sinking of the fault block under Jackson's Hole.

Five canyons—Moran, Leigh, Cascade, Avalanche, and Death—cut through this block almost to the level of the valley floor. The glaciers which formed these canyons retreated about nine thousand years ago (a moment ago in geologic time). At the time of their retreat, the snouts of the glaciers had pushed out of the canyons onto the valley floor. They had been grinding away the canyons for a quarter of a million years. What they had been grinding on, the schists, gneisses, and granites that make up the Teton fault block, are rocks too old to imagine. The granite is two-five-zero-zero-zero-zero-zero-zero-zero-zero years old. The gneiss into which the granite intruded is older but probably not older than the oldest known rocks, some three-five-zero-zero-zero-zero-zero-zero-zero-zero years old. The Tetons are a recent form out of the oldest stuff.

When the glaciers melted back, the rock shards, which had been pried off the mountains and frozen into their snouts, were left on the valley floor as terminal moraines. Lakes formed behind the semicircular dams thus created. Even the ungeologic eye can see what had happened in the formation of the mountains. The mountains look new and sharp, ground to shape, not ground down. To common sense, the geologists' talk of numbers of years gone by seems wild. But anybody can pick up a rock from the lakeside, observe that the rock was part of a dam, and guess that the rock was once part of the mountains. He won't know its name or its age but might guess that, like tempered steel in a fine old tool, it has been heated and hardened and has endured. The rumor from the geologist is that rocks fifteen miles below the surface are heated to seven hundred degrees and folded like plastic. It is unsettling to think about things like that going on as nearby as the next town. Even geologists don't think about it all the time. The new and the ancient, the volatile and the stolid, unimaginable forces and unimaginable repose, it's all carved in the landscape.

Cascade Canyon is the most extensive of the canyons, the peaks which flank it, the highest, the most jagged, the most climbed; and its lake is Jenny Lake. The view from the door of the ranger station was across the lake and up the canyon. At the mouth of the canyon, the right wall is Mt. St. John. St. John is a complex mountain containing many pinnacles and spires that encircle a high canyon gorged out of the mountain near the summit. The glacier that did this had just started its career when the last ice age ended. The canyon is called Hanging Canyon. In it are three small lakes, whose waters descend in falls and cascades into Jenny Lake at a point halfway along its northwestern shore.

The left wall of the mouth of Cascade Canyon is Mount Teewinot, whose base forms the southwestern shore of Jenny Lake. Teewinot is a simple mountain, pyramid shaped, with a pointed summit scarcely big enough to allow one person to stand on it. Simple geometry to the left, rugged crags on the right, deep canyon between, lake at my feet to reflect it all: I could move my gaze from one aspect to another of this mountainous terrain, set there as if to be an image of itself.

The outlet of Jenny Lake, Cottonwood Creek, wanders south parallel to the range until it reaches a point below the mouth of the next great canyon, Avalanche. There it turns abruptly left to enter the Snake River. The Snake River has worked its way west across the valley floor toward the mountains because the fault block beneath the valley is still tilting toward the mountains. As the Park Service has tried to channel visitors away from Jenny Lake, flood control engineers have tried to contain the river within dikes, to keep it from moving closer to the mountains. It's not easy being a Department of Interior.

South of the lake, between the base of Teewinot and Cottonwood Creek, lies a large meadow called Lupine Meadow because it is blue with that flower in most Junes. Nine hundred and forty-six steps down Cottonwood Creek from the lake, on the west side of the stream, in a grove of trees between the creek and the meadow, were the five log cabins where the climbing rangers were housed. Connie and I, with our two children, Melanie and Kirk, lived in the middle and largest of the cabins for five summers. In our bedroom window, through the firs, pines, cottonwoods, and aspens, shone the rising moon and the rising sun, reflected off the waters of the creek. From our breakfast table we looked across the meadow half a mile to Mt. Teewinot, which rose directly without foothills to its summit one mile above us. From the chopping block outside the kitchen door, where I split the wood for the stove, I could look south to Buck Mountain. From the chopping block outside the living room door, where I cut the wood for the fireplace made of stones from the creek, I could look north to Mt. Moran. I am still looking forward to the day when Connie completely forgives me for taking her away from that place, a quarter of a century hasn't been quite enough time for her to do that.

The duties of the Jenny Lake rangers were to keep the peace and safety in this area, as any peace officers. Then there were the intricate problems of seeing that the area was used in a manner designated by Park Service regulations and that concessions conducted business as they had agreed to under the terms of their permits. We went on road patrol (that is, highway patrol) and ambulance runs and patrolled the backcountry on climbing patrols, hiking patrols, and horseback patrols. Our responsibility in the developed part of the park was confined to the area near Jenny Lake and the next lake north, String Lake, where there was a picnicking and swimming area. But anything at all that happened to people in the mountains and canyons, from the north boundary to the south boundary, was our concern.

The job that took most of our energies, mental and physical, if not most of our time, was registering, advising, signing out, and signing in the five thousand climbers that visited the park every summer. On the average of once every ten days, we would rescue one or more of these five thousand or evacuate a body. Among seasonal employees in the Park Service, we were an elite. We had a greater variety of duty and more autonomy than other seasonals anywhere in the service. It was a huge responsibility, which could not be borne by a seasonal who thought of it as a summer job. In the past now almost forty years, the position of ranger in charge at Jenny Lake has been held by three men (four including Tim Bond), Dick Emerson, me, and Bob Irvine.

Geology and landscape concentrated people and their activities, and therefore our responsibilities, at Jenny Lake. This and history, specifically an episode in World War II, explain why we had so much autonomy. Doug McLaren, our district ranger, was a Tenth Mountain Boy. That is, he served in the Tenth Mountain Division in World War II. This was an army division made up of skiers and climbers. Since skiing and climbing were in their infancy before the war, nearly every American skier and climber eligible for military service ended up in this division. They trained in the Colorado Rockies and on Mt. Rainier and eventually went into combat in the Italian mountains. These mountain troops were an odd collection that likely was possible only in the army of a democracy. They were an elite, an aristocracy of the mountains. But since most of them were in the enlisted ranks, they were an elite at the bottom. The Tenth Mountain Division was the only army division where the average IQ of the enlisted men was higher than the average IQ of officers. After the war, these men often ran into each other in the mountainous areas of the country. It would be interesting to know how many ski areas were started by former Tenth Mountain Boys. Their camaraderie, natural to mountaineers and redoubled by their war experiences, continued. Dick Emerson was a Tenth Mountain Boy, as was Ernie Field, chief ranger before Russ. Doug, Dick, and Ernie had formed the Grand Teton Rescue Team in 1948. They had established the regulations and traditions which were known as the Climbing Regulations.

The regulations required a climber in the park to register as a climber, to sign out for each climb, and to sign in when he returned. There were three purposes to these regulations: facilitating search and rescue, providing information about the routes to climbers, and record keeping. There was often a fourth purpose in the mind of the ranger talking to the climber, preventing innocents from going to slaughter. Technically, the ranger could deny permission to climb. In practice, this wasn't done, except when it would be impossible for us to perform a rescue. (It sometimes happened that the team and all available backup people would be out on a difficult or extended rescue and climbers wouldn't be signed out until we were back in.) Instead of denying permission, we attempted to talk people out of doing routes we felt they weren't ready to attempt. The practice of using persuasion instead of authority was the work of Dick Emerson, who coined the phrase, "let the mountains teach them." Doug told me the phrase when I took over at Jenny Lake, and I passed it on to all who worked with me in the station.

There had been a few experienced climbers who had resented the regulations, but most of that had passed by the time of my tenure. The exceptions were a few northwestern climbers who had gotten soured on the Park Service while climbing Mt. Rainier, whose rangers subjected climbers to military-type inspections and included practices such as jumping on your ice axe.

My favorite of the early Park Service attempts to regulate climbing activity was the system in use at Devil's Tower. Devil's Tower is too small an area to be able to staff a rescue team, and it's also a long way from any of the concentrations of climbers in the Rockies, like those at Jackson, Laramie, and Boulder. Nevertheless, it was a fairly simple matter to get permission to climb there. All you needed was a note from someone who had already climbed the tower. It was first climbed free by Jack Durrance. He had been brought out from Hanover to rescue a man who parachuted onto the top. I climbed Devil's Tower with Jake Breitenbach my first time. Jake had gotten a note from Jack Durrance, the dean of the Dartmouth mountaineers, while visiting him to pay homage.

It was sometimes argued that the Park Service ought not to rescue injured climbers. (I never heard it argued that they should not remove bodies from the mountains.) But the American temperament will have to change before that solution can be seriously considered.

The system developed at Grand Teton Park by the Tenth Mountain Boys eventually prevailed. The key was to hire experienced climbers as rangers because the system depends on mutual respect between climber and ranger. While Dick was at the ranger station, he put up such routes as the Direct North Face of the Grand and the South Buttress of Mt. Moran. His suggestions about how to climb in the Tetons were hearkened to. There were no serious problems with managing climbers in the mountains. The same could not be said of activities in the valley.

At the same time that climbing activity was on the increase, car camping was as well. Sites at Jenny Lake became a scarce resource. As campers far outnumbered climbers, friends of climbing within the Park Service foresaw complaints about climbers occupying all the sites. We knew that if these complaints reached Congress, climbers would lose. The ten-day camping limit at Jenny Lake was not strictly enforced with regard to climbers or people doing extensive hiking in the backcountry. Since this group made up five percent of the people who used the campground, according to data gathered by Dick (who was a sociologist in the off-season), there was no reason to enforce it. Still, the campground filled earlier and earlier in the day. People who were turned away were not happy about being shunted off to one of the overflow campgrounds, especially as these were essentially fields with latrines. They hadn't come to the "wilderness" to live like migrant workers.

By establishing a climbers' campground at the site of an old CCC camp on the south end of Jenny Lake, with a camping limit of thirty days instead of ten days, the park attempted to avert complaints about the climbers. The facilities were no better than in the overflow campgrounds. Climbers at first objected to their exile, suspicious that the park was as eager to get them out of sight as it was to help them. But the "C-Camp" soon became home. One reason the campgrounds were in demand was that some phrase merchant in the Park Service had come up with Mission 66. The National Park Service had a dual and potentially contradictory function: to preserve some of the wilderness and to make it available to the visitor. Mission 66 was a plan to consolidate and expand the wilderness holdings of the Park Service and to attract more users to the parks. Since this was an expensive idea to implement, the image of the visitor in the minds of policy makers changed from "people with interests in natural history" to "vacationing taxpayers." Mission 66 was effective in getting appropriations from Congress. Taxpayers, supplied by a new industry in car camping equipment, began to pour into the parks.[1]

The other function of the Park Service, protecting the wilderness, was nearly buried under new campgrounds with showers, new highways, new architecturally elegant visitor centers to replace the log cabins, and new parking lots. The time came when the park had to pave the most used trails in order to keep the terrain from being destroyed by unmoccasined feet. Then a time came when you could not find a place to look at the mountains without there also being a sign in the view prohibiting something which common sense had once prohibited. Finally a time came when you had to reserve a backcountry campsite as you would a hotel room in St. Moritz. The time had passed when a ranger could engage visitors in a casual conversation and, in the course of a half hour, tactfully teach people who hadn't camped before such basic practices as how to build, maintain, and control a campfire. Some of what used to be accomplished by conversation could be accomplished by signs, displays, and brochures. But planting every campsite with a sign reading, for example, DO NOT BUILD LARGE FIRES ON WINDY DAYS was not an imaginable alternative for financial, if not for philosophical and aesthetic, reasons. So, on windy days, we patrolled

---

[1] I may be giving too much credit to Mission 66. The people might have started pouring in anyway. I might not be the only one who noticed the significance of Alaska statehood. This latest rush wasn't for land or gold but for a mythical experience, the wilderness experience. The new frontiersmen were consumers of experience.

the campgrounds for fires that were too large or for untended fires that the wind blew up again because they hadn't been doused. On one such patrol, I came upon a fire that I saw from a quarter of a mile up the road. I turned on the red light and drove forty miles an hour in a fifteen-mile-per-hour zone to get to it. There was no one at the campsite or in any of the neighboring sites, although there was a pickup camper parked in the spot for the campsite. I put out the man-tall flames and was starting to leave when I heard someone talking in the camper. I knocked on the door, and a man holding a hand of cards opened it. I told him that I had put out his fire because of the wind. "Oh," he said, "sorry, I always like to have a fire when I'm camping."

As people switched from backpacks to trucks to carry their camping gear, thieves trailed them into the parks. Looking for crooks, as we called it at Jenny Lake, became part of the duty and may have subtly changed our manner of greeting visitors.

When Congress began looking for pockets out of which to pay for guns and butter, the Park Service got hit with two successive 25 percent cuts in operating money, but the people didn't stop coming. The only hope for new money was for police work, not for catching crooks, for riot control. Every spring, before rescue practice, we got riot training from the FBI. Budget money was made available for riot guns, gas, helmets, face masks, handcuffs, riot batons, radios, and patrol cars. Rangers were taken out of the backcountry, and the backcountry ranger stations were closed. The only increases in ranger positions were at the entrance stations and on road patrol.

There was one new position, law enforcement specialist. The idea was to have somebody who knew about the Miranda decision, constitutional protections, paper work, and all that. Ours was a law student from a nearby university. He had ideas of his own about what a law enforcement specialist was supposed to do. Park policy was that no ranger could wear sidearms during daylight hours and only road patrolmen, actually on road patrol at night, could wear their sidearm in any case. Our law enforcement specialist thought the daylight hours were over when the first shadows from the peaks hit the valley floor. At four in the afternoon one could find him sauntering through the cocktail lounge of the Jackson Lake Lodge, boots spit shined, holster spit shined and heavy with pistol. The pretty waitresses were well protected.

The other place one could find him was lurking around the Jenny Lake Campground and the Climbers' Campground, hoping to catch a climber smoking pot. There was a suspicion that the "boys at Jenny Lake" might be lax in enforcing the controlled substances law.

The training sessions provided by the FBI were held at the park. Police, sheriffs, marshals, deputies, and tribal police from surrounding counties attended. To be fair to the FBI, they gave us good training in subjects and skills we might need. They were thorough and fair about the Miranda decision and other search-and-seizure decisions and about methods of interrogation. They were officially and personally disgusted by police brutality, which they knew, and we knew, was not unknown in the areas represented by those present in the class. They advised us never to pull the pistol out of our holsters unless we were going to use it and taught us how to disarm an armed man without using our guns and how to subdue someone without injuring him. Because of this training, I was later able to subdue a berserk man who was armed with a club. I didn't put a scratch or a bruise on him, didn't threaten him or swear at him. All I did was subject him to a little pain, which was gone in two seconds but, fortunately for both of us, not forgotten. In an hour, he calmed down, and two people, at least, were grateful for that training.

But while our FBI teachers could talk about armed robbery philosophically, murder tragically, con men admiringly, and one man, who'd killed a planeload of people for the insurance money, sympathetically, rioters in their eyes were demonic. One agent said to us repeatedly, "You've seen them, these characters with the fur-lined jockstraps." It took me a while to figure out what he was talking about. The reason that I had trouble catching the image he had in mind with his reference to fur-lined jocks was that in the movies they showed us of riots, the rioters were college kids at Ft. Lauderdale and kids from Boston at Hampton Beach. When he said that he had seen them around Jackson, it finally dawned on me that he was talking about climbers. He must have seen some climbers and imagined he had seen the Weathermen at their summer retreat.

The local police had never seen drunk college kids on vacation or unemployed factory workers from the East, nor did they expect to, but they dearly wanted to try out their high-powered training and equipment. California was closer, thus the annual rumor that the Hell's Angels were on their way to Yellowstone. It was silly to think that the Hell's Angels would visit a region like northwestern Wyoming, where rifles mounted on the cab window of your rig are as much standard equipment as spare tires, but the local police hadn't seen Hell's Angels either. They could imagine whatever they wanted to.

One day a motorcyclist wearing a black leather jacket with something akin to "The Devil's Imps" written on the back rode through Jackson. No person had been so attended to since President Kennedy's visit to the valley. The biker was followed by our south district road patrol to the north district. Their road patrolman followed him to Yellowstone, where he was met by another patrolman and tailed again until he left the park at West Yellowstone. We had reversed the tradition of the Texas Rangers, who, when called into a town to stop a riot, dispatched only one ranger because there was only one riot: we dispatched a mob of rangers to stop one rioter.[2]

---

[2] Eventually a crook was caught in the act by a ranger. The crook was robbing a parked car, which is what crooks in the park mainly did, and the ranger was Rick Reese, a Jenny Lake climbing ranger. Rick was staked out in the String Lake parking lot wearing Levis and a t-shirt. He had been armed with a can of Mace, but it fell out of a hole in his pocket while he was pursuing the fleeing crook, so he made the arrest unarmed. This happened after I had left Jenny Lake, but I was very pleased that Rick had been able to help out the law enforcement enthusiasts who had spent so many thankless hours trying to nab our friends the climbers for us.

There were changes taking place in climbing and climbers as well as in rangering and rangers. When I first heard of the Tetons, from upperclassmen in the Dartmouth Mountaineering Club, they were the ultimate goal of American mountaineers. By the time I arrived in 1958, the Tetons, though still a worthy goal for recreational climbers, were being demoted from their status as a rock-climbing range to a mountaineer's practice area. Before World War II, Exum, Petzoldt, Fryxell, Coulter, and Durrance were the prominent names in the Tetons. After the war, the famous climbers were Ortenburger, Unsoeld, and Emerson. In 1953, Emerson led the Pendulum Pitch on the North Face of the Grand free, in company with Unsoeld and Ortenburger. That same year he led the technically much more difficult and imaginative Pendulum Pitch on the South Buttress of Mt. Moran. With the first, he put a period on the exploits of the past masters. With the second, he anticipated Yosemite standards.

The distinction between the really serious climbers and the recreational climbers was that whereas recreational climbers climbed in order to be able to continue to work, the leading climbers worked in order to be able to climb. In both cases, it was climbing that made living worth the effort. Up until 1950, as serious as climbers were, climbing was about as prominent in American life as curling. Then, in 1950, the French climbed Annapurna. To young climbers, the French climb was akin to the help the French gave the colonies in the Revolution. In the spiritual recession which followed World War II—the guilt of the Holocaust, the knowledge that under the mushroom cloud Churchill's inspiring words are as insane as Hitler's—the story of the French heroism on Annapurna gave us a vision of how one might live.

By any realistic assessment, the war that brought us the Holocaust and Hiroshima is the most horrific war in all history. The future can be confidently included within the purview of this assessment because if there is a third world war, it will end history. Yet World War II appears to us as "the last good war." Why? I think it is because, in addition to its unspeakable horrors, it provided a few contexts for acts of individual heroism and a few circumstances of camaraderie (without these, courageous acts are only stunts). Prominent among them were those recounted in stories of the French Resistance, stories that are important way out of proportion to France's military contribution to the war, which was little more than providing the battleground. What makes these stories important is that aesthetics and ethics, or beauty and truth, if thou wouldst, are at least as important as raw physical courage in making them for us instructions in living. The climb of Annapurna, done mainly by men who were too young to have participated in the resistance, showed that one could aspire to and get a kind of fame we feared lost from the world. The book *Annapurna* we took as a text of moral instruction.

The famed men of American mountaineering after the 1950s were Fred Beckey, Yvon Chouinard, Layton Kor, Jim McCarthy, and Royal Robbins. Beckey, originally from the Northwest, was really from all the wilderness mountain areas in North America. Chouinard was a cross between a Teton climber and a Yosemite climber. Kor was from Colorado and the southwestern desert. McCarthy was from the Shawangunks outside of New York City. Robbins was from Yosemite. If I were trying to compile an exhaustive account of climbing leadership, spheres of influence, or degrees of skill, there would be other names: Frost, Weeks, Steck, Roper, Gran, Pratt, Rearick, Kamps, Evans, and the quiet, almost superhuman John Gill, plus another thirty or so whose work will be remembered for one reason or another. But Beckey, Chouinard, Kor, McCarthy, and Robbins were our heroes. They brought the standard of American climbing to European levels of proficiency, imagination, and daring by their climbs in other regions of the country, and they came to the Tetons to rest. In other parts of the country they climbed with passion; in the Tetons they climbed with affection. Their presence kept the Tetons at the hub of American climbing because if you wanted to know what was happening in American climbing, you had to go where the stories were being told, and that was at Jenny Lake.

What primarily distinguished these climbers from earlier climbers was higher standards of performance and skill, not a generation gap in values. There was a little of that, having to do with the use of direct aid, for example, but in the end the best climbers moved in the direction of older climbers by placing a high value on eliminating direct aid from any pitch they could. There existed a continuity of values between this generation of leaders and the older leaders. Both were born before 1945.

In my time in the ranger station, climbing got better, equipment got better, the rescue team got better, but rangering became more complicated. An incident early on was to portend times to come.

One day Sterling greeted me with the news that Ken Weeks was in the camp, AWOL from the army, intending to stay that way. Weeks had registered for climbing under a new name, and we were to remember to use that name. My badge hanging heavy from my shirt, I stood there pondering. Not turning him in was an easy decision to make. Falsifying records was harder. Although I hated the army, I wasn't a conscientious objector. It seemed right to me that young males should be required to serve their people. In war? I had no opinion about war. It seemed to me a phenomenon beyond the ken of ethical speculation. All I had to go on was personal friendship, a sense of duty, and my memory of my experiences in the army. The old soldiers spoke of better times, but in my experience, the unstated purpose of my military training was to reduce everyone to a condition of moral despair such that death in combat might come as a release. If Weeks wanted to refuse that, at the risk of prison, I would do my part. Ken was in the campground for a month when two of my superiors picked him up and turned him over to the FBI. I was told that the FBI had located him, but I wasn't told how. Maybe somebody said something, there in the Tetons or back in his home town. Maybe his mail had been opened.

One day, while Ken was being held in the county jail, Sterling, Lyn, and I went down to talk with him from outside the jail. We came with a length of small line, a length of plastic tubing, a jug, and a six-pack. The six-pack and the plastic tubing went into the jug; the line, one end tied to the jug, was passed to the cell. That day was better for Ken than most of his days to come for a long while.

Later we heard that Weeks made four escapes from the stockade, hiding all day in a snowbank in Colorado, in the winter, on one escape, and was finally sent to Leavenworth. There they broke him, physically, and he served his time without further protest.

Nobody had told me that catching AWOLs was part of rangering. But there was a price I had to pay. I had a secret which had to be kept from my superiors; there was a lie I might have to tell. Nothing was said to me by my superiors about my part in Ken's desertion, but it was clear that there were circumstances in which I could not be trusted to perform my duties as a federal enforcement officer.

Pig Pen was another warning of what was to come, a transitional figure. Pig Pen was a rock climber but one of the first for whom climbing was secondary to living in the C-Camp and carrying on his experiment with an alternative life style. He was of a good family and attended prestigious Reed College in Portland, Oregon. At Reed he found that he was allowed to go barefoot year-round. Because Reed regarded itself as a haven for geniuses and because the academic pressure there was intense, unconventional behavior had long been tolerated. If Einstein could wear sweaters with holes in them and not worry about his hair, Reed students could go barefoot. An inevitable consequence of going barefoot is dirty feet. On Pig Pen, the dirt migrated upward. Unremarkable as a climber, Pig Pen was remarkable for his dirt.

Pig Pen did have climbing boots and a pair of socks he never washed. Hikers and climbers from Cascade Canyon and Symmetry Spire congregated on the dock at the mouth of Cascade Creek to wait for Mann McCain's launch to take them back across Jenny Lake. The water in the lake was so pure that we used to drink from the lake while we waited. One day, inspired by the sight of a dozen people drinking from the lake, Pig Pen decided that it was time he washed his socks. A yellow-gray cloud several feet in diameter emanated from his socks and hung in the water beside the dock. So vivid was the memory of the washing of Pig Pen's socks that I was never after able to take an innocent drink of water at that place.

Pig Pen was a transitional figure in that he was a good-natured sort with wit and he got some fun out of his little sorties against conventionality. He probably became a brain surgeon and is now being made completely antiseptic twice a day.

Each year, there were more characters in the C-Camp who regarded it as a port of refuge for grievances they harbored against their parents and the world. Inevitably, even climbers who had no grievance with the world were seen as rebellious youth. There were no showers at the C-Camp, as there never had been at Jenny Lake. Climbers had always worn old clothes. Army surplus field gear was standard, a legacy from the Tenth Mountain Division. Nobody paid any attention until not washing and wearing odd-looking clothes became a symbol of political and social revolution. Most climbers didn't mind being taken for hippies and refused to take steps to correct the misperceptions of them. What could they say, that they weren't really unconventional?

The standard in climbing skill rose to the degree that it couldn't be met with a seasonal commitment. An alternative and impoverished lifestyle developed. An ambitious climber could afford the time neither for work nor college. (The largest group of dropouts from Dartmouth, between 1953 and 1959, were members of the Dartmouth Mountaineering Club. There were many more who didn't drop out from Dartmouth but dropped out after Dartmouth. Only Carlos Plummer seemed to feel no conflict between being a climber and pursuing a conventional career—providing you count two trips to Antarctica, including one for twelve months, as a conventional route for a hard-rock geologist to take in the pursuit of his career.) Commitment and poverty are old comrades.

A curious thing about us was that we could not frankly acknowledge our leaders and heroes as that. When Royal Robbins walked through the camp, he left a wake. People who were sitting down would stand as he passed and then, as if puzzled to find themselves on their feet, would stretch or find something in their gear to fiddle with. But one story about Royal that I heard frequently was how he declined an invitation to engage in a push-up contest, was later discovered in the brush doing push-ups, and still later suggested a push-up contest. People got a perverse delight in telling this story, as if by undercutting Royal's stature a little, they would raise theirs by just that much. It was like Seareach taunting Odysseus or Unferth taunting Beowulf. We could thereby count his accomplishments as part of our own, and I think deep down we did. Maneuvered into a position where he could not honorably decline, Royal had a responsibility to all of us who valued the standard he made for us to win the contest. But we had no straightforward way to thank him for what he did for us. Similarly, I have heard many ungenerous remarks about Chouinard's commercial success, far fewer about the fact that he decided, on ethical and aesthetic grounds, to switch from the production of pitons to the production of jam nuts. That kind of decision is supposed to be as impossible as deciding not to use the longbow in battle, but he did it.

Nevertheless, our moments of pettiness did not prevent bonds being forged between us that were impervious to the divisive pressures of personality, social class, geographic origin, age, politics, and condition of economic survival in an industrial culture. We were almost a kind of community, the kind of community that gathered annually at the Green River Rendezvous four generations earlier. Our gathering place was the C-Camp at Jenny Lake, and the rise and fall of this community happened within the nine-year history of the C-Camp. That rise and fall was coincidental with the emergence, growth, degeneration, and demise of the Teton Tea Party.

The first Teton Tea Party I attended was in 1958. We built a campfire in the rocks under the new bridge over the Snake

River and sat around a fire listening to and singing folk songs. I walked out of the firelight to take a piss in a night clear, cold, and quiet except for the river hushing its way under the bridge. I recalled the night I'd spent by Dinwoody Creek near the Wind River. This time the black between the stars didn't scare me. I had comrades murmuring and laughing back in the circle of the lodgepole and cottonwood fire. Bill Briggs was there as well as Tim Bond and three or four other climbers who were also folksingers, about a squad of us. The musicians outnumbered the listeners. On the campfire was a kettle of Teton Tea, a mixture of wine and tea from a recipe that had been in Brigger's family in Maine. It all seemed natural to us, the fire, the spiked tea, and, oddly, guitars, banjo and autoharp—about as unhandy as gear gets in a camp of climbers.

Unsoeld carried a harmonica into the mountains. In the middle of the approach to the Lower Saddle, just as the clients were arriving at full understanding of what they were going to have to put up with in order to get up the Grand, where the trail gets as steep as it can get without requiring the use of hands, Willi would whip out his harmonica and play it all the way up the steep section. You would think that this trick of Willi's might have become a tradition. Or yodeling. But not so—it was hot wine spiced with tea and folk music. Within ten years, Teton Tea was being sold in coffee houses in Seattle and San Francisco.

The songs at the first tea parties were the songs Briggs had picked up in the 1950s. He'd gone to the British Isles and picked up climbing ballads. He knew songs from the Alps, comic songs from Appalachia, and songs from other places that were sung loudly and laughingly solo or in chorus. During the growth in popularity of the Teton Tea Party, those songs were displaced in the repertoires by plaintive laments of losers who deserved better, songs claiming spiritual identity with those oppressed by love, chance, the law, or politics.

Jake hated these songs and protested bitterly at what was happening to the Teton Tea Party. As Jake pointed out, there wasn't one of us who didn't consider himself to be living the best possible life, so why sit around a campfire in one of the most beautiful mountain settings in the world listening to sad songs?

Jake did not complain about the lamenting songs until the Teton Tea Party got institutionalized. When we said that Jake's judgment was too harsh, he pointed out that it had been he who, in 1956, had carried Brigger's guitar up to the Garnet Canyon Meadows for a party high in the mountains. By 1965, two years after Jake's death, there were as many as 150 people attending Teton Tea Parties presided over by Bill Briggs. By then, Brigger had to give a little talk, at least once a summer, on the history and development of the Teton Tea Party. By then, the "tea" itself had degenerated to where frozen raspberries were added to the recipe.

Something more was going on than music. Teton Tea Parties became quasi-religious ceremonies, and not only were the majority of the participants not folk singers, they weren't even climbers.

As Brigger presided over larger and larger audiences, he had less and less control over the purpose of the Teton Tea Party. He had been energetic in organizing them because he loved to sing and play and loved to entertain. His own preferences hadn't been for the kind of songs Jake objected to but for happy songs. He was always on the side of good spirits and cheer, and that never changed. But the pressure from the audience was in another direction. I think that he got hooked on the possibility of transforming a hundred rapt, sad faces, in the next instance, into a hundred happy faces singing along. Later, Brigger became a Scientologist.

In this and other ways the C-Camp became a zoological garden displaying human specimens. People from town would drive through the camp, with their doors locked, to see what the world was coming to. Bearded, dusty, unmarried males and females sleeping in the same tents and doing God-knows-what after dark, cooking utensils scattered about the sites because there were not enough tables, two latrines for 130 people, the C-Camp and its inhabitants became one of the sights to see.

Tolerance for what the hippies were up to was but one sign of a growing estrangement between climbers and the parent culture. We at the ranger station tried to keep the zoo from getting any worse. Our registration and sign-out system worked because of the network of friendships we maintained as climbers. Because it was impossible to devise a set of regulations which effectively covered all known or imaginable circumstances, the administration of park policy depended on our personal authority. Several forces were at work which undercut that authority.

Experimentation in chemicals that "expanded the mind" began early among the climbers and, with a few exceptions, was over before it became part of the counterculture. Unfortunately, a well-known climber and a ranger, both of whom were friends of mine, continued their explorations with peyote after it was made illegal, then widened their field of inquiry into LSD. This put me in an awkward position. I had in the past trusted my life to each of these people, but even if there weren't personal reasons for covering for them, I would have lost contact with other climbers if I had enforced the law, or so I felt. Even climbers who themselves didn't experiment with drugs saw an analogy between climbing and "consciousness expansion."

There were others, less heroic than Ken Weeks, who tried to find sanctuary in the park. The authentic freaks found us. The word that we were not strict in enforcing the camping limit filtered out to them. A group of people arrived who registered as climbers, signed out on a climb, went hunting for mushrooms, returned to camp, and lit up a joint. Later, they signed back in as having made an unsuccessful attempt. They had us. Could we require a fixed percentage of successful ascents for climbs of minimum difficulty? Neither could we mobilize peer pressure. Whereas I once knew nearly every climber who visited the park, by 1967, when there were often a hundred people in the campground, there could be eighty people I had never seen nor heard of.

Charlie Brown (his true alias) was a bona fide, leather-and-beads-garbed, candle-and-belt-making freak. In spite of myself, I wondered if he'd ever worn a fur-lined jockstrap. Charlie

Brown found the C-Camp, pitched a tepee, and moved in, with various of his anemic-looking friends. Charlie's speech was punctuated with "man" when he spoke, as often he did, of matters somewhat mystical, his manner indicating that he was on the point of a profundity beyond language and grammar. Charlie failed in his stated purpose to live a secluded life. While professing rage at the Sunday tourists circling the camp, he was always on hand to give them a show.

In a fit of magnanimity one day, Charlie ran through the C-Camp screaming "free pot for everybody." This was too much for one of my colleagues. He packed Charlie up in the ranger pickup and drove him to the park boundary. As much as I loved the idea of a campground without Charlie Brown, I couldn't let this pass. This particular ranger smoked marijuana himself. I suspected him of getting his supplies from the C-Camp, and I suspected that was the reason he wanted Charlie out of there. He was afraid that Charlie would blow the whole thing open. I told my colleague that unless he wanted to bust Charlie for possession, he had to go and bring Charlie back. He brought Charlie back.

Within a week, Charlie had carved Fuck You Tourists on the back of the C-Camp sign. Charlie could find himself in the Teton County Jail for that, and I didn't think that Charlie was made of the same stuff as Ken Weeks. I made him erase his message by reducing the thickness of the sign by the depth of the carved letters—with a small, dull chisel. Finally, Charlie went two weeks without even pretending to climb, and we had him. Even so, the ethics remained cloudy because we selectively enforced the limit of stay.

Charlie relocated in the Wind Rivers and gave the Forest Service down there fits when he announced that he was going to winter over in the mountains "like the Indians and the mountain men," which shows how much Charlie knew about the Indians and the mountain men. The last I heard of Charlie Brown was that, under his real name, he was a candidate for mayor of Berkeley, California. I never found out how he did.

Hemming showed up from Europe. Relations between us were a little tense. He had joined John Harlin in Europe. Harlin had a Himalayan expedition in mind. Gary had written to Barry, Jake, and me. Harlin had vetoed the inclusion of Buckingham in the invitation for reasons that were not specified. I never answered Gary's letter. Gary also disapproved of my getting married and returning to school. He accused Connie of having trapped me. Connie hit him. Gary approved of that.

We were drinking beer in my cabin one evening when Gary got into one of his moods. To keep him from erupting and waking Connie and the kids, I suggested that we go out and look at the moon. We could hear the singing at the tea party in the campground. A coyote howled from the lower slope of Teewinot. I observed that the coyote was probably offended by the quality of the singing in his meadow. Then Hemming and I attempted to imitate the howl of an aesthetically pained coyote. Perhaps we were too subtle. We silenced the coyote but not the tea party.

In the end, the antics of the revelers, pleading from the ranger station, and hints dropped by Brigger's fellow guides persuaded Briggs to move the parties out of the C-Camp. It was not hard to foresee that the C-Camp itself would go the way of the Teton Tea Party.

As the standards continued to go up and more climbers aspired to be included among the best, tensions arose which could not so easily be dispelled, particularly concerning the ethics of climbing. The problem lay in the fact that climbing ethics were rooted in climbing aesthetics. This is hard to describe in a way that doesn't sound silly, but after you've climbed in one area a lot, you have the feeling that the mountains tell you how they ought to be climbed. You climb in a certain way because of the nature of the rock or terrain, the weather, the history and tradition of the place, and something of your own which asks for something more graceful than just surviving. If it works, you feel that you have done something beautiful. When you've got that feeling, you've got the right way to do it. You hear the mountain's message by how you feel. The person who does this climb first, or best, is seen as the lawmaker (or lawgiver, depending on the status of one's authority problem). A lot of other things—style, personality, how many other people can or want to do what you did—determine whether or not your notion of right is accepted. The aesthetic appropriate to different regions differed and so did what was "right."

To many outsiders, the California climbers appeared arrogant. I believe they were the opposite. They developed a profound sense of humility in the shadow of their great walls, out of which grew a strict code about how a climb should be conducted. Their disapproval of siege climbing tactics and the excessive use of bolts was not a way of showing off their superior skills, but ethical wisdom. This ethical wisdom was not contained in a set of precepts; it was contained in a set of experiences that only the walls themselves provided. Any wall could be climbed eventually by some means. The point was to climb the wall by the right means. To learn what was right meant that you humbled yourself not before Royal Robbins but before where he had been and how he got there and what he had learned in getting there. These days there is talk of our need for an ethic of place. That is precisely what we were about.

It was true that if a god had coated the Yosemite walls with grease, thereby creating a fair approximation of Northwest conditions, technique would have been less refined. But once the more refined technique was found, it became the standard. Not only did northwestern climbers have to climb Yosemite walls by Yosemite standards, they had to try to climb their own walls by those standards. It didn't seem fair; it wasn't fair that the Californians were the best climbers because they learned in Yosemite, but even those who protested knew somewhere in their heart that this was the way it had to be.

Difficult as it was to learn, knowing and doing what was right was an easier problem for climbers than for other visitors to the parks. By 1966, the results of Mission 66 were in. The campgrounds were packed by 10 A.M. All parking spaces were full all the time, and people began parking everywhere. The trails in the mouth of Cascade Canyon were as crowded at times as the boardwalks of Jackson. I couldn't go anywhere in my area of responsibility at any time without seeing a violation of park regulations. Observing people breaking regulations obviously also became a part of the experience of visitors sensitive to the values the regulations were intended to protect. The park was full of the guilty and the angry, not unlike the country.

There was an older seasonal naturalist who had worked in Rainier and Teton national parks for twenty-five years. He not only had complete knowledge of the flora and fauna of the area but was loved by visitors for his humorous and kindly style in teaching it. The press of people in the park eroded his good nature. One day a woman came up to him with a bouquet of flowers she had picked. The vision of thousands of people stripping the terrain of flowers was too much for him. "Can you tell me what these flowers are?" she asked. "Let me see them," he said pleasantly. He took the bouquet in his hands and slowly tore it to shreds and dropped it at her feet. "Pretty, weren't they," he said.

He didn't come back the next year. How could the Park Service have lost a loyalty as long-standing as his? What could have driven him to an anger that was, for him, violent? My mission was that of a mediator between the regulations, the ambitions of my superiors, the visitors, the climbers, other rangers, and my own view of what people ought to get from a visit to the park. It seemed less and less possible to succeed in my mission.

There had been two new chief rangers and two new assistant chief rangers since Russ. Doug was still there, and Dunbar, but they were less able to protect us from the changes taking place in the Park Service. Being permanent park rangers had come to mean that they wore a uniform at a desk; we didn't see much of them. They still worked as much as fifty unpaid hours of overtime per month and still provided the taxpayer with the best value for his dollar of any government service, but they were known in the Park Service as "homesteaders," members of the service who stay in one place. Homesteading was frowned upon by the personnel theoreticians who thought on the military-corporate model. To get a promotion you had to transfer, and if a promotion wasn't available, you were expected to transfer anyway, laterally. Neither of them uttered a word of complaint to us, but we could see that they had problems of their own. There was no superior we could talk to with complete openness.

By 1966 there was open warfare between the road patrol and the Jenny Lake rangers.

In 1966, the Park Service decided to close the Climbers' Campground. I was almost relieved. The Jenny Lake Campground was more pleasant than the C-Camp. By passing sites from one climbing party to the next, with our collusion, certain sites could have climbers in them all summer. And the freaks were kept out. Kept in our hands, the system not only would work, it would be an improvement.

Chouinard had been in Europe in 1966 to learn about ice climbing. In 1967 he stopped by the Tetons and stayed at the Jenny Lake Campground. He showed me his new axe. I loved to hear him tell about how he thought his way into the design solutions he came up with. He explained why the curve was as it was; the shapes of the point, pick, and adze; the dimensions and the metallurgy; and who he had talked to in Europe to help him in his thinking. I loved the pictures he made in my mind of the crusty, venerable, mountain-hardened men he had sought out, questioned, and listened to, storing it all in his head, hands, and feet for when he got back to his mountains and his forge.

I asked Yvon if he'd seen Gary.

"Gary's a French national hero, or at least a Parisian hero. It's an experience to walk down the street with him. Girls and reporters trail along."

"Because of the rescue on the West Face of the Dru?"

"Partly, but something the French admire even more happened. Hemming fell in love with a seventeen-year-old girl from a respectable Parisian family. The father was not pleased and locked his daughter up in her bedroom on the second floor of their house. The house had a wall around it. Gary climbed over the wall and up the side of the house to her bedroom. The old man called the police, and Gary went to jail. The press loved it. They call him the beatnik of Mt. Blanc. Girls wrote letters to him. He slept under the bridges in Paris. The press started telling where he was sleeping, and the girls started to come down to the bridges to find him. It got so that Gary had to give out false information about where he was sleeping."

Chouinard was not in a campsite of his own but was staying at a friend's campsite. That night, the road patrol busted Yvon for camping in an undesignated site. The campground was our responsibility. Even if he had been in an undesignated site instead of, as was the case, under a bush at the edge of the campsite, the usual thing would have been to issue a warning. Chouinard they cited to appear before the chief ranger. I asked to speak to the chief ranger. I explained to him that Chouinard's stature among climbers was great, that he was staying at the site with the permission of the people who were registered for the site, and that this action couldn't be interpreted as anything but harassment. Our job at Jenny Lake would become impossible if this sort of thing kept up. The chief ranger was unmoved by my plea; Chouinard had to appear. Yvon had more time in the Tetons above the ten-thousand-foot level than the chief ranger had in his Tetons desk chair, but he lectured Chouinard in the most patronizing manner and, in effect, dismissed him from the mountains. Although it was only temporary and not a serious inconvenience, the message sent and received was that the police would be watching him. It wasn't the Jenny Lake rangers but the cops who'd be negotiating the chief ranger's wishes with the climber.

The next step would be a tightening up of the camping limit. After the incident with Chouinard, it was clear that the decision had already been made. The effects would be subtle but far-reaching. There were only a dozen climbers who stayed in the Tetons for more than two weeks, climbers who had determined to serve a full apprenticeship in the Tetons. The limit would not affect the statistics much. But those climbers who stayed a month, or an entire season, were important to the spirit of the place. Some of them aspired to be guides and were systematically doing the more difficult routes. Some just loved the Tetons and thought of them as their home range. If they weren't allowed to be there, no climber could think of himself as coming home to the center of American mountaineering; every climber would be paying a visit with a limited welcome.

Worst of all, the continuity of storytelling would be broken. With each day numbered, climbers would not be able to afford a day just to talk and think. The oral tradition would stop, and it was the oral tradition that made the Tetons home to climbers.

Shawangunk climbers would have gone to the Bugaboos in June and have come to the Tetons in July. A party from Colorado who had been in the Bugaboos two seasons before and in Alaska in July would stop by in August. Three weeks later, a group of Californians who had escaped the Yosemite heat by going to the Cirque of the Towers in the Wind Rivers would run up to Jenny Lake before returning to Yosemite for the fall climbing season there. All their stories were stored in the memories of those climbers who were staying for the season or passed along by climbers whose stays overlapped each other's. The technical details of the climbs would be recorded in the mountaineering journals that winter, but however artful the prose (and it got artier as the decade progressed), it would be pale beer compared to the gossiping, laughing, gesticulating storytelling of the campground.

The quality of the journal articles themselves would suffer if these stories were silenced. They were oral first drafts getting honed in the retelling. It was often true that a climber did not understand the significance of his story until it got tested before an audience of climbers. Barry, Bill, Jake, and I knew that we had to get off Denali by going over the top. We even knew that there was a sense in which we'd intended it to be that way. But it wasn't until Yvon made his remark, about the commitment we had made being a first, that we could think of our experience as having made a contribution to our mates.

It was not entirely a coincidence that I, ranger in charge at Jenny Lake, was also a student of Chaucer. Keeping stories alive in our memory is part of my work. The other part of my work was rescue. I hadn't quite yet come to the end of that work.

CHAPTER 10

AT THE HEIGHT

ate in the 1967 season, J. J. Cook, "Cookie," invited us on a moonlight float trip down the Snake River. We were a diverse group that had been drawn to the valley under the Tetons. Cookie was a fly fisherman and river guide, whose daughter married the maharaja of Sikkim. There was my wife, Connie, a native of Jackson, whose mother kept the stage station on Teton Pass; her father had driven the freight wagons from the train, over the pass, into the valley. Professor Crabtree of the Stevens Institute in Hoboken, who was originally from Kansas, provided commentary. Zaidee, Jim Huidekoper's almost grown-up daughter, was there too. Her dad was a rancher who had been a peer of one of the Kennedys at Harvard.

Also traveling with us was a bottle of Hudson's Bay rum.

Down river, Cookie got too close to the bank. "Man the scuppers, we're going ashore!" yelled Crabtree. I chuckled about that. Then I thought of it again and chuckled and giggled some more. Everybody else had stopped chuckling some time earlier. Everybody else had stopped nipping on the rum some time earlier too.

Then I got maudlin.

Teewinot, Owen, and the Grand, called the Cathedral Group, viewed from the northeast, were faintly backlit from the sun down over the horizon. I was in the grip of a complicated mood. I knew the mountains and didn't, loved them and feared them, felt gratitude and fulfillment and loss and regret. I started talking to the mountains loudly with a drunk's postured seriousness. The vision of how it was going to be between me and the world was beginning to cloud over, leaving me with an unfocused sense of grievance, so I did the natural thing. I said something mean to my wife. I told her that I loved the mountains as much as I loved her, and if it weren't for the fact that she were so beautiful, I'd leave her in a minute and go off into the mountains. I'd had the mood to just up and head for the hills twice before: while standing on the deck of the USS *Albany* off the Azores as a midshipman in the navy and when looking at some hills while on an artillery maneuver at Fort Sill, Oklahoma. The mood seemed to be compounded of mountains, water, and a sense of doing the wrong thing.

Connie wasn't fooled by the beautiful part. I was being a bastard and there wasn't much she could do. What can you say to a drunk in a rubber raft?

I noticed that my companions regarded me as a drunk who bordered on being unfunny. I determined to show them that I was serious about staying in the mountains. We stopped on a sandbar, and I announced that I was going to spend the night there, my last night alone with the mountains or something such. To prove to my companions that I could take care of myself, I gathered wood for a fire. I wasn't particular about what I gathered; damp seemed as good as dry, and damp was handier since to get dry wood I'd have to swim for it. I carefully laid the fire and struck match after match after match. When the matches were gone, I allowed myself to be talked into getting back into the raft, feeling shrewd because I knew that I wasn't nearly as drunk as they thought I was. When we arrived at the landing, I proved how sober I was by refusing to abandon ship. I did finally agree to get out long enough so they could load the raft on top of the car and me into the raft.

It was after 1:00 when we got back to the cabin. Ralph Tingey was there, and I explained to him about how I wouldn't abandon the raft, and he explained to me about how there was a party calling for help on the North Face of the Grand, and suddenly I wasn't so drunk any more.

I've often wondered what my mates were thinking at that moment. I don't mean about going on a rescue with a drunk; I mean about going up on the North Face for a rescue. To the degree I was able to think, my thoughts wandered between disbelief and relief. Ever since I had been a ranger, the image of a North Face rescue had been there. It obviously had to happen someday, we said. Once a climb only the most experienced were audacious enough to undertake, the North Face was by the mid-sixties being done by aspiring young climbers in the third year of their apprenticeship in mountaineering. It had become the test which established mastery over the old mountaineering skills. Inevitably, we felt, someone would take the test before they were fully prepared—out of eagerness to move into the current realms of glory, blank wall climbing, gymnastic climbing, and, already on the horizon, vertical ice climbing.

Yvon Chouinard, among others, warned ambitious young climbers that the relative absence of technically difficult pitches is itself one of the dangers of the North Face. Bad weather or a minor injury would create a horror show survivable only by those with seasoning that cannot be acquired in three years. It would have been presumptuous for a youngster, no matter how technically gifted, to have accused Chouinard of being a nervous Nellie, so his admonitions helped. Nevertheless, warnings inspire as well as caution: we had the North Face in mind as one place where an injury or death would certainly happen. After eight years, we had lost all confidence in our ability to predict who would not get into trouble, but we had lots of faith in the force of numbers. Nothing good resulted from more people. Given the number of people coming to the mountains, sooner or later everything imaginable would happen.

In the years since I had moved into the ranger station, and especially since Dunbar Susong had become the assistant district ranger, we had improved our equipment. We had acquired, for example, an Austrian cable-rescue rig like those used on Eiger North Face rescues. More important, we had the team.

Never before could we have mustered a team like that of 1967. In the years of working out techniques, gathering material, and building up manpower, our argument had been What if there is a North Face rescue? The seven of us who would go up on the rescue had all climbed the North Face. It was as if the mountain had kindly waited.

It would have to wait a bit longer. There was nothing I could do at the moment, and fortunately for the good name of the Park Service, and of my children, not much anybody could do. I had to get some sleep and sober up. I gave just a fleeting mental grin at myself for the recent sentimentality about my beloved mountains. In eight years on the rescue team, I had never let my guard so far down. That wasn't by any means the first night I had partied, but it was the only time I ever allowed myself to forget that within the hour I might be on my way up on a rescue. Again, it was as if the mountain had been waiting.

I told Ralph that we'd check it out with the spotting scope in the morning and went to bed. Whether that decision was made because instinctively I knew it was the right one or merely because I was so hopelessly befuddled that it was the only thing I could do is one of the things I'm fated never to know. Had I been sober, I might have reasoned that we could commit ourselves to a full-scale operation or send out a two-man scouting party. The only standard procedure in competent rescue work is in where you store your gear, but usually a report of a party in trouble that is based on indirect evidence, such as a report of a shout heard from a cliff or a party overdue, merits only the sending out of a scouting party. As it happened, had we done that, there would not have been any net loss of time, but we might have burned out two of our strongest climbers, Rick Reese and either Ted Wilson or Ralph. But no one argued that we send out scouts first. The mood of this one was different.

Ralph had given me, in the most objective terms, the information he had acquired and sorted during the previous three hours, including lights he had spotted at the place the party was reported to be, and he was careful to point out that there was nothing conclusive. Yet, it was obvious that he was convinced. The spotting scope could confirm his assessment, but it could not deny it. There would be no risking losing a day while we accustomed ourselves to the sensation that this was it, as had happened on the Appie rescue. We would go whether we picked them out in the spotting scope or not. We'd go together, and we'd ask for a helicopter—as soon as I sobered up.

Ralph, still shaking from two hours of sitting in the mist-chilled meadow, woke me up with the news that he'd seen the party. We started organizing. He took me out to the scope. The moment I looked into the scope, I realized what a difficult task I had given him. It had taken him thirty minutes to locate them. The scope was at the limit of its capability. The slightest movement, a passing breeze or car, distorted the field of vision. His precise memory of the route had allowed him to methodically search it, not merely pitch by pitch, but almost move by move. To sweep that scope fifty feet at a time would have been precise work. Ralph had had to move its field of vision no more than fifteen feet at a time. After he spotted them, he watched for an hour. There was no doubt: only one of the figures was moving. They'd be on that ledge until we moved them off it. We assumed that it was the girl who was hurt. She weighed 120 pounds as against the man's weight of 170.

Did we have enough evidence to justify chartering a helicopter? There was a note of pleading in my voice as I asked Doug for one. I'm afraid of helicopters. When in one, I cannot shake the impression that I am being wafted into the air thousands of feet over very unyielding metamorphic rock by a dragonfly with a thyroid problem. But given a choice between a few minutes of fear and five thousand feet of heavy carrying, I'd take the fear. If I hadn't, I would have been overruled by the rest of the team anyway.

I like a helicopter pilot who doesn't waste time trying to reassure his nervous passengers. With the exchange of a few brief sentences, ours saw that we understood the problem. Even a helicopter is not independent of the winds and what the various shapes of the mountains can do to them. Once he understood that we didn't expect him to take off and make a beeline for the ledge upon which were our clients, our pilot was interested in hearing what we knew of the terrain and air currents in the vicinity of the Cathedral Group. The Grand and Owen are on a north-south line, with the Grand to the south. Owen and Teewinot are on an east-west line, with Teewinot to the east. In the middle of this triangle of summits is a glacier, Teton Glacier. The North Face falls directly to this glacier. Outside this triangle is a series of canyons. To the east, of course, is Jackson's Hole. Our cabins were on the east side of the meadow at the base of Teewinot. North of Teewinot and Owen is Cascade Canyon. West of Owen and the Grand, behind them from our perspective at our cabins, is the South Fork of Cascade Canyon, with a basin called Dartmouth Basin at the head of it. South of the Grand is Garnet Canyon. The col between Garnet Canyon and Dartmouth Basin is called the Lower Saddle. The most popular routes up the Grand start from this twelve-thousand-foot saddle that is big enough so that a hundred people could all find level places to bivouac. The Exum Guide Service hut is on this saddle, as is a roughed-out heliport.

To fly directly up the glacier would be equivalent to paddling a canoe up a rapid. Our pilot chose to approach from the back. He picked his way up Cascade Canyon and then turned south up the South Fork, feeling out the terrain and looking for updrafts which would lift us to our maximum safe altitude of thirteen thousand feet. It was like putting in a kayak upstream of a rapids. Mt. Owen and the Grand are almost joined by a huge buttress with the descriptive title the Grandstand. The Grandstand is the back wall of the Teton Glacier as viewed from the valley. It was a possible route, not a preferred one. We merely glanced at it, intent on finding and really seeing what still was no more substantial than a report of shouts in the mountains and two watery shadows wavering in the lens of the spotting scope.

The same imagination which for years had me falling off the North Face of the Grand in my dreams had me, in the few seconds between the time we thought we should spot them and when we did spot them, hoping that we hadn't really seen anything, that nobody had fallen off the Grand, and that I was just having a hangover. I was having a hangover all right, but there were also two people on a ledge.

The first thing that we noticed was that it was the man who was down. The girl was trying to jump up and down for joy but was considerably inhibited by the two thousand feet of exposure to the glacier below the ledge on which she was leaping about.

With me in the helicopter was Rick Reese, tacitly acknowledged by all of us as the strongest climber on the rescue team. I was to assess the condition of the party and try to talk to them through a battery-powered bullhorn (part of our riot control equipment). Rick was to look over the route. The implacable steepness of the North Face is relieved by four prominent ledges called the First, Second, Third, and Fourth ledges, as you ascend the face. Also, as you ascend, the ledges become shorter and narrower and slope fairly steeply eastward toward the valley and also northward toward the glacier. So, while these ledges are a break in the steepness of the face, they're not the sort of place where you'd want to let your attention wander.

Our two victims were at the lower end of the Second Ledge (altitude 12,800). This meant that they would be relatively easy to get to. The Second Ledge connects to another ledge that crosses the West Face and ends at the Upper Saddle (altitude 13,000). The Upper Saddle is on the Owen-Spalding Route, the regular route between the summit and the Lower Saddle. Over the years we had carried maybe a ton of wounded humanity off the mountain via this route. It was tedious, not without problems, but reasonable and familiar. What I mostly thought about that way off was that it involved murderously backbreaking work because it was seldom steep enough or on the fall line enough to permit a straightforward lowering. If we took that route, we'd be bearing the weight of the victim mainly on our arms and backs. Our other options were on very unfamiliar terrain. We had long ago formulated a plan to be used in the event of a North Face rescue. If the party were on the First Ledge or below, we would lower. If they were above the Second Ledge, depending upon how high they were, we would either raise the litter toward the summit until we could go down the regular route or lower it to the top of the Second Ledge and traverse around the connecting ledge to the regular route. We had covered all the eventualities except the one which we now faced. Their position on the lower third of the Second Ledge was equally remote from the connecting ledge and the First Ledge. In terms of our planning the route of evacuation, our victims were in no-man's-land.

Raising and traversing techniques are rarely used in rescue work. When they are, as on an Eiger rescue, it's apt to be world news. Raising requires some device for gaining mechanical advantage and is practically impossible except on vertical or near vertical rock where the litter can be held away from the face by one or two men. An overhang is ideal. Traversing, especially an ascending traverse, requires an almost unbelievable amount of physical energy. The angle doesn't have to ease from the vertical much before the litter bearers begin to feel that they both are lifting against gravity and are in a tug-of-war against the raising device, which feels as if it is trying to pitch them forward on their faces, and are at the same time keeping their balance sideways. It's like trying to both lift and drag a heavy rock while standing sideways on a steep slope.

Although raising and traversing are not to be considered in usual circumstances, we were hoping that one or the other of these would be possible. Our sensible reason for so hoping was that we didn't want to enter ourselves and the litter into the hail of rocks whistling, spinning, and cascading more or less constantly down the face. Gravity was normally our ally, in lowering we cashed in on the potential energy the victim had stored in climbing to the site of the accident. But on this face, gravity would be firing rocks at us.

I think there was also a less sensible reason for hoping we could raise or traverse: we hadn't done much of it. Maybe it was an opportunity to outwit nature, to cheat a little. Maybe we wouldn't have to be competent, disciplined, hardworking, and brave—just clever.

Rick was not encouraged. It was a long way from where they were to the top of the Second Ledge. It was also a very long way down to the glacier.

I had no more reason for cheer based on what I could perceive. I could not make them hear me above the roar of the helicopter and so was unable to determine the exact nature and extent of his injuries. I hoped the victim could be loaded into a one-man carrying seat and be carried off at least the worst of it on the back of a rescuer, Rick, to be precise. The man merely raised one arm, slower and more weakly than I wished, and let it drop. His back didn't appear to be injured, so we would take along the carrying seat. If he could stand the jostling, the rescue would be greatly simplified. I wished that his wave had been more enthusiastic.

As soon as we realized that we weren't going to find out anything more, perched there in midair, we told the pilot that it would be fine with us if he got the hell out of there. He had not been having an easy time with the down, up, and cross drafts. I had been trying not to picture the consequences of a falling rock taking a bad bounce off the face and nicking a rotor blade, a possibility which the pilot most likely did not suspect. I did not distract him by mentioning it.

As we soared past the North Ridge and down across the West Face, Rick and I turned our attention to the questions of logistics. What quantity of what type of gear would we have to get to the ledge by what means? Later, the problems would become, cumulatively, technical, physiological, and—after a certain point in time, technical difficulty, or terror—psychological. The point of logistics is to anticipate these problems. Get it right technically and the physiological and psychological problems are less likely to accumulate. It would be nice to have to take only the carrying seat. It would be a disaster if we took only the carrying seat and had to have the litter. This sort of uncertainty fixed the terms under which the mountain would meet us for the next two and a half days. We'd never see clearly beyond the immediate step.

Since we couldn't decide whether to take him up and out or down and out, we had to have gear brought to the Upper Saddle that would allow us to go either way. That was simple enough, in theory. The catch was that we could have no more gear than five of us could transport on our backs from the Upper Saddle to the Second Ledge. We could not be completely equipped for either eventuality nor could we carry as much food as we wanted to. The idea was to get to the site as quickly as possible without expending all our energy. Ted, Mike Ermath, Rick, and I would move what we had with us from the Lower Saddle to the Upper Saddle and across the West Face to the accident site.

Ralph stayed at the Lower Saddle to lead the less experienced support team up to the ledge with equipment we would radio for on the basis of further knowledge. Bob Irvine was already on the mountain someplace, climbing with Leigh Ortenburger. This meant that by the time we got to the accident site, we would have men and equipment in the valley, at the Lower Saddle, at the Upper Saddle, and strung out along the trails and route in between.

I couldn't see that my years of experience and preparation made any difference than if this had been my first rescue—the reverse, in fact. I had already made a mistake in vetoing the suggestion that the bolt kit be brought because I thought I knew the mountain well enough to be sure that we could find blocks enough to put rope slings around or piton cracks enough for anchors and thereby avoid the time-consuming job of drilling holes in the granite for bolts. Eight years earlier, I wouldn't have dared make such a judgment. From the helicopter, we had seen that we would need the bolt kit.

I made no mistakes on personnel. The choice of Ralph to lead the less-experienced support team was perfect. Ralph was a sleeper. Slightly built, a devout Mormon, and a doctoral student in Arabic at Johns Hopkins, he was less intimidating than the grouchy old salts like Bob Irvine and me or than the dashingly impressive Rick Reese and Ted Wilson. Yet he was a better technical rock climber than any of us. The combination of his reassuring bearing plus his obvious competence was just what the younger climbers would need to feel confident and perform at their best. Because they were bigger than Ralph, they would want to carry their weight; because Ralph was less known to them than us, they wouldn't do something stupid trying to impress him. Most important of all, what they didn't know, Ralph would tell them, and they'd know he was right because he would be. I did not know that the support team needed such sophisticated leadership because I did not know the support team. With Ralph there, it didn't matter that I didn't know them. Maybe I had learned some things.

The trip from the Lower Saddle to the Upper Saddle we'd all made uncounted times before. When we left the Lower Saddle with a heavy load, we turned our minds off and turned them back on when we got to the Upper Saddle. Had we become so indifferent to the scenery? No, it's just that if we'd turned our minds on while carrying those loads, what would have come through was not the scenery but the pain. We had been told by climbers at the Lower Saddle that Leigh and Bob had not come down from the summit. I was not surprised when, at the Upper Saddle, some climbers told us that Bob and Leigh had heard the cries for help, had judged them to be on the Second Ledge, and had already set out on the same route we had judged to be the best one. I smiled as I pictured those two mathematicians sitting on top of the Grand systematically sorting out the possibilities while the frantic cries for help rang through the peaks.

I had trusted that we would find Bob and Leigh, all five of us had, although we had two technically competent but young climbers with us, Hugh and Larry Scott, in case we didn't. The Scotts reacted well to warming the bench; their day would come if they stuck around long enough. They understood why we wanted only the most tested of us there, and they were as happy to find that Bob and Leigh were where we hoped they'd be as were the rest of us.

We went around the mountain to join Lorraine Hough and Gaylord Campbell on their ledge. Gay had suffered much and was suffering still. He had a double compound fracture of the lower leg, splinted between an ice axe and an ice hammer. There were loose pieces of bone floating in the flesh.

So much for the carrying seat. The seat would have to be taken back and the litter brought around the mountain. The two heavy and awkward reels of steel cable would have to come up from the Lower Saddle to the Upper Saddle and over. We would lower.

The traverse we had just come over was longer and more difficult than we had expected. I had been on it before but always from the perspective of a difficult climb behind me. It had an altogether different character when contemplated as a route for transporting heavy and awkward equipment. Ted went back for ropes—alone. We had used all ours as fixed handlines, including a chewed remnant of Gay's climbing rope. Ted had volunteered. It was a compromise of safety for speed, but as he pointed out, the ropes were needed and he could do it. As he left, my glance fixed on a white powder mark nearby. There had been many of them on the ledges along the traverse. I had kept them in the periphery of my consciousness. These powdery scars were caused by falling rock. There were hundreds of scars. Any of the rocks that produced them would have been big enough to knock Ted off the mountain.

While Ted was on the traverse, we expended an hour and a half of time and a great deal of Gay's remaining energy and tolerance for pain replacing his makeshift splint with an inflatable splint.

Ted returned, weighted down and unbalanced by three ropes. Nearly everyone in America has seen a picture of the Grand Teton, whether they know what it is they're looking at or not. The Grand Teton and the Matterhorn are our visual definitions of mountain; pictures of both are everywhere. The right side of the usual view of the Grand is the North Face. The West Face is behind. These are the steepest, darkest, and coldest parts of the mountain. From the West Face there is no visible evidence that there are humans on earth. You can't even see the potato fields in Idaho, just mountains and desert. When Ted returned from traversing these two faces alone, he remarked, "Now I know what Hermann Buhl meant by solitude." Ted had gotten about as far away from the hearth as humankind can venture and stay with us.

We murmured our appreciation to Ted and spent another half hour of daylight taking stock. Lori had to be escorted off the mountain. Leigh was the logical one to do this, and Bob said as much. "I don't see how we can possibly ask Leigh to help us. We're getting paid." The $2.40 an hour plus overtime wasn't the issue. We had contracted to do this. Gay thought that a large rock had come off the mountain, shattered on the ledge beside him, and cartwheeled him down to Lori's ledge twenty feet below. There were certain facts that made it appear to us that that might not be exactly what happened, that Gay may have fallen while improperly protected, but it could have. In any case, there was no denying the fact that rocks would be coming off the mountain. This operation was going to have a high element of objective danger. Leigh's skills could do very little about that. He was on vacation—out on a pleasure climb. He had done all that duty, friendship, and reason bound him to do. I recalled my first rescue, the evacuation of Tim's body. Leigh had volunteered for that one. He'd been with me earlier in the summer when we'd run on to a rescue situation while out on a climb. I recalled a couple of times we'd been on this side of the mountain together, putting up new routes. I looked across to the summit of Mt. Owen and tried to pick out the ledge below the summit on which he and I once bivouacked, delayed by one of Emerson's notoriously modestly rated 5.7s. I either had to ask him or insist that he leave. I couldn't leave it up to him to volunteer. Cashing in all the chits I had and taking out a mortgage for the shortfall, I looked straight at him and asked him to stay with us. It was much easier than the time I begged for a hamburger in Texas.

How were we to get that mass of gear across from the Upper Saddle? Would Ralph, Hugh, and Larry bring it over on our fixed lines? They had the technical skills, but would they know where to look for invisible ice on rock? Could they tell gravel that would hold one's weight from that which would not, or which loose blocks are usable and which are not? Would they instinctively make the right move in a bombardment of rock? The fact that I had these questions did not reflect on the abilities of the Scotts. All these things are things you learn without knowing how you learned them. One day you dodge a rock and realize you knew to dodge right instead of left. The rock had hit and gone by before you had a conscious thought. It happens a couple more times and you begin to believe that you know. But you can't explain what it is you know or how you came to know it. You feel unable to help someone who doesn't know. We decided to play it safe this time; we'd pushed luck enough with Ted's solo traverse. Rick, Mike, and I would take Lori across and return with Ralph and the gear. The team at the Upper Saddle would escort her on down to the Lower Saddle, from where she could be flown out in the morning. Bob, Leigh, and Ted had been worked hardest that day, so they'd stay with Gay. We would either return by moonlight or bivouac somewhere on the way. One more thing, a radio call for morphine. With such pain, there was a possibility of shock.

As we discussed his fate, Gay joined in. I tried to be polite. From my point of view, very little of what we had to discuss was any of his concern. His job was to deal with his pain as best he could and to avoid dying of shock, if possible. We'd take care of the business of getting him off the mountain. But I knew he'd not be able to accept that point of view, if for no other reason than the boredom of thinking about one's own pain and nothing else. So I tried to appear attentive to his remarks and avoided contradicting him when he made suggestions that couldn't or shouldn't be acted upon. I'd learned another thing in eight years; argue only if you have to. If the decision is yours to make, the event and not argument will determine who's right.

At 10:00 P.M., Mike, Ralph, and the two Scotts were bivouacked on the West Face with the gear we came for. Lori was on the way down, and Rick and I were making the last radio contact from the Upper Saddle. A new helicopter had been procured, operational to twenty thousand feet. Doug would try to drop the medicine, morphine, and antibiotics to the site. That failing, he'd lower medicine and the bolt kit to us by rope from the helicopter. Rick and I were staying at the Upper Saddle. We were sure a drop was possible there. Doug, who by this time had been directing rescue operations for a decade and a half, had thoughtfully driven up to our cabin for the radio contact so that Connie could listen in.

The transmission over, I had nothing to do until dawn except try to sleep. The operation thus far had been far from perfect, but had there been any fundamental mistakes? The bolt kit had been a mistake, but not one that caused any delay. We couldn't get a prescription for medicine until we could radio down the victim's condition, and I knew that we could get the bolt kit by whatever means we got the medicine. Not committing ourselves to the litter and cable rig from the beginning was another matter. I was badly hungover, I had little sleep, and I was scared, any one of which undoubtedly affected my judgment. But I also lacked an adequate philosophy for coping with technology. I was never able to rely on the helicopter wholeheartedly. As had happened many times before, I wondered if it might not be better to not use it at all. I knew what muscles could do, and I was, after eight years of practice, confident of my ability to judge skill. Suppose I'd just sent an advance team of two or three and . . . the possibilities began to multiply. I was tired of tactics and second-guessing myself. Here we were. It was a beautiful evening, cold and clear. The setting was spectacular. We were just seven hundred feet below the summit. The bivouac site was fairly comfortable as bivouac sites go. It was wonderful to be able to sleep. Who would have thought you'd be allowed to sleep on a North Face rescue?

I slept from 11 to 3. By 3 A.M., the heat stored in the mountain granite had gone. That is a very bad time for humans. I awoke wide-eyed and shivering into my North Face nightmare. The stars had begun to dim without the sky becoming perceptibly lighter. The Anglo-Saxons had a word specifically for this time of day, *uht.* Their word *uhtceare* translates "care before dawn" or "star-dying fear." The buried awareness that another party was climbing the face below us surfaced in my thoughts.

I wondered dimly whether we would kill one of them with the rocks we would be knocking off and dozed off for a few minutes. I awoke again feeling that I had not completed a thought—oh yes, the other party. I recalled out of childhood a gravel bank and a strange boy, rock in hand, arm cocked. The image was vague, but not the panic. The sky was perceptibly lighter. The sun would rise at least once more.

The sky was already pink when we heard the helicopter. We scrambled out of our bivouac garb, embarrassed to be caught unready and uneager. The party on the face didn't have a radio and so did not know that a medicine drop was to be made. They were less prepared than we were. Leigh woke up, out of what Bob and Ted insist was a snoring sleep, to the roar of the helicopter. Before he could assimilate the clamor into his consciousness, there was an object flying through the air at him. Leigh flinched and made a basket catch. They had morphine at last. Doug had brought enough extra to make a drop to us if the drop on the face had failed, but it hadn't, so we had only equipment to transport.

Getting back to the site took two valuable hours of sunlight. Taking the Scotts part way along the traverse with us enabled us to retrieve two 150-foot ropes. As Larry Scott untied the upper end of the second rope and cast it off to me, the logistics phase of the rescue ended. We were cut off from our supply line. We had a lowering block and two 300-foot reels of steel cable, two 150-foot nylon ropes, three 120-foot ropes, sundry hardware, and a lot less than the recommended minimum daily requirement of food. (It was two years before Ted confessed that he had turned down a stack of sandwiches, prepared for us by the park wives, because he could not bring himself to add another ounce to his pack.)

Fortunately, we could get started before having to commit ourselves to a line of descent. Whatever we did ultimately, we first had to negotiate the four hundred feet to the First Ledge. An indication of how we had to change our concept of scale is the fact that this first, easy, and obvious step in what we had to do was the longest technical rock lowering in the history of the team. We eased ourselves into it by lowering the first one hundred feet using rope, which we had done hundreds of times, instead of the cable, which we'd done only in rescue practice. Ted was litterman for that one hundred feet, and it exhausted him. Ted had been our morphine substitute. He'd stayed up all night talking to Gay, nursing him.

By unspoken agreement, we parcelled out the worry. No one can deal with all the fears; each has to pick a big worry and let that mute the others. Mike was our safety inspector. He questioned and double-checked all knots and anchors.

The cable presented some interesting problems—interesting to Bob, who gravitated to the problem. It turned out that the slightest slack, such as one strand rolling off another on the drum, resulted in a bone-shaking and terrifying jolt to Gay and his litterman, Mike on our first use of the cable. Nylon rope is forgiving. It is soft and strong and will stretch half its length again before failing. None of us knew how much a steel cable would take. It was stronger than our ropes—we knew that—but it looked very tiny; and it appeared to have no resiliency. Resiliency is a quality a climber is conditioned to regard as essential. To us, the steel cable felt like it would be stubbornly unyielding to a certain point and then pop. The cable slipping off an overhang, the litter dragging slightly on a rock, or a slight change in angle or weight left a little slack in the cable, which would be taken up all at once in a drop at the litter. It seemed like a foot of drop each time, but it was only an inch or two. The litterman seldom knew when a jolt was coming. Imagine if your chair dropped an inch to the floor sometime soon. The causes of the jolts were deduced by Bob, and we had the choice of believing him or worrying about it ourselves.

We belayed the litter with rope, to back up the lowering cable. Our belay technique seemed marginal. We would have preferred to have had the rope run through a friction device, but we didn't. That meant that if the cable failed, the belayer would suddenly have three hundred pounds of weight to support, more if his rope wasn't taut. His rope couldn't be taut, because that caused the cable to bounce. It was in the best interests of the litterman to have the belay rope slack, as long as he was a litterman and not a falling object. It was in the best interests of the belayer, whose job was to never forget that litter and litterman could become falling objects without notice, to keep the rope taut. It was a regrettable conflict of interests.

Rocks started booming down. The litterman tried to secure, or knock off, as many rocks as he could before he got below them. Inevitably he missed some, and the running cable sent them after him. We were lowering the Stokes litter in a horizontal position, both because of the nature of Gay's injury, and because that way he could only look up. When you're helpless, there's something to the warning not to look down. That meant that he lay face up to the rocks. The litterman tried to shelter him with his body, which was more reassuring than effective. It's amazing that he did not take a serious hit. Still, the lowering to the First Ledge wasn't too bad.

Leigh, knowing well why I had asked him to stay on, had proceeded directly to the First Ledge to search out a way off the mountain. Every climber knows that Leigh Ortenburger was the author of *A Climber's Guide to the Teton Range* and assumes correctly that he was a very experienced climber. Many climbers know also that his guide established a new standard of accuracy and thoroughness. What perhaps only I knew was how reassuring such a historical perspective can be in a situation like the one we were in. There were possibly a hundred climbers in the country who were technically better than Leigh but not one I would have rather had there. We didn't know yet what we had to do on that mountain, but we had with us the one man in the world who knew exactly everything that had been done on that mountain.

I regarded Rick as my personal reservoir of strength. From him came the energy to overcome inertia. His mind, his muscles, and his wit were constantly at work.

Ralph was the spirit of sacrifice, quietly doing the unwanted work as if feeling privileged to be there.

I puttered about, muttering to myself or to anyone who would listen to me.

Once on the First Ledge, forward motion mired down in indecision. Even the morphine couldn't keep Gay happy as we talked first this way and then that. Leigh had scouted out the possibility of reaching the Grandstand with 600 feet of cable. That is, we could drop straight off the Ledge to the north. I could estimate a 120-foot rappel within a margin of 10 percent. I had no confidence in judging twice that distance, and I could not contemplate looking down five times that and having any notion at all about what I was looking at. Usually I knew how far up I was because I knew how many leads had been made. I had a lot of practice judging distance looking up. Even on a tall building where the surface is uniform, looking up feels very different from looking down. On a mountain, the two perspectives are totally foreign to each other. A 10 percent error in 600 feet is a five-story building. I was prepared to believe that Leigh's estimate was very close, but we couldn't see any ledges below us on the alleged 600-foot wall. The litter would be down there, and we wouldn't be able to rappel down to it. Even if Leigh was right, the advantages of a single 600-foot lowering appeared to be outweighed by the disadvantages.

The advantages were three. One, we'd only have to set up one really solid anchor. With the time that would save, we could set up an anchor that could hold the entire rescue team and gear if need be. Two, the wall was vertical to overhanging, meaning there would be little bumping, dragging, grunting, and sweating and fewer rocks pulled down. Three, it was an elegant solution. Just cast off and drift down the mountain in the invisible gravitational current, like a spider descending from the ceiling.

The principle disadvantages were that after lowering the litter, the six remaining at the top would have to descend the North Face route, following the First Ledge down to its lower end and then descending fairly straightforward but rotten rock a thousand feet or so to the glacier. Then they would have to climb back up the Grandstand a thousand feet to the litter and take it back down. Second, the litter would have to be lowered unbelayed. The rockfall would be less, but the ones that came would be coming from a long way up. However strong the cable, stretched taut over the lip of an overhang and taking a direct hit? or if it didn't reach and they had to dangle there for six or eight hours? I remarked to Leigh, "The man who went down that six hundred feet wondering if it would reach, listening to rocks sail by him, might never get entirely back to us." He agreed that this was a possibility. We dropped rocks off and counted the seconds. Some said six seconds, some said eight, an uncertainty of two hundred feet. We were also uncertain about what would happen when we came to the end of the first reel and had to join the second three hundred feet of cable to it. Most of all, I, at least, did not want to split the party. The regular route it was to be.

We stuck to that plan for one hundred feet down the First Ledge. Then Leigh made the first move in what has become one of the legendary feats of American mountaineering. He had gone down the ledge, looked over the edge, and announced in a tone of undeniable authority that, one, we could get to the Grandstand in two 300-foot lowerings and, two, the rest of us could follow the litter because there was, in addition to the ledge 300 feet below us, a smaller intermediate ledge exactly halfway down the first 300-foot pitch. It was inadequate for the litter, but adequate for the rest of us. This meant that we could tie our 150-foot ropes together, hang them double down to the intermediate ledge, rappel 150 feet to that ledge, retrieve our rope by pulling on one strand, and repeat the process to join the litter at the 300-foot level. If there was no comparable ledge in the lower 300-foot segment, we could use the two 150-foot lengths as one fixed and irretrievable 300-foot strand. We would have to abandon them and somehow get off the Grandstand with two 120-foot ropes (we'd had to cut the third one for slings), but the problems on the Grandstand were more manageable. Suddenly, Leigh's view seemed reasonable.

The debate this time was shorter. These discussions, I now realize, were as much acclimatization time as they were times of rational deliberation. We needed to accustom ourselves to the scope of the thing. A kind of pressure had been building in me since dawn. It took a long time to get across the traverse, and the traverse had to be counted as not even part of the problem but blessedly easy access to the accident site. I began the day with a feeling akin to being late for an appointment. The constant reviewing of the options had made me uncertain about decisions already made. No decision had been self-evident. Furthermore, the whole world seemed to be tuned in. Radio communication in the park had been shut down so that the channels were free for our use. We knew that everyone we knew who could get near a radio, including our families, was keeping track of us. We were asked many times for estimates of our progress, information needed in order to coordinate our support below, should we ever reach lower slopes, and my estimates had been consistently too optimistic. I even found time to worry about my upcoming doctoral examinations. I hadn't covered half the material I had planned to that summer. The Climber's Camp had been closed, and an era was ending for climbers in America and for me in the Tetons. Relations with my superiors were not good. Things weren't so good in the country in 1967 either. My big tests were coming all at once; the values and efforts of a lifetime were being tested, and I felt unprepared.

Certain worries I could, and did, enumerate to anyone who would listen. It seemed to help them to have me complain. Emerson discovered on the Everest expedition that if A expresses doubt, B expresses confidence. I didn't want to face the fact that we were going to have another bivouac. I didn't like being out of food or worrying about the other party, which had climbed up to us and had started the descent back down the regular route. I found their shouts of joy, when they arrived safely on the glacier, obnoxious. Irvine and I had enjoyed grumbling to each other for years. Now he was being excessively chipper. Sleeping bags had been flown up to the base of the glacier on the strength of one of my optimistic predictions. A team had assembled there ready to bring them up to us, but we weren't going to get anywhere within reach. Most of all, I didn't like the sound rocks made as they came by with a slicing whir or hit with a crack. I didn't like where I was, what I had done, or what I had yet to do. But Leigh's solution was a thing of beauty, and we'd do it.

Now we truly were racing against the descending sun, trying to get down before it did. Leigh tested his claim, that the unknown distances were known to him, by rappeling into the unknown in search of the two ledges. He went on and on. We were fishing for a ledge with him as bait. He radioed back, "I've got one!" The first three-hundred-foot lowering would work. As we got the litter down to the three-hundred-foot ledge, it appeared that we were holding our own against time, if the rest of us were fast enough in getting down as well.

I was one of the last down to the intermediate ledge. I was shocked to find that the ledge was a large detached flake with a flat top. The last man off a rappel has to go without a belay. I assigned myself that duty as a sort of punishment for having made so many bad guesses that day. I studied the flake I was on, and my curiosity was rewarded with the discovery that the flake was not part of the mountain! My hands became moist. The flake was delicately balanced, a piton driven behind it would pry it away from, and possibly off, the wall. I was not at all delicately balanced. Every time I moved, the cable reel in my pack tried to pitch me off the wall. I was sure that soon my legs would begin trembling uncontrollably, sewing machine legs, as we called it. It happens sometimes when you overload on oxygen and adrenalin. I had to stand balanced on that flake because when I leaned against the wall, I thought I could feel the flake move outward. I had to lean against the wall because soon my legs wouldn't support me and I would fall off the mountain.

My eyes wouldn't focus on one thing. The knot at my waist. It's untied! The carabineer. It's open! The piton. It's pulling! The gap behind the flake. It's wider! I wanted to check everything at once. I jerked my eyes from one to the other so fast I didn't check any of them. I started the rounds again, knot, carabineer, piton, piton crack, rope. I felt as if I was standing on grease. I couldn't see anything wrong, which made it worse. Where is it? What's going to do it?

I felt as if I were floating in my boots. My boots. They're untied! They weren't. Boots untied! Jesus Christ, what am I going to do, cut the rope and jump off? I won't have to. I'll be shaking so hard I'll shake myself off. But I'm not shaking, idiot. I wasn't. While all this was happening, nothing was happening: I'd glanced around twice and shifted my weight once. I laughed and that was it. For years, I had awaited the moment when I would not be able to will myself to do what I was afraid to do. All that while, something had happened. Over the years I had learned the right habits. Rock was rock, mass and gravity were mass and gravity, balance was balance, a knot was a knot, routine was routine. I didn't have to understand anything. All I had to do was what I'd done hundreds of times before. I had no extraordinary mental resources, just discipline born of experience and mindless habit. Aristotle said virtue is habit. It had taken me twenty-three years to learn how to rescue my brother properly.

Not that everything became suddenly peachy. I got down to the big ledge and found that the anchor that had been laboriously placed wouldn't do. It was thirty feet too far to the east. Thirty feet horizontally along the ledge here meant a vertical difference of sixty feet down on the Grandstand. The cable might reach, but the rope wouldn't, because some rope had to be used in knots and in belaying. Someone suggested that the litterman rappel off the end of his belay rope and hang from the litter for the last few feet. It was too late and we were too tired for anything as fancy as that, but I found the idea attractive. Bob quietly and firmly objected. He was right. That did not change the fact that I had never wanted anything in the world more than I wanted to get down to that Grandstand before dark. The drill bits were dull; we would lose an hour drilling new holes. I got two solid whacks on my hard hat from falling rocks just for aggravation. The new holes would have to be drilled thirty feet to the west, on what we hoped was the other side of an intervening rockfall area. I decided to be the hero. I should have been thinking, and I knew it, but I wanted to pound on the mountain for a while. I didn't pound long enough and ruined the first hole by driving in the bolt before the drill hole was deep enough. My friends were standing over on the ledge, with the valley becoming dark behind them, waiting for me to do my job, and I was just flailing away at it. Finally, I called on the reserves and asked Rick to drill the holes properly. The mountain may have gotten me on the run, but I knew it couldn't get him off balance.

Then things started to work. Rick got the anchor in. Leigh tested his theory that it was three hundred feet and not more to the Grandstand, as he had tested the upper half. He went over the edge. If he was wrong, he would have to climb back up three hundred feet. The friction of a single rope with the weight of three hundred feet creates a tremendous amount of heat. Because two ropes had to be tied together, no mechanical device, like a rappel bar, which would absorb and dissipate the heat, could be used. Leigh had permanent burn scars from that rappel. But when he stood finally on the Grandstand, the end of the rope dangled chest high. The distance was within three feet of being exactly three hundred feet, a margin of error of one percent, half that for the whole six hundred feet. As they say, not bad for government work.

Mike joined Leigh; he too was burned. The sun was well down. I offered to let someone else take the litter, but they declined. Since I'd been babbling about little else for the past two hours, they'd guessed that I badly wanted off. With that rappel to think about all night and falling rocks to keep them awake, they couldn't have expected to get much rest, but my need was greater.

I caught a glimpse of the last red as Gay in the litter and I, attached to a sling outside, went over the edge of an overhang and rotated freely four feet from the wall. The head lamp I had borrowed from Gay was almost out. Leigh's penlight, two hundred feet below, looked like a single ray of light pointed at the heavens. My sling seat cut into my legs, and I thought about circulation and retaining consciousness. I had eaten only four bites of cheese, two bites of candy, and half a C-ration can of beans that day. I was, nevertheless, happy. I was on a grand piece of rock, massive, uncluttered, and overhanging for the last 260 feet.

I was proud of my skills with the litter and would like to have shown Gay how smoothly I could get him down. There was more important work to do. The litter could not be allowed to swing too far to the east, or it wouldn't reach. I had to concentrate on that. For the first time, I began to warm to Gay. Up to this point, he had contributed far too much to the discussions about the tactics of the rescue for my taste. His interest in the matter was understandable, but I'd rather that victims be spectators. There's something to be said for my position, too. The victim's judgment is not unbiased.

Dangling from the end of that tiny cable, smaller in diameter than a pencil, we were similarly in a largely passive situation. We chatted about what was happening to us and got so we could anticipate the jolts in the cable. Gay felt that he could distinguish between a jolt caused by a strand rolling off another strand on the reel and a jolt caused by the friction of the cable over the terrain, which created varying tensions in different segments of the length of the cable. He'd had a lot of time to ponder about what caused the jolts. We sounded like two sidewalk superintendents at a construction site.

We approached a bulge not far above Leigh. By hanging from my slings underneath the litter, I could reach the rock with both hands and feet. Scratching and crawling, I pulled the litter a few precious feet westward along the wall. Gay, though he was being badly bumped, reported my gains and spoke words of encouragement. Suddenly there was nothing for me to grasp, and we pendulumed sickeningly eastward, but then stopped and swung back. "It caught! Right there!" cried Gay. I struggled back into a vertical position and saw that the last three inches of a projecting rock held the cable in exactly the right position. Now we could talk to Leigh in normal voices, and I was almost ebullient. Leigh said, "M'God, Sinclair, is that dim glow your head lamp? I thought you were smoking your pipe." I had actually started to smoke my pipe during the lowering, but the stem was too long. By neglecting to bring a short-stemmed pipe, I had missed my chance to become a legend. Leigh had cleared out a place for the litter under an overhang. With the radios to carry our instructions, we swung Gay into position a few inches at a time as neatly as would a dragline operator. We propped a couple of rocks under the foot end, and with the cable for a belay, he was safe for the night, with his head and torso protected, though his legs were exposed. Thoughts of the full length of cable exposed all night to unknown and unseen quantities of rockfall gave me a second's pause. I had an image of the cable being severed near the top, its full length whipping down the face to jerk the litter out of its bed, but fretting about things like that was no longer as entertaining as it had been on the detached flake. I jammed another rock in beside the litter and let it go at that. There couldn't be any such thing as absolute safety.

Objectively speaking, we weren't in all that terrific a position. Four men were perched on a sloping, wet ledge, at the wrong end of a three-hundred-foot, overhanging, flesh-burning rappel, with the singing of falling rocks to lull them to sleep. I derived a small amount of comfort from the thought that all four, Rick, Ralph, Bob, and Ted, were Salt Lake City climbers, if not the fathers, at least the uncles of the new generation of hard men coming out of that area. They weren't all Mormons, but they were all clean-cut and uncynical. Their virtues would protect them. Mike was alone, one hundred feet below us, where he had gone to explore the route. We had been slow, but not because we didn't keep pressing. Mike had gone down alone while we were fiddling with the litter. We'd made use of every second of daylight.

I too had lowered my weary bones into better bowers. Leigh and I were on a little platform scratched into the debris in the moat between the face and a snow patch. I was at the edge of the platform. (I'm certain Leigh planned that while I was busy with the litter.) When I dozed off, my hand slipped from my lap and hung in space. I didn't like that sensation. My legs were cramped, and when I dozed, my feet slid into the snow. When they tingled with cold, I woke up and wiggled my toes to

Photograph by Leigh Ortenburger, courtesy of the family and estate of Leigh Ortenburger.

NORTH FACE OF GRAND TETON
X: Accident Site
A: Three-Hundred-Foot Lowering from First Ledge
B: Three-Hundred-Foot Lowering to Grandstand

restore circulation. Rocks dropped in occasionally. One hit the snow between Leigh's foot and mine and filled the neck of my down jacket with snow.

"What's that?" I said, as if I didn't know.

"I dunno," muttered Leigh, as if he didn't either, and went immediately back to sleep. If the rocks wanted us to pay attention that night, they'd have to hit us. My dreams were of YMCA showers with steam rising from the floor, a way of accounting for the tingling in my feet.

The next day we found that the mountain hadn't done with us yet. The rappels were sloppy. Without the two long ropes, we'd lost flexibility in setting up belay positions. The fussing to set up a solid position seemed interminable, like the rappels of beginners. We were a long way down the mountain now, so there were plenty of places for the rocks to come from and plenty of time for them to achieve terminal velocity. At one point, out of sheer perversity, I calculated the amount of rock falling around us. During one lowering, two hundred pounds of rock landed within thirty feet of me. I didn't see how we could escape taking a hit. This continuous assault from above, combined with fatigue and hunger, developed in us a condition which can be called rock shock. The most dramatic instance of what we'd become like occurred after Rick made the last, difficult overhanging lowering from the Grandstand to the snow at the top of the glacier. As the helicopter, carrying Gay to the hospital, started its engine, the roar crashed down on us from off the mountain walls. Those of us who were still on the mountain instantly cowered as if overtaken by the largest and last rockfall, believing that the mountain had waited until this last moment to get us.

The last two rappels, with the taste of beer practically in our mouths, turned out to be three.

It was here that we regained a small measure of dignity. Someone suggested that we just leave the ropes on the last two rappels in order to save time.

"No need to leave ropes behind," said Leigh. He wasn't thinking of their value. They were so chewed up they'd have to be discarded anyway. It was a question of style. The mountain had thrashed us to the bones, but in our retreat we would walk, not run.

The helicopter returned and carried, in relays, to the meadow outside our cabins, knowledge in Leigh, strength in Rick, reason in Bob, foresight in Mike, selflessness in Ralph, and compassion in Ted, courage in all, my comrades, who had made this the noblest adventure of my life, and given me, finally, self-possession.

Photograph courtesy of the National Park Service

NORTH FACE RESCUE TEAM, SHORTLY AFTER RETURN FROM THE GRAND TETON. L to R, Ted Wilson, Pete Sinclair, Ralph Tingey, Mike Ermath, Rick Reese, Bob Irvine. Leigh Ortenburger not pictured.

CHAPTER 11

COMING DOWN

he day after the North Face rescue, we had to pack up for Seattle. We had to get the kids in school, and I had to finish preparation for my doctoral examination. We wondered if we had spent our last summer in the cabin. This thought paled the flush of victory.

Two weeks after we got back to Seattle, Rick Reese and Rich Ream, a friend of ours from Jackson, came out. We got in touch with Dick Emerson, who was also teaching at the University of Washington, and decided to attempt Mt. Rainier. Rick and I had climbed together only on rescues. I had long wanted to climb with Dick. Not only had he preceded me at Jenny Lake and established the tradition I had tried to maintain, I had climbed a number of his bold and elegant routes.

It was raining as we set out from the ranger station at Paradise. The rain intensified as the wind piped up. The rain drove at us horizontally, and although we were wearing waterproof ponchos, we got wet. We continued to climb after each of us privately had concluded that there was no chance we'd get up the mountain. The average age of the party was thirty-seven. It took Rick, the youngest and strongest, half an hour to figure out that he had to be the one to decide. He did at last, and we ran down the mountain.

At the time we turned back and a few hundred yards from where we turned back, a strange sequence of events was getting underway. A party of three climbers descending from Camp Muir was joined by a fourth climber who had decided not to try to get to Camp Muir. They got off route descending a glacier to the east of us. One member of the party fell eighteen or twenty feet into a crevasse. Another climber walked up to the edge and fell in too, whereupon the climber who fell in the crevasse first announced that they were doomed, although neither was hurt or in any further danger. The fourth member, the newcomer, found this talk spooky.

"Hey, wait a minute, don't say that. I'll just run down to Paradise and get some help." Which he did.

The third member of the original party stayed and found the easy way into the crevasse, a good place to be, in fact, because it protected them from the wind. He lit their stove and heated some soup. He was even able to light a candle. He tried to get his two friends to zip up their down jackets and put on their gloves, to no avail. They had made their decision. The first one died at about 11 P.M.; the second two hours later. The third member of the party stayed in the crevasse until dawn. The next morning the rescue team found him standing in the sun beside the crevasse, his hands in his pockets.

During the initial hours of this incident, we were back at the Paradise Ranger Station telling war stories. The Rainier rangers offered us the upstairs of the station as a place to dry out. We opened a bottle of wine and told Dick what we'd been up to at Jenny Lake and asked him about the old days. By the time the fourth member of the crevassed party arrived back at Paradise, we were in the mood for a rescue. We offered our services to the Rainier rangers in the event that any technical help was needed. They put us in reserve. We stipulated that we would be glad to work on the search and on the technical phases, if there were any, but that we were not interested in hauling out bodies.

In the morning, the four of us with a Rainier guide and Ron Shrigley, a naturalist we knew from the days when he had worked in the Tetons, were dispatched to pick up a litter and gear that the main team had cached part way up the trail. We were to take the litter up to the crevasse and bring down a body.

It was either that or go home, and it turned out that we were still in the mood for a rescue.

The storm had marked the end of summer. The rain had turned to snow in the night, and we set out in a morning sparkling in light, new snow. The air was sweet and cold. We grumbled a bit about the fact that one fourth of the rescue team, we, got to carry one half the gear. On the other hand, we could name some rescues where the organization had been worse. As rescues go, this one had proceeded like clockwork. That gave us confidence in the people we would be working with, most of whom we didn't know.

In truth, there was no place we'd rather have been that morning, body or not. Rick, Dick, and I were eager to try their equipment. For litters, they used modified ski patrol toboggans which were broken down for carrying and mounted on a wheel for trail work. In the Tetons, we used the military surplus, wire-mesh Stokes litters modified by Dick a decade and a half earlier. They were excellent for rock but terrible on snow, which the mesh scooped up and compacted underneath the victim, crushing them against their retaining slings.

The timing continued to go as if the operation had been rehearsed. We got there just as they finished removing the bodies from the crevasse and were starting to load one on the litter they had brought up. It was logical that the Teton rescuers handle one litter and the Rainier rescuers the other.

Before that conclusion could be arrived at, there was a period of standing around and how-about-this and what-do-you-think-of-the-other. Rescuing in the Northwest had been mainly done by huge volunteer rescue organizations. There were several of these, so many that there weren't enough victims to go around. The Rainier people, tired of the politics of parceling out the rescues equitably, had begun to develop their own team. They were a new team, and we were a team with nearly two decades of experience and reputation. We didn't want to usurp their leader's responsibility on his own turf; he didn't want to give us orders. With two bodies, the situation was easily resolved.

Having shown that we were circumspect, it was time to get on with the contest. Both teams began the descent by anchoring with an ice axe implanted in the snow, then lowering the litter the length of a climbing rope, then setting up another anchor and so on. The Rainier team, with more practice on glaciers, were going to get ahead of us if we stuck to that technique. We shifted to the "moving belay," a technique we used in the Tetons when the slope was too steep to comfortably walk the litter along but where we wouldn't go very far if we lost control. It was not a technique that would have evolved on a mountain like Rainier with its steep glaciers and huge crevasses. But the terrain we happened to be on then was uncrevassed and similar to the snow-covered scree slopes of the Tetons. We let the litter slide out of control for a ways, and then, by digging in our heels while holding the belay rope, grabbing the side of the litter, and generally having a good time rolling in the snow, we'd bring it to a stop.

In this manner, we built up a small lead over the Rainier team. That gave Rick time to come up with a better solution. What was wrong with our technique was that it looked sloppy and unprofessional. We appeared to be getting the litter down more by luck than by skill. What was wanted was a way to go fast with the litter in control at all times. Rick's solution was to sit on the chest of the victim and ride the litter down the mountain, digging in his heels to brake it. Two could control the litter this way, one on it and one glissading behind holding the belay rope in case the litter flipped.

The other team did not adopt our technique. They might have thought of their corpse as a person. For some, it may have been their first encounter with that fear which comes when you confront your own death in another's. That fear never completely disappears, but a time comes when it is not the only thing. We could not put on grave countenances for the death of two people we had never seen alive. It seemed proper for us to live those moments together on the mountain as joyously as we were able. We laughed, yodeled, and leaped in the bright sunlight, sky, and snow. As we neared Paradise, we saw on the trail below us a group of park employees approaching. Several hundred yards behind them was another group of people carrying TV cameras. There were TV news trucks in the parking lot. When the park people reached us, we turned the litter, now mounted on a wheel, over to them, dropped down off the trail, skirted around beneath the people carrying cameras, and slipped into the parking lot. Rick took a snapshot of Rich, Dick, and me. I have it still, Rich was gray-haired, Dick was getting there, and with me, it looked like baldness would win. We had our arms around each other, we were holding a beer, and we were grinning. It was the best possible end to a rescue and to the rescue careers of Dick Emerson and me, his successor—and I thought so at the time.

Although I knew that was my last rescue, I was in no hurry to notify the Park Service. I had other things to think about. I passed the exams for my doctorate and would spend one more year at the university as an instructor, to work on my dissertation.

Since meeting Ade Murie at McKinley, I had stopped in to see him at his cabin in Moose whenever he and I were in the valley at the same time. I respected him long before I understood him. He was a scientist in the old sense. He refused to involve himself in the political issues surrounding scientific work, but he was not indifferent to the issues. He urged me to get to know his brother Olaus. Ade was proud of the political work Olaus and Mardie had done in the Wilderness Society. Ade thought I should write articles expressing to the world at large what I felt about the importance of the wilderness. I did some of that, but I felt he ought to be the one writing the articles.

Ade didn't stay completely free of environmental politics. He wrote an article critical of the Park Service practice of spraying trees to kill the pine beetle. He cited studies which indicated that spraying actually prolonged the infestation cycle. He also suggested that the Park Service had lost track of its mission by following the counsel of foresters who were educated in agricultural colleges. The squatters were winning over the mountain men again.

The Park Service eventually did stop spraying. If I wrote an article, I wanted it to work like that.

I had talked to Ade about my fears that serious climbers would be forced from the park on grounds that climbing was "a special use." He observed that climbing was "not a special use but a use." He said that human culture would not be worth having if each of us were allowed to do only what all of us could do. Then he pointed to two stacks of typewritten sheets on his table. "Here are two versions of a report I have to submit to Washington. One is so critical of management practices at McKinley that if I submit it, I'll probably never be allowed to return to Igloo Creek. The other one is not a false report, but it doesn't say much and wouldn't accomplish much."

"Have you decided which one you will send?"

"No. They have been right there for a week." After a pause, he said, "I do not think one ought to destroy one's usefulness."

My moral dilemma seemed small compared to Ade's. I didn't have any usefulness to destroy. My exams out of the way, I wrote an article as critical of the Park Service as I could be and yet remain within the framework of respect that I held for the service. The effort to be both critical and respectful was beyond my powers as an essayist. The article was published in *Ascent.* Royal Robbins thought the article was intelligent and thoughtful; my superiors thought me disloyal. One thought I was trying to incite a riot.

Also during the winter of 1967-68, Barry spoke to me about joining him in starting another guide service in Jackson's Hole. The new ski area, which was just outside the park's south boundary, wanted Barry to station a guide service there. It had been difficult for us who had come there in the late 1950s to keep a foothold in Jackson. Frank Ewing had succeeded. The Barker-Ewing float trips on the Snake River became the model for such operations. Dick and Frank had strong amateur interests in natural history. They hired guides with similar interests, and their trips were floating field trips in natural history.[1]

Jake started a climbing shop. He died on Everest.

Dick Pittman, who ran the climbing shop for Jake when he left for Everest, was killed in an avalanche on the ski area. (Frank and Pitt were together, working on the ski patrol. Frank was caught too but survived.)

Barry had tried a lodge and a motel, which had not worked out for him.

As have Americans from the beginning, we were working on our version of utopia. Nobody said it out loud, but we were trying to live according to the heroic virtues: courage, friendship, self-possession, piety toward the gods of nature, and loyalty to each other and to a code of behavior while competing to achieve the highest standards of performance we could aspire to. These are among them, although they are not a list like the Ten Commandments or the Beatitudes. The heroic virtues are contained in the stories of the heroes, the whole stories—Achilles's wrath as well as his self-possession, both, in the mixture they have in his story.

Robbins, Chouinard, Beckey, Kor, and McCarthy were our Achilles, Odysseus, Nestor, Ajax, and Diomedes. If there was a violation of ethics which he sensed but could only say in a way that would be misunderstood, Robbins, like Achilles, greatest among the warriors, brooded in his tent before issuing forth to chastise the offender by showing him, in action, what ought to have been done.

Chouinard, like Odysseus, was inventive and resourceful, visited many lands and learned their customs, and was listened to in counsel. His articles on climbing in Yosemite and on ice climbing were proclamations of the directions to be taken by American climbers.

---

[1] It is now possible to book passage on a luxury liner with college professors on the staff and go to Antarctica.

Beckey was Nestor, storytelling, worried about the signs from the gods (the weather), there a generation before us, ageless, still doing it.

Kor, like Ajax, was the biggest and the strongest, unswerving in his performance of great deeds, and impatient of too much counsel. One day in the Tetons, Layton prevailed upon a girl to translate a French climbing article for him. The girl began translating the opening paragraphs, which were setting the scene existential. Kor said, "Skip all that flowery crap and get to the good stuff." She skipped to "at the top of the dihedral was a ceiling with a crack leading to the left." The giant Kor sat hunched over, his ear bent toward the slight girl on the log beside him, his expression rapt.

McCarthy, who was slightly wounded in Yosemite but undaunted, was, like Diomedes, good natured, competitive, and spirited.

All of these men have survived. None of these men, at the time of their greatest climbs, were professional guides. They must have sensed that it would be a mistake to make the exercise of their virtues their paying work. Those of us who did become professionals, the guides and rangers, found that the more we worked, the less we climbed in a serious way.

Royal once invited me to go climbing with him and his wife, Liz. I told Royal that I wasn't in his class and that I was afraid that I would embarrass myself and hold him up. He told me not to worry, he'd do the leading and I could learn something about Yosemite technique. It was a great opportunity for me. He and Liz packed in to the Lower Saddle, and I was to go up after work. Just before I got off work, I had to go out on a search for a lost person. It wasn't a long search. I could have left that evening by ten and reached the saddle not long after midnight. I would once have done it with glee. But when the search was over, I went to bed.

The same sort of thing happened to the guides. There were so many complaints of burnout from the guides that we investigated their operation and submitted a report to Exum and the Park Service. Among the problems we identified were too many people being served, too much routine in the work of the guides, and a feeling among the guides that they were not getting their fair share of profits. We were proud of our "insights" and surprised that few improvements followed upon our revelations. Ortenburger read the report and thought us wrong about the money the guides got: "A person can live on what they make." Even if I had thought of it, I could not have responded that the guides were not receiving a just reward for their virtues. That was not Greek, or Viking, or Blackfoot, or mountain man. That was the good old American notion that virtue ought to have a cash value.

Since we couldn't tell Glenn that the guides themselves had asked us to look into the operation of the guide service, Glenn thought that we were gratuitously nosing around in his business at a time when he was already feeling harried by the same things that confused us: more people, different people, changes in the park, changes in the world. Glenn was made to see himself as management, and he was not pleased to be viewed as other than the senior climber among us. Relations between us became less warm; there was one more person eyeing me suspiciously.

Barry had not burned out as a guide. He kept driving. Barry had gone to Yosemite. He had gone to Antarctica and, with John Evans, had done the first ascent of the highest peak on the continent. He returned to the Himalayas on a mysterious mission financed by some part of the government. Teamed with him in establishing a new guide service, I felt I might get it back again and it would be like it was on Denali. He hoped to avoid the labor-management problems besetting the Exum Guide Service. Barry hoped to attract clients who wanted to do difficult climbs. It happened in Europe; maybe the time had come for it to happen in America.

I let the deadline for notifying the park that I was returning pass. I couldn't tell Connie that we would not be returning to the cabin on Cottonwood Creek. The park called to ask if I was coming back. I wavered. The only response I'd received from the park about my article was a government publication listing regulations for what federal employees could and could not publish. There was no note and no name attached to it to tell me if anybody in particular wanted me to hear these stern admonitions.

I told the person on the other end of the line that I had been wondering whether or not I was welcome back. There was a pause. The rescue team was to be given the Department of Interior Valor Award. We were to be flown to Washington, where Secretary Udall himself would present us the medals. We were the first seasonal employees ever to be given this award. Was I welcome back or was I to be allowed back because of the award?

"We just need to know whether you are coming back or not so we can get set up for the summer."

"No, I will not be back. I'm going to guide for Barry Corbet."

Then, in March, Barry was paralyzed in a helicopter crash. I would operate the guide service for him.

The award ceremony in June was a great moment for us. We missed Leigh, who because he was not an employee of the Department of Interior, could not be a recipient of the Valor Award. I also wished Connie could have been there to witness her husband's triumph, but we couldn't afford it.

We devoted the morning of the day we received the award to visiting monuments and memorials. Naturally, we climbed the Washington Monument—inside. Our school textbooks had not prepared us for the encampment of black people under a line of trees beside a reflecting pool. I wondered what the man who had designed the place would have thought if he had seen those people not reverently pacing along the walks under the carefully spaced trees, admiring his pools, but living there. They stood and sat outside of their tents and shelters, cooking and chatting as if the pools were a stream that crossed a meadow. The children at play especially transformed the place. I had an urge to swim in the pools.

The auditorium in the Interior Building was bigger than I had imagined it. As we filed on stage to receive our citations and medals, I became again a small town boy graduating from a city high school. During the photographing, Secretary Udall asked me if I was returning to Jenny Lake. Even the secretary of interior knew about Jenny Lake. I hated telling him no. At the reception afterwards, I saw Russ Dickenson again. He was courtly and did not put me on the spot. Also at the reception, I found that some Park Service people had read my article without thinking me disloyal. Later, I found that my article was even commended to the secretary himself. However, he was not to remain in office for long.

The evening of feasting and drinking we planned for ourselves did not live up to Jackson's Hole standards. Mike's brother, Fritz, he who had spent the night on the ledge above Tim Bond's body, traveled between Washington and Europe for the State Department or something and had arranged to be in Washington to see us get the award. (When we went to his room, he asked us to stand inside the doorway for a moment. He had to lock the attache case lying on his bed. He apologized. It was a rule he had to follow.) Fritz steered us to a good restaurant he knew of. For drinking, we ended up in a joint that had not bad-looking, but less than gorgeous, topless dancers. Our party was a little bit conspicuous. We men were either in new suits or in the suits we'd worn at our weddings. The wives were from west of the Mississippi, but not so far west as California. I had the feeling that we were entertaining the dancers more than they were entertaining us.

They danced to music so amplified that my ears hurt deep inside and I thought that I might be injured. I had to go outside for a break. A cabby had brought us to this place. There was no other place of any kind, not even a drugstore, open near it. We had seen no other places of entertainment on our way to here. Laramie, Wyoming, on a Sunday night was as lively as Washington, D.C. It was raining. I had been remembering Leslie Gore.

Gore and I had teamed up in Fort Devons during the last months of our hitches. The first sergeant did not like us. I was an Ivy Leaguer, and Gore was the only black in the battery with a college education. Gore and I made quite a pair. I wore, left over from my OCS days, body-tight, tailored fatigues so starched that I had to pry them open to put them on. I was the sharpest soldier in the battery. While in OCS, I had spit shined each of my four boots for thirty-eight and a half hours. I had only to rub them with a cloth before inspection for the sergeant to see his face in them. Before I came, his had been the shiniest boots in the battery. The thing the sergeant liked least about me was the fact that I had not washed out of OCS but had left on a "one-five-alpha," lack of motivation.

Gore had an opposite appearance to mine. He was short, thin, had an ascetic expression and casually observant eyes. His fatigues had come from a bin in the supply room. Whereas I was wedged into my fatigues, he was comfortably contained by his. Gore in a field jacket looked like a black English professor in a Harris Tweed. Gore did not observe the subtle racial boundaries that allowed other blacks in the battery to be friendly with whites while soldiering but not to be social friends. Whites and blacks went separate ways at the post gates; Gore and I went to town together. The sergeant thought us queer.

The sergeant called us the "college boys" and gleefully assigned us to the "ash and trash" detail as often as he could without leaving himself vulnerable to an investigation by the inspector general. We loved this detail. What the sergeant didn't know was that it took less than an hour to collect all the ash and trash in the regiment and we spent the rest of our afternoons in the post library. Gore, who had more experience with this sort of thing, taught me to grumble and pout just enough so that the sergeant would continue enjoying assigning us to ash and trash but not so much that the sergeant would think we were ready to complain to the I.G. In a normal rotation of details, we would have been assigned to ash and trash once every six weeks. We trained the sergeant to assign us every week. After a while, the sergeant suspected that we did not hate the detail. But he so loved saying "The college boys, ash and trash" that he could not stop.

One night, Gore took me in to Boston, to Storyville, where Gerry Mulligan and Chet Baker were playing. They were still in their twenties at the time. We caught the end of a set and waited and waited for the musicians to reappear. Gore said they probably got stoned and went to another place to hear some other musicians, black musicians. When they returned, Mulligan and Baker were giggling so much that they couldn't hold their instruments to their lips. When they started playing, they played for two hours and twenty-five minutes without stopping—not even, for the first forty minutes, between songs. There is amplification and there's amplification.

That had been ten years before, in June, 1958, when I had last seen Gore. Then he had been from Washington, D.C. It was only 10:30 in the evening, not as late as the rain and deserted streets had made it seem. Next to this joint, which I now remembered from Wrightstown, New Jersey; Lawton, Oklahoma; and Ayers, Massachusetts, but not from Storyville, was a phone booth. The Gs in the chained directory were intact. There were Gores. There was a Gore, L.

There were five rings before a woman answered. She had a sophisticated southern voice—that fit, but it was hard to say whether it was middleclass black or upperclass white.

"Does the Leslie Gore who was in the Fourth Regimental Combat Unit in 1958 live there?" I knew she could tell I'd been drinking.

She laughed. "No, I'm afraid you've got the wrong Gore. I'm sorry."

Soothing voice. I believed that she was sorry that I could not find my friend. I apologized for disturbing her so late, and she forgave me.

Back inside, everybody had had enough. We hated to give up our hopes of a real party, but we were tired, and Fritz and I both had to catch early morning flights. The next morning, I had to hurry to make my plane and didn't have time to find a *Washington Post.* They had run an article about the rescue at the time it had happened, and it seemed likely that one of their photographers had been at the auditorium. As it turned out, there was other news, which the cabby told me on the way to the airport; an Arab had shot RFK. I thought of Al Lowenstein, who had been important in solidifying Robert Kennedy's campaign. To do so, he'd had to abandon Hubert Humphrey, to whom he had been a foreign affairs advisor before taking up Michael Scott's cause in Southwest Africa. The vice president had written a personal note of commendation to each of us on the rescue team.

Before getting on the plane, I took the box with my medal in it out of my traveling case. I put the box back in the case. I took the coins out of my right pocket and put the medal in that pocket and carried it there where I could feel its heaviness as I walked onto the plane and sat in the plane. Its weight and size reminded me that it was there. I did not dare to take it out of my pocket to look at, as if the object in my pocket were a shameful object or some secret I was slipping out of the capital with.

I was going up to Connecticut to see my mother and father. This was my first return to the East since my mother's operation the spring before I went to work for the Park Service. As we neared Hartford, I put the medal back in its box. People don't just go around carrying medals in their pockets. What if there were an accident? It would be almost as embarrassing as having dirty underwear.

Peter Koedt and I got the guide service going in 1968. Then he went to Canada to keep from being drafted.

For the next summer, 1969, I convinced one of my oldest climbing buddies, Ray Jacquot ("Jake"), to work with me. Two of my former colleagues at Jenny Lake, Ted Wilson and Jim Greig, joined us, as did another long time Teton climber, Jack Turner. Jack had nearly finished his doctorate in philosophy from Cornell but had no prospects for an academic job. Jacquot and I were luckier. Academic jobs became suddenly scarce in 1969, but Jake and I had both been offered jobs at the University of Wyoming. Everybody but Ted Wilson was in some stage of being a college professor. (Ted, who had also been doing graduate work at the University of Washington my last year there, took a different route; he became a college administrator after he stopped being mayor of Salt Lake City.) It looked as if, as one of our clients remarked, we were trying to start a college instead of a guide service.

Now that it was clear that I would be a college teacher, I got interested in the psychology of learning. There was a lot about the topic in the popular press, and I read piles of it. I discussed what I'd been reading with Chouinard. He visited our instructional area and helped me figure out instructional sequences which grew out of the terrain itself rather than out of a list of techniques and skills thought to be basic. Yvon pointed out that what was basic was learning that our feet could do more than we were accustomed to thinking our feet can do. Rather than begin a class by teaching the bowline, we began the class by having our clients climb for an hour on easy terrain without using their hands and with the guide disturbing their thoughts as little as possible during that time. It was an extension of the Dick Emerson principle, "Let the mountains teach them." We taught knots and rope handling when we moved to more difficult terrain, the point where clients could see that having a rope and knowing how to use it might be handy.

In 1954, the summer between high school and college, a group of us who worked at a Boy Scout camp as counselors and instructors went to the White Mountains of New Hampshire after the camp season ended. The past summer, we had been content to set speed records up the trails to the summits. This summer, we were to try for a record on the Imp, a pinnacle with a steep trail. We also took along a rope.

There were four or five of us led by "Rip" Van Riper and Al Viola, who were already in college. Rip was at Dartmouth, where I was headed. His roommate, who was a real mountaineer, taught Rip to rappel and gave him a general notion about belaying. One side of the Imp was a cliff; Rip thought we could rappel and belay on it.

We set the record and turned our attention to the cliff. It was much higher than it looked from the valley. From the top of the cliff, a granite slab let down, like a coal chute, along the base of a small wall. Fifty or sixty feet down, the slab ended and we could see only the trees in the valley several hundred feet below. Al wanted to climb down to the edge of the precipice to take a look. He tied himself to the end of the rope and climbed down, with Rip tending the other end of the rope. When Al got to the edge, he whistled and then laughed at what we had imagined we were going to do. While Al climbed back up, his rope dislodged a loaf-of-bread sized rock; it bounced once and caught him square on the hip. Al crumpled to his knees, dizzy and nauseated by the pain.

I don't remember how or why I got myself down to Al. But I remember every detail of my getting back up the slab. When the nausea passed and the pain subsided, Al was able, with help from the rope, to slowly work his way back up by leaning against the wall to his left. I worked out to his right along a small ledge on the slab. Nine feet above me was another small ledge. There was nothing to grab with my hands until I got up there. It appeared that climbers did not haul themselves up mountains hand over hand after all. Above my left knee was a niche in the slab six inches long and the width of a half-dollar. By standing tiptoe on my right foot and bending my left knee up to my shoulder, I could get my left foot on this niche. As soon as I put my weight on my left foot and raised my right foot off the ledge, I knew I was doing something wrong. I was on the point of tipping over backwards, but it was too late to change my mind. I had to keep muscling up on my left leg and did. Now I could reach the higher ledge with my hands. Unfortunately, this ledge sloped outward a bit; I could not grip it tightly enough to haul myself up on it. I would have to rely on my feet. There was another niche up about two feet from the one I was standing on, this one the width of a quarter. But I had been taught something: take small steps. Exploring further, able now to see small features on the surface of the slab that had been invisible to me, I discovered an intermediate foothold that was the width of a dime. Much too small. A slight tremble began in my left leg. I couldn't stop there long. Al was painfully hauling himself up to my left. Everybody was watching him and had not noticed where I had gotten to. I glanced down, very briefly, and then looked at the intermediate hold again. I put my foot tentatively on it. My foot didn't slip off. I put some weight on it. It didn't look right, but it didn't slip and the trembling stopped. I tried putting most of my weight on my hands. That was terrible! My hands were insecure on the sloping ledge, and now even my left foot, with most of my weight off of it, felt insecure. Could I really stand on this intermediate hold? and then what? There were more holds. Once I got used to thinking of something the width of a dime as a hold, there were many holds. I put thoughts of the consequences of a slip out of my mind and climbed up to the ledge.

In doing so, I drew Rip's attention. He sternly ordered me to stay put until Al was up and they could get the rope to me. The rock above was easier than what I'd already climbed, but I gladly obeyed. I was scared. I felt foolhardy and embarrassed but also exhilarated. I bowed my head so that they would not see my grin. I would do more of this. When I got to Dartmouth, I decided, I would get to know Rip's roommate, Jake Breitenbach.

Hemming returned from France in 1969. He went first to see Barry in Denver. He wanted Barry out of his wheelchair and ordered him to stand up. Barry tried; that was easier than arguing with Hemming. They ended the evening by playing Russian roulette. Gary still smiled like a little boy, but his games had become earnest.

Gary came then to Jackson's Hole "to see his mates." Connie had just given birth to our third child, and Gary spent an afternoon with Connie and Summer Dawn. Gary and Connie at last became friends. The next afternoon, Gary came out to the guide shack to see me with Muffy Corbet, Barry's former wife, and a bottle of brandy. Our conversations weren't like our conversations of old; we didn't talk of what I wanted and he demanded from the world. As he left to go up to Jenny Lake to visit with the Exum guides, he said, "When are you going to get guts enough to talk to me?" I laughed. Some of the old Gary was still there. "Oh, we'll get around to it," I said.

The next morning, Rick Reese called me from the ranger station to tell me that he had just found Gary's body in the trees behind the guides' camp. Gary had shot himself in the head. I sought out Briggs, the one I thought might have the best insight on what had happened to Gary. He thought it was essentially an accident, and I concurred. Gary hadn't received an expected letter from a woman he loved, he'd been drinking, he and Muffy had words, and he picked a fight with one of the younger guides and, as always, lost the fight. It was too much for one day. It was an accident that it had all happened on one day.

Or was it? When Gary returned from France the first time, he told me that he had tried LSD. It was in the Shawangunks. When it got dark, he had climbed the cliff band and stood on top looking over the campfires below and "had seen the other side."

"It would have been easy to step over, to cross the boundary. I almost did. I don't know why I didn't."

I did not take that as suicide talk but as literary and spiritual talk. It wasn't from Sartre or Camus that Gary and I and others got our first exposure to existentialist thought. It was from Maurice Herzog's foreword to *Annapurna*: "In overstepping our limitations, in touching the extreme boundaries of man's world, we have come to know something of its true splendor. In my worst moments of anguish, I seemed to discover the deep significance of existence of which till then I had been unaware."

After the above, Lucien Devies goes on:

> *It takes courage to draw the veil from those moments when the individual approaches nearly to the universal. That wonderful world of high mountains, dazzling in their rock and ice, acts as a catalyst. It suggests the infinite, but it is not the infinite. The heights only give us what we ourselves bring to them. Climbing is a means of self-expression. Its justification lies in the men it develops, its heroes and its saints. This was the essential truth which a whole nation grasped when it offered its praise and admiration to the conquerors of Annapurna. Man overcomes himself, affirms himself, and realizes himself in the struggle towards the summit, toward the absolute. In the extreme tension*

> *of the struggle, on the frontier of death, the universe disappears and drops away beneath us. Space, time, fear, suffering, no longer exist. Everything then becomes quite simple. As on the crest of a wave, or in the heart of a cyclone, we are strangely calm—not the calm of emptiness, but the heart of action itself. Then we know with absolute certainty that there is something indestructible in us, against which nothing shall prevail.*

When Connie last saw Gary and when I last saw him, he was at peace with himself. Had he achieved that "absolute certainty that there is something indestructible in us, against which nothing shall prevail"? One is permitted to hope so.

The next season, 1970, Carlos joined the crew. The clan was gathering, but it was too late. Barry sold the business because he was not going to get out of his wheelchair. I stayed for half the summer, to provide some continuity, and returned to our cabin thirty miles from Laramie.

There is a small mountain range in that part of the Rockies that Jacquot and I loved. It has three small faces, and Jake proposed that we climb these faces together but unroped. They hadn't yet been soloed, and no one had climbed all three faces in one day. We were in top shape. Without hurrying, just as a consequence of being unroped, we established speed records on the three faces. We were alone as we made each move unprotected, but we were also together in the mountains. I felt as if my spirit was returned to a former glory.

After that climb, I decided to take a break from climbing to see if I could sort out my thoughts. I also left Wyoming. An innovative college, Evergreen State, opened in Olympia, Washington. Willi Unsoeld was on the planning faculty and got me the job. Willi continued to climb and included the teaching of climbing in his academic work. To Willi's surprise, I avoided doing this. I had written up some of the techniques I had discussed with Yvon, citing some of the educational psychologists I had been reading as authorities for the pedagogical principles I used. Outward Bound, whom Willi worked for before coming to Evergreen, used this material as part of their training of instructors. The techniques work, but I came to wish that I hadn't that small role in proffering climbing to people who hadn't found their way to the mountains unaided.

In a later year, I saw a television program about using rock climbing to rehabilitate juvenile delinquents. I recognized the principles Yvon and I first worked out. The climber-therapists were effective teachers, but what they were doing made me uncomfortable. The kids were really kids, two of them were too young even to be Boy Scouts. There were shots of them terrified and crying. They would have been crying for their mothers if they'd had any. The teachers, a man and a woman, taught the kids how to be confident, after making them terrified.

At the evening campfire, the kids were encouraged to recount the day's events. I had also formalized this part of the fun of climbing, made it an instructional technique. What the kids told about was not the thing itself, the pitches on the rock, but their internal experiences and the effect they opined these would have on their personalities. You could see them conning the instructors. Given what the purpose was in taking these kids out of their reformatory for a weekend of climbing, none of this was inappropriate. And if you've gone that far, why not TV? Although I had a part in bringing this about, it still didn't seem as if it was what the mountains are for.

Things hadn't gone this far in 1972, when it dawned on Willi that I was serious about not including the teaching of climbing as part of my academic work. He confronted me in my office one day.

"Pete, I know what you're doing."

He was one up on me already. "What am I doing?" I asked.

"You're doing what I did a couple of years ago. I too felt I was too old to climb. I got tired of being scared, tired of the cold, tired of trying to stay in shape. But my kids got old enough to climb, and it's wonderful being with them."

I didn't deny that he was right about me, to him or to myself, but I've thought there was something more. Willi was later killed on Rainier. Devi Unsoeld, his daughter, died before that on Nanda Devi. Mark Emerson, Dick and Pat's son, died still earlier. It may be that there had gotten to be too many deaths. Still, that's not all of it. There are worse ways to die being invented every year.

I taught my son Kirk very little about climbing, but he learned anyway. Perhaps he didn't have any choice. It may be that Willi felt that Regon, Devi, and Krag (but not Terres, who did not become a climber) didn't have a choice about learning to climb and felt it was his responsibility to help them as best he could. Did Willi have a choice? If not, it wasn't because of his competitiveness, which was considerable, nor his stubbornness nor his fear of getting old: if he could not help but keep going back, it must have been because though he had learned that the mountains were sacred, he was not yet certain how we are to hold them sacred.

DECEMBER 17, 1992, M/V *Le Conte,* OUTBOUND FROM SITKA TO PETERSBURG

0740. The sky is clear again, the temperature in the upper teens, cold enough so that the snow and ice on the decks is not slippery. I woke up this morning at about 0440, got up because we were due to stop in Kake, and found Chatham Strait to be carpeted with moonlight. From Petersburg I will go to Juneau, from Juneau to Sitka. My destination is where I started. I am here because I want to be here on the waters of these straits, circled by these mountains. There are 18 passengers aboard this, one of the smallest of the Alaska Marine Highway System's ferries, after 100 to 150 passengers on their last run. I cannot imagine a better place to end this story.

The solstice nearing, the horizon is pink all across the southeast quadrant on into the southwest quadrant: the sun's setting anticipated in its rising. The mountains of Kupreanof, Baronof, and Admiralty Islands a snowy ring behind and to port, the mountains of the continent a sharp-edged silhouette forward.

I began writing this story twenty years ago, when it was clear to me that this story had ended. The beginning pages are pretty much what they were then, including the perhaps immodest

title. I may have written this story in order to understand what I mean by the title. Our time has been such that innocence is often thought of as an enviable state, even a virtue, rather than the absence of experience—or worse, a failure to have, in gaining experience, exchanged innocence for wisdom.

What I thought I knew when I started this story is that no climber of the then present or the future could have what we had. That saddened me a little; I pitied those to follow in equal measure to my gratitude that I had been there in the golden age of American mountaineering, and I still do. I am not talking about our first ascents—most of which belong to Fred Beckey, anyway—I am talking about a quality of the experience which I believed could not be explained but which might emerge from the stories I knew. Innocence is what you leave in your wake when you know the story.

I have written that we were inspired by the story of the French expedition on Annapurna. We were the last generation who could be so inspired because we were also a generation that aspired to be heroes but ended up in the hero business. It is my hope that we are not judged as having failed in character, but as having lost our way as a consequence of the time, a time in which we imagine—as is customary in our culture at the end of the millennium—the end of history. And now we know we will not need the aid of supernatural powers, or even natural powers, to bring it about. You could say that we've got it down to a science, and all the technical difficulties are solved.

My theme might come clearer if we think beyond the end of history—which could come as easily from a scarcity of potable water or arable land as from the fiery holocaust—to what happens next. Will this bald eagle I see soaring on a cold thermal above a clearcut on the north shore of Kupreanof survive?

It is likely that there will be surviving individuals of Homo sapiens, *but they will soon become a different species, as Faulkner has taught us by asserting the opposite in his "last ding-dong of doom" speech. ["It is easy enough to say that man is immortal simply because he will endure: that when the last ding-dong of doom has clanged and faded from the last worthless rock hanging tideless in the last red and dying evening, that even then there will still be one more sound: that of his puny inexhaustible voice, still talking. I refuse to accept this. I believe that man will not merely endure: he will prevail . . . . The poet's voice need not merely be the record of man, it can be one of the props, the pillars to help him endure and prevail."] What will really happen is that those who will prevail will be those who survived only by having erased their memory, who tell no stories to each other or their children. Their lives will be of an eternal present, as are the lives of our brother and sister animals. They will communicate with each other directly by gesture and image, in waking dreams of a kind that will undoubtedly be compelling and beautiful. Their tools will be as aesthetically pleasing and as well made as anything made by their progenitors—and certainly more than adequate to the purpose of providing food, shelter, clothing, and protection from large animal predators (including their own kind)—but they will not make poetry. Their gesticulations will evolve into dance. With their voices they will make music taught to them by the birds, those survivors of the dinosaurs, and other animals, music they will learn from wind and surf and thunder and songs they will make with the instrument of their own voices, but no lyrics. Such people would live lives that vacillated between euphoria and ecstacy, with occasional lows of mere serenity, for the price of giving up language and that part of memory which only language can make, which, in the event of the end of history, will have been proved to be of no use to us.*

Even in their killing they will be, as are our fellow species, a species of the truly innocent, and they will truly not be us.

DECEMBER 18, M/V *Le Conte*, OUTBOUND FOR SITKA VIA SKAGWAY
We slowed in the night because of snow and fog, making it a risk that I might miss my plane. Instead of disembarking in Juneau, where I'd be sure to catch the plane, I decided to continue on up the Lynn Canal. I haven't finished the story.

At dawn the mountains are but misty forms of gray and white, with a distinct and straight black line the tide has made at the base between the snow and water. It's as if the mountains were laminated onto the beach.

That day when Willi came into my office, I didn't say anything to him. He was trying to goad me with the talk of being tired of being cold and scared, plus appeal to me as a teacher and a parent. I almost said, Willi, it's over. That was the question between us. He wanted to show me that it wasn't over. It couldn't be over, we hadn't got there yet! There he was, toeless, his hair passing gray and headed for white, constant pain, permanent limp, and he's trying to tell me it's not over. He sometimes seemed to me more like a charismatic preacher than a philosophy professor, but he was a truth seeker. He'd push you like that, get in your face, see if he could get you mad enough to say what you really think down there where the pain is hidden. I wasn't mad, but I wasn't laughing at him either. The truth is he didn't know it wasn't over, and I didn't know that it was. Maybe I was just through. It is over in climbing, but maybe it is somewhere else now or will be? I do know that for me it ended in Wyoming, where it began.

I was the only member of the faculty sitting among the two hundred students surrounding a flagpole. We had lowered the flag to half-mast. We had heard that in Denver the mayor himself had lowered the flag to half-mast when the news of what had happened at Kent State came in. I was staring at the right hand of a Wyoming highway patrolman, which was about six feet away from me and six inches above eye level. The hand was curled around the stock of the shotgun, the index finger twitching on the trigger guard, not the trigger, thank God. But why is he trembling? What is he afraid of? Not these kids? Then I knew. He was afraid of what he imagined he was about to do with that shotgun.

Wyoming was just another state in the union after all. I had hoped not.

It was January, 1959. My clothes and climbing gear were in my army duffel bag, my sleeping bag, books, and miscellaneous in an army surplus frame pack. I wore my long, almost to the ankle Harris Tweed overcoat. The combination made me something of a spectacle, but it couldn't be helped. I was coming to Wyoming for good this time. Of the accumulated stuff of my first twenty-five years, I carried everything I could not abandon. Wearing the overcoat was the easiest way to carry it. Besides, it was my only winter coat, and I was hitchhiking.

My father gave me a ride over to the Albany Turnpike, slipped me two hundred dollars and let me convince him not to wait until I got a ride. Albany, Buffalo, Cleveland, South Bend, and Iowa City in a day and a half. I stayed overnight in Iowa City with a college student who'd given me a ride from Joliet. He envied me and thought there was something remarkable about me. I suppose there was. I had quit the track team, dropped out of college twice, dropped out of NROTC and Army OCS, and still believed the world was full of prospects.

I took the Greyhound from Iowa City to Rock Springs. A cat skinner in a pickup gave me a ride to Farson. A rancher in a white Olds picked me up there.

The rancher's sheepskin coat lay in the back seat, but he'd kept his Stetson on. He was in his early fifties, average height, broad across the shoulders, no gut. I wouldn't say he had a drawl, but a more pronounced, less slurred way of speaking. He was from the other side of the Wind River, up near the Bighorns, a place with a wonderful name, Ten Sleep, Wyoming, where he owned a sheep ranch. You just know that a sheep rancher from Ten Sleep, Wyoming, is one of the world's good guys, however few they are.

Our conversation was unhurried, well spaced by time looking at the high desert we drove across, dazzling white with new snow, dotted with gray-green sage bushes, bounded east and west by the Wind River and Salt River Ranges, no houses, cabins, shacks, sheds, pens, or fences, one sheep wagon. I guessed the rancher to be a man who read much and was probably expert in some single bookish topic I'd have to know him a long time to find out about.

"Out here, do they ever call a sheepherder a shepherd?" I asked.

He smiled at the notion of it, not at my greenness, knowing I was not that green. Country feller smarter than he looks. Eastern boy letting him know he's smart enough to know that.

The rancher passed the Big Piney cutoff, went on up through Pinedale to Daniel Junction, thirty miles out of his way, to let me off there.

To the west about five or six hundred yards was the Green River. To the northeast, thirty miles as the eye looks, were Gannet and Fremont Peaks. When I had come to Wyoming in August, I'd been on the other side of the range coming up the Wind River. The foothills on that side blocked the view of these peaks. A rancher had given me a ride then too. As I thought about it, it occurred to me that other than Buckingham, these ranchers were the only two native Wyomingites I'd conversed with, even though I'd been in Jackson for all of August. Buckingham didn't count; he was going to graduate school at Princeton and didn't even have a Wyoming accent. The Teton County Sheriff had an accent; he was the first person to greet me when I arrived in Jackson. That wasn't a conversation but a brief interrogation on the boardwalk; he was interested in the Gypsies. I hadn't been surprised or offended. The sign on Togwotee Pass had said YONDER LIES JACKSON'S HOLE THE LAST OF THE OLD WEST.

As the sun hovered above the Salt River Range, Jackson's Hole seemed yonder indeed. This was Wyoming in the winter—no tourists, no college kids at their summer jobs, almost nobody going up the road. Those that did went west or south at the junction, not north. It was Friday, but there'd be no mail truck, because it was New Year's Day.

What had the rancher been thinking of? There was nothing at this junction, no gas station or store, no ranches in view, either. We talked about there not being much traffic this day. He said, "Oh, somebody'll likely help you out. People around here are just folks."

Down the road to the east, toward Pinedale, was a little old log cabin and some outbuildings. I was at the junction for a couple of hours before I realized that people lived there. I paid more attention to it as it became evident that the next vehicle going along Highway 189 might well be the mail truck the next morning, headed the other way. If I hadn't frozen to death, I could catch it coming back in the afternoon.

By sunset, I'd done considerable thinking about my position. It would have been better if nobody was in the cabin. Then, after dark, I could slip into one of the sheds, crawl in my sleeping bag, and wait out the night. There were at least five people in the cabin: papa, mother, two young boys, and an almost grown girl. I'd also figured out why the rancher left me at the junction and not back in Pinedale. A person headed my way could easily pass me up while I was near a town. But any driver at all going up this road in the late afternoon would know that they were probably the only car headed for Jackson. They'd almost have to pick me up.

Having recognized my true relationship to any drivers coming up this road, I then had to acknowledge the true nature of my relationship to the people in the cabin. It was the scale of the neighborhood that prevented me seeing sooner that I was on their turf, and not only was I in a position that demanded charity but the nearest and probably only people in a position to provide it was this poor family eking out a survival existence on this barren plain at seven thousand feet, next to the Continental Divide.

The mountains moved closer, as they do toward dark, but still I couldn't make myself do the right thing, which was to walk right up to the cabin and ask for shelter or at least a glass of water, to give them an opportunity instead of making them seek me out.

It was the girl who came. She walked right up and looked straight at me. "Pa says you'd better come in and have some supper." Then she looked pointedly at my duffel bag on the ground, turned back toward the cabin, and stood without glancing back, waiting to move until I picked up the duffel bag. I picked it up.

So I had supper and spent the night. Pa, in season, was a logger in the mountain forests. Daughter was smart as well as pretty. She'd already been awarded a scholarship for college next year. Mother was the reader. Mother made real good elk stew. They were proud of daughter, they were proud of themselves, the cabin was warm, everybody was in good spirits, everybody was living well.

Before I went to sleep, I thought, "They did me, a stranger, honor by sending her instead of the boys. How extraordinarily courteous these people are, and how easy it seems for them to be that way!"

That's how I hoped it would be, just that simple.